LIGHTNING
Fire from the Sky

Jerry – 11/08

Best wishes

Craig B. Smith

LIGHTNING
Fire from the Sky

BY

CRAIG B. SMITH
ILLUSTRATIONS BY KURT MUELLER

DOCKSIDE SAILING PRESS

Newport Beach, California

Dockside Sailing Press
www.DocksideConsultants.com

Library of Congress Cataloging-in-Publication Data

Smith, Craig B.
Lightning—Fire From the Sky/ by Craig B. Smith;
Illustrations by Kurt Mueller.

Includes bibliographic references and index
ISBN 978-0-615-24869-1

1. Lightning

2008935929

Book design by Nancy J. Smith

Printed by BookMasters Inc.
30 Amberwood Parkway, Ashland, Ohio

This book is dedicated to all those who have survived a lightning strike but continue to struggle with the after effects.

Contents

	Page
Foreword by Dr. Martin Uman	v
Preface	vii
Chapter 1: Thor's Anvil	1
Chapter 2: That Bolt from the Blue	19
Chapter 3: When Lightning Strikes Twice	52
Chapter 4: Crabs and Lions Beware: Health Impacts of Lightning	74
Chapter 5: Reasons for Keraunophobia	108
Chapter 6: The Lights Flickered and Then Went Out	121
Chapter 7: Dodging the Electric Bullet	156
Chapter 8: Predicting the Unpredictable	200
Chapter 9: The Bell Ringer's Deception	217
Appendixes	
1. Units of Measure, Conversion Factors, Data	245
2. Glossary of Special Terms	246
End Notes	249
Annotated Bibliography	272
Permissions/Credits/Acknowledgements	279
Index	282

Plates, Figures, and Tables

Plates
1. Lightning Strikes Near Dana Point, California During a Winter Storm
2. Fulgurite
3. Lightning Strike on Empire State Building, New York
4. Rocket Launch Tower
5. Lightning Strike in Desert Near Lake Havasu, California
6. Lightning Strike on the Eiffel Tower, Paris, 1902
7. Spider Lightning Over Norman, Oklahoma
8. Lightning Flash Density Chart for the United States
9. Lightning Flashes Over Dana Point Harbor, California
10. Lightning Damaged Tree, Lewis Creek Trail, California
11. Lightning Strike on Queensboro Bridge, New York City
12. Oil Storage Tank Damaged by Lightning
13. Cloud-to-Ground Lightning, Oro Valley, Arizona
14. Test House Lightning Protection System

Figures
1. D'Alibard's Electrical Apparatus, 5
2. Diagram of a Tesla Coil, 8
3. Sketch of a Van de Graaff Generator, 9
4. Circuit Diagram of a Marx Generator, 11
5. International Center for Lightning Research and Testing Site Map, 16
6. Sketch of Cloud Showing Charge Distribution, 24
7. Various Types of Cloud-to-Ground Flashes, 33
8. The Stepped Leader, Dart Leader, and Return Stroke, 34
9. Sketch of the Atmosphere Showing Ionized Regions and Hop Transmission Paths, 45
10. Thunderstorm Day Map of the United States, 61

11. United States Lightning Deaths by Month, 1959-1994, 73
12. Simplified Electrical Model (Equivalent Circuit) of the Human Body, 82
13. Detailed Equivalent Circuit of the Human Body, 86
14. Soil Voltage Gradient (Step Voltage), 91
15. Sketch of the Human Heart, 94
16. Normal Electrocardiogram and ECG Showing Ventricular Fibrillation, 95
17. Various Lightning Strike Positions, 108
18. Lightning Entry Points in a Building, 158
19. Area Protected by Lightning Arrestors, 159
20. Lightning Strike at Kennedy Space Center, 215

Tables
1. Typical Ground Flash Incidence Rates, 63
2. Lightning Casualty Rates, 66
3. Effects of Electric Current on Humans, 75
4. Economic Losses Due to Lightning, 122
5. Aircraft Crashes Attributed to Lightning Strikes, 145
6. Personal Safety Guidelines, 228

Foreword

I greatly enjoyed reading Craig Smith's fine book on the building of the pyramids—*How the Great Pyramid Was Built* (Smithsonian Institution Press, 2004), his first serious venture into literature after a distinguished career in engineering and engineering management. Craig's writing style combines a personal literary flair with an attention to quantitative detail and innovative organization. *"Lightning: Fire from the Sky"* is Craig's third book and, in writing it, he has wandered onto my turf. Lightning is a very complex business about which there is probably as much unknown (or poorly understood) as known (or relatively well understood). For example, we really do not understand the exact mechanism by which lightning is initiated in the cloud, and we only crudely understand how lightning decides what to strike on the ground. Nevertheless, we have a general qualitative overview of all lightning processes and a fairly good quantitative knowledge of some of these processes. In his book, Craig takes us on an engaging trip through all aspects of lightning behavior at a level that all can understand. Of particular interest to me is his fine treatment of death, injury, and disaster by lightning, much of it told by the victims. Lightning victims who read the book will find comfort in shared experiences, albeit negative ones, and a better idea of future expectations for a resolution of medical problems. Physicians can benefit from his discourse since few have had enough experience with lightning victims to know the optimum therapeutic approaches. Finally, everyone can be better educated about lightning with the result that death and incapacitating injuries will be reduced, one of Craig's main objectives. Understanding lightning is becoming more important, as lightning becomes more of a problem with technology's progress to more and more sophisticated low-voltage electronic systems that can easily be damaged by transient lightning currents, voltages, and electric and magnetic fields. Lightning is still producing surprises, like the newly discovered and largely unexpected emission of X-rays from propagating lightning channels (leaders), X-rays that have similar properties to those your dentist and doctor sends through you, a subject that is covered in Craig's up-to-date treatment of lightning.

-Martin A. Uman

Biographical note:

Dr. Martin A. Uman is one of the world's foremost authorities on lightning. Currently, he is Distinguished Professor of the University of Florida's Department of Electrical and Computer Engineering. He has written five books on lightning as well as many encyclopedia articles and many technical papers. He has several patents related to lightning detection and was instrumental in helping establish the National Lightning Detection Network. Dr. Uman is a Fellow of three professional organizations: the American Geophysical Union, the American Meteorological Society, and the Institute of Electrical and Electronics Engineers. He is the recipient of the IEEE Heinrich Hertz Medal for "outstanding contributions to the understanding of lightning electromagnetics and its application to lightning detection and protection," and the AGU John Adam Fleming Medal for "outstanding contribution to the description and understanding of electricity and magnetism of the Earth and its atmosphere." Dr. Uman is Director of the International Center for Lightning Research and Testing, located at Camp Blanding, Florida. At this large and one-of-a-kind facility, Dr. Uman and his colleagues fire rockets trailing conducting wires into storm clouds to create lightning strikes to experimental test objects, including instrumented buildings and power lines.

Preface

Somewhere in central Florida, a kingfisher dives from the top of a dead tree into a pond and emerges with a minnow. Back on its perch, it tilts its head and swallows the fish, then fluffs its feathers to cool in the 95-degree heat. Above, a column of warm air slowly pushes its way into the atmosphere. Heated by the midsummer sun, and laden with moisture that has evaporated from swamplands and golf courses, this juggernaut weighing 10 million tons rises one mile, and then two, into the clear Florida sky. As it climbs, it creates a virtual chimney, sucking more warm air with it. Two miles up, the temperature drops to around 45 degrees, and now, gathering mass and speed, the huge column of moist air pushes into the upper atmosphere. At five miles up, the temperature is well below freezing. Some of the water vapor condenses into microscopic drops of water and becomes ice crystals.

Far below, a golfer eyes the sky. The first large drops of rain have fallen. As the cloud above him continues to build into the ominous form of a thunderhead, parts of the cloud are actually rising faster than the raindrops can fall, and as a result, some drops are stripped of part of their moisture. The violent forces and friction leave sections of the cloud with a positive electrical charge and other parts with a negative charge. Charge accumulates until the voltage is so high—a potential difference of millions of volts—that the electrical resistance of the air is broken down, creating a path of ionized air. Ionized air readily conducts electricity, acting as if a copper wire was dropped through the cloud. The massive amount of electrical energy stored in the cloud flows down this invisible conductor. In a fraction of a second, the huge electrical current raises the temperature tens of thousands of degrees, vaporizing air and water, tearing apart the molecules of oxygen and nitrogen and producing multiple rapid flashes of light. The process within the ionized air is so violent that the vaporized gases are blown away from the current's path at supersonic speeds, causing a loud crash of thunder as the sound barrier is broken. After the flash, nitrogen molecules are fused, as are oxygen.

Below the storm, the kingfisher seeks a sheltered perch. The golfer sees the lightning flash and 20 seconds later hears the peal of thunder. From this he knows that the strike was only four miles away—time to hurry to the clubhouse and call it a day. He knows what lightning can do to a man holding a metal golf club—or one who is not!

This violent confluence of natural forces is repeated about 100 times per *second* in the atmosphere, somewhere on the earth. In the United States, where lightning strikes 25 to 30 million times per year, there are hundreds of lightning-related deaths and injuries every year. When large electrical currents course through the human body, cells are vaporized and nerves and organs destroyed. Even if one survives a lightning strike, the future could hold years of debilitating injury. Thirty percent of lightning strike *survivors* never completely recover and eventually die as a result of their injuries. As you read this paragraph, there were 10 lightning strikes somewhere in the United States alone.

Besides the risk to humans, lightning annually kills large numbers of farm animals, ignites destructive forest fires, poses a threat to aircraft and boats, and is the proximate cause of more than 60 percent of the outages experienced by the nation's electric utilities. The cost to the electric utility industry alone exceeds $1 billion per year. During the launch of Apollo 12, lightning briefly disrupted some of the spacecraft's instrumentation systems, but the astronauts were able to override the problem. In 1987, an unmanned Atlas Centaur missile launched from Kennedy Space Center and carrying a United States Navy communications satellite was struck by lightning, damaging the flight control system and causing the missile to fly erratically and to begin breaking up.

As a safety precaution, the missile was destroyed over the Atlantic and the payload was lost.

It is no wonder that thunder and lightning have burned their way into human cultures, leaving an indelible mark on myth, religion, literature, superstition. When faced with powerful natural phenomena that could be neither understood nor controlled, humankind has assigned to them supernatural origins, made them part of a pantheon of deities.

Lightning is associated with thunderstorms, and certain regions of the world are more prone to thunderstorms than others. In the United States, central Florida has the greatest incidence—more than 100 thunderstorm days per year. The southern belt of states—Louisiana, Mississippi, Alabama, Georgia, South Carolina, and Florida—have a frequency of around 60 to 80 thunderstorm days per year, as does the region of northern New Mexico and southern Colorado. The Pacific Coast, however, may see only five days with thunderstorms per year.

For prehistoric humans, thunder and lightning were feared, but also brought the boon of fire. To the ancients, thunder was the voice of the gods, and lightning was the expression of their displeasure. This ancient belief has come down to modern times—"may lightning strike me dead." Aristotle (384-322 B.C.), writing 300 years before the birth of Christ, described cloud formation in terms of moist and dry exhalations, stating that when air in the process of cooling is forcibly ejected from one cloud and strikes another, the impact is what we call thunder. Lucretius (98-55 B.C.) postulated that thunder was caused when high winds buffeted clouds and caused them to clash together. The first experiment to prove the electrical nature of lightning was devised by Benjamin Franklin in 1750; however, it was not until a Pennsylvania thunderstorm in 1752 that he performed the famous kite experiment. The following year, G.W. Richman, a German physicist, tried to duplicate Franklin's experiments and was killed when struck by lightning.

Only in the last century has the science of lightning been explored in depth, thanks to the advent of high speed photographic techniques and improved detection systems. Most research is ground-based, but has also been performed using balloons, rockets, and especially instrumented aircraft that fly into and over thunderstorms. The space shuttle has been used to make lightning observations from outer space, proving that lightning discharges can occur in the stratosphere. Although thunderstorms are the most common source of lightning, it can also be produced by sandstorms and snowstorms. Pliny the Younger (62-113 A.D.) wrote of the terrifying spectacle of Mt. Vesuvius erupting and destroying Pompeii, observing that "a black and dreadful cloud, broken with rapid zigzag flashes, revealed behind it variously shaped masses of flame: these last were like sheet-lightning, but much larger." As Pliny observed, lightning can take on various forms, in part depending on weather conditions. Besides the familiar jagged flash, it may appear as a bright sheet of light, a ribbon, a string of beads, or a round ball. While we are most concerned with ground strikes, there are also intra-cloud strikes and cloud to cloud strikes. Strikes can go from cloud to earth or vice versa. (See Plate1.)

In the most common form of a ground strike, the initial ionized path is called a *stepped leader*. Traveling at a speed of around 224,000 miles per hour, the stepped leader delivers negative charge to the ground. It is followed immediately by a very luminous return stroke, a wave front of high electric field intensity traveling at one-third to one-tenth the speed of light from the ground back up to the cloud. The current as measured at the ground is typically in the range of 25,000 to 30,000 amperes but can be as high as 100,000 amperes. (Compare this to 10 amperes, for a household toaster, or 100 amperes for an entire home.) The return stroke travels through a channel estimated to be about an inch in diameter. Depending on the availability of charged particles, this process may repeat with additional strokes. The average lightning flash has about four strokes, each with a peak power of 3,000 to as much as 20,000 megawatts—equivalent to the output of 20 large nuclear power plants, although only for the very briefest of durations—10 to 30 microseconds.[1]

Other forms of lightning include flashes or discharges with upward leaders, often rising from tall buildings; intracloud discharges, sheet lightning, which is a form of cloud illumination caused by lightning; bead lightning in which the channel to ground appears to break up into segments ten or twenty meters in length; and ball lightning in which lightning takes the shape of a luminous sphere with a diameter of a foot or so that persists for a few seconds.

The North American Lightning Detection Network has added to knowledge of the incidence and effects of lightning. The network has 180 sensors located throughout North America that continuously monitor electric and magnetic fields over a wide area. Besides measuring the intensity of the strikes (peak current), the system determines the location of each strike by triangulating readings from several sensors at different locations. NASA has future plans to place a lightning mapping system in a geostationary orbit in space. Such a system would be capable of detecting ground discharges and various forms of cloud discharges over a large part of the earth's surface. The additional data that will be obtained should prove useful in improving weather forecasting and for issuing warnings of severe storms.

With the greater understanding of lightning phenomena that exists today, it is possible to design improved lightning protection systems. The nation's electric utilities are conducting research on extremely rapid switching circuits that will detect the presence of lightning and conduct it to ground via a safe path before it damages electrical distribution equipment. For the protection of human beings, common sense still is the best safeguard—stay out of open areas during thunderstorms.

Still, it is not always possible to tell. There have been lightning strikes from cloudless skies. Thunder is not always an effective warning, because if the strike is more than 10 to15 miles away, thunder cannot be heard.

Gretel Ehrlich, walking her dogs in the Wyoming mountains one August afternoon, saw the thunderclouds build, heard one distant thunderclap. She did not hear thunder from the ground strike that hit her and tossed her body to the side of the trail like a limp doll, because she was unconscious before the noise reached her. Somehow, when she regained consciousness, vision blurred, legs partially paralyzed, having difficulty breathing, she managed to stagger back to her ranch house and dial 911 before passing out again. In the local hospital, which was ill-equipped to deal with lightning injuries, the medical technicians tallied up the damage. The lightning strike had caused ventricular fibrillation and cardiac arrest. Possibly due to the fact that the strike flung her to the side of the rocky trail, her heart started again, although the blow also caused a concussion, broken ribs, a damaged jaw, and lacerations above the eye. Her body was covered with fernlike burn patterns—the lightning's tattoo. She had paralysis below her waist and up through her chest and throat. Incredibly, after just an overnight stay, she was discharged from the hospital! After recuperating at home for days, she had no energy and seemed to get worse. In desperation she called her parents, who flew her to a hospital in California that was better equipped to treat her injuries. There she finally received the comprehensive medical examination that is mandatory for lightning victims: CAT scans, X-rays, EKGs, and an EEG.

Ehrlich suffered from fainting spells and a lack of energy. Medical tests showed that a part of her brain had been burned out by lightning. It was the part of the brain stem that tells the blood vessels to constrict and tells the heart to increase its rate of pumping. With this damage, the other parts of her circulatory control system—the part that tells the heart to slow down—ran unchecked. After more than two years of treatment Ehrlich was able to resume a somewhat normal life. Had she stayed in Wyoming and not sought further treatment, it would have simply been a matter of time before she succumbed to a slow death from a fatal arrhythmia, becoming part of the 30 percent post-lightning strike morbidity statistics.[2]

North Carolina—the site of roughly 50 thunderstorm days per year—hosted the Second Annual Lightning Strike and Electric Shock Conference in 1992. Dozens of survivors of lightning strikes and electric shock gathered to share their experiences and to act as a support group for each other. The conference broke up for a day because of violent lightning storms in the area. The medical doctors who came to present lectures found some attendees traumatized and dispensed tranquilizers to those in need of them.

I attended the 14th annual meeting of this group. It was a moving experience: no self-pity, just a determination to deal with their injuries as best they could. Most of the participants reported that their physicians did not know how to treat them. More than one said their physicians thought they "made up the story" of what happened, and treated them for unrelated illnesses. Most had ongoing disabilities from the strike. Fear of lightning, indelibly burned into their brains, was now a permanent part of their lives. As one man said, "I had to come to grips with the fact that I'm not the person I used to be."

Lightning is all around us. Sometimes it makes its presence known through booming thunder, and other times strikes beyond the sound of the previous thunder, suddenly, deadly, without warning. As children, we ran to our parents for comfort during violent thunderstorms, when the crashes literally rattled the windows of the house. As adults, we no longer fear the thunder, and in fact can enjoy the spectacle of the distant sky illuminated by a violent thunderstorm. But we must still respect and fear lightning, as one of nature's most potent and violent forces that can strike randomly at any time, anywhere.

Why This Book Is Important
If you want to be perfectly safe from lightning, construct an underground room using reinforced concrete or concrete blocks with a continuous web of steel reinforcing that is all bonded together. Place the structure about 10 feet underground, and above it and around it place a mesh or grid work of copper bars (each square of the grid about 6 feet on a side. Attach radial bars that extend out 100 feet horizontally under the soil, one at each corner and one in the center of each side of this copper cage surrounding your underground structure. Ensure that any electrical or telephone connections coming into your underground structure have surge protection devices and are likewise bonded to the grounding system. Better yet, have no penetrations whatsoever into your underground shelter.

In the center of the structure, at least 6 feet from every wall, place a large, comfortable, non-metal frame bed. Make sure that you never leave this bed, and I can assure you that you'll never get hit by lightning.

Now, should you decide to leave your underground bunker, there is of course a possibility that you could be hit by lightning on the surface of the earth. If you make certain that you never leave the underground structure when a thunderstorm threatens, your odds of getting hit by lightning are rather small. If, on the other hand, you leave the shelter on a summer day, or suppose we say on a July day in Florida, you have greatly increased your risk of getting hit by lightning, particularly if you decide to leave the shelter to play a game of golf.

Of course, no one wants to spend their life in an underground bunker. The point I'm trying to emphasize is that it is difficult to be 100% certain of avoiding a lightning strike. Most of us go through life without worrying about lightning.

However, as we shall see in the examples cited in this book, people are actually struck by lightning in almost every conceivable circumstance of their day-to-day lives, from calmly eating lunch in the safety of their home to sitting at their office desk in a high-rise building, to working outside or attending athletic or sporting events.

My perception of lightning was dramatically altered while researching this book. Originally, I thought of lightning as a remote, unusual phenomenon, of interest due to the large release of power that accompanies a lightning strike, the damage it could cause, and the rare fatality. During my early work on the book, I was amazed at the number of people who have had a close experience with lightning. I had just to mention the topic and the stories came pouring forth. A neighbor's mother was struck while talking on the phone. Another friend experienced a near miss when lightning shattered a nearby tree. Another recounted how her grandmother was knocked unconscious while milking a cow. All of her hair was burned off. She eventually recovered, but the cow was killed. Dozens of such stories altered my perception. Suddenly, lightning injury was no longer a remote, rare phenomenon— it was close and personal. The book includes a selection of personal accounts as told to me by lightning strike survivors.

My research revealed new facets of great importance to a general readership. First, the chances of being struck by lightning are much greater than is generally believed. On average, several people—perhaps dozens—are killed by lightning, somewhere in the world, every day of the year. In the less-developed parts of the world, where the populations are largely rural, thousands will die needlessly. In the United States, several hundred people will die from lightning strikes this year. As many as one thousand will be struck; the actual number is not known with accuracy because there is no standard reporting system. The official statistics understate the actual number of victims. Even more disconcerting is the fact that 30 percent of those who initially survive a strike will die of their injuries within a few years.

Tragically, many of these deaths could be avoided by prompt and appropriate medical care. Unfortunately, few medical practitioners know how to treat lightning victims— not just their physical symptoms, but the neuropsychological effects as well. The cost of lightning deaths and injuries— productive careers cut short, horrendous medical expenses, disruption of families, bereavement, and loss—is much larger than might be expected. A sobering aspect of this is that most deaths and injuries are avoidable. Observing commonsense rules to avoid exposure is a starting point; deployment of a new generation of detection and warning devices would further reduce the human and social costs of lightning injuries, and improved medical care would drop death rates.

Government agencies in the United States, notably the Federal Emergency Management Agency and the Occupational Health and Safety Administration, have few provisions for lightning hazard education, and little in the way of standards for training.

There is a huge cost due to lightning damage of electric utility systems. Yet, through solid engineering, research, and information exchange, utility engineers have been able to devise protective systems that have reduced outages despite the fact that the systems have expanded and grown ever more complex. Still, much more needs to be done; the problems are far from being solved and we are not immune to future blackouts.

A parallel effort is urgently needed in the public sector to increase awareness of individuals, to expand the usage of lightning detection systems, and to better prepare medical practitioners to deal with lightning victims. Hopefully, this book will help raise international awareness of the importance of this problem.

1

Thor's Anvil

It was in very ancient times, long before recorded history, when humanlike creatures roamed primeval forests of dense fern and ancient trees. Clouds formed and thunder more terrible than we have ever heard rocked snow-capped mountains. A terrifying bolt of the bluest light shot from the sky and ignited a huge conifer that blazed like a torch for hours and finally crashed to the ground in a shower of smoke and sparks. A shadowy figure emerged from a nearby cave, shivering in the cold and petrified with fear, and found warmth near the dying blaze. In a moment of boldness, she seized a flaming branch and carried it into the cave. A new era in human history began with this simple act—protection against fierce predators, the ability to fashion better tools, protection against inclement weather, and the ability to preserve food. So Prometheus exists—in the form of a random lightning strike.

Lightning has both fascinated and terrified humans since prehistoric times. The ancients associated lightning with the gods—the Greeks, with Zeus, the sky god, discharger of thunderbolts; the Romans, with Jupiter; the Vikings with Thor. So pervasive was the effect of lightning on human thought that the Etruscans wrote a book on the interpretation of thunder and lightning: the *Libri Fulgurates*. Lightning is mentioned a number of times in the bible—as noted in this Old Testament verse:

"(The Lord) causeth the vapors to ascend from the ends of the earth; he maketh lightnings for the rain; he bringeth the wind..."[1]

The Romans personified Jupiter as the light of the moon and sun, a flash of lightning, the peal of thunder. Thor, god of the ancient Norsemen, was personified in thunder and lightning, which was said to emanate from blows on his mighty anvil. Indra, storm god of ancient India, was responsible for life-giving rain. The invincible power of his thunderbolts was sought after in battles; he was imagined to be a giant, capable of eating herds of cattle and drinking barrels of wine. Shango, a god of Yoruba tribesmen in Nigeria, created thunder and lightning by hurling "thunderstones" to earth. Priests searched the area where strikes occurred in the hope of finding these stones, attributed with mystical powers. When lightning strikes sandy soil, the high temperature created by the lightning current fuses the sand into tubular glass structures called *fulgurites*. (See Plate 2.)

For the Maya, there was K'awil, god of lightning, a figure with flames shooting from his head. For the Inca, a snakelike god called Illapa moved into the heavens and created thunder and lightning and was believed to be the god of waters. Every ancient civilization—from the Greeks and Persians to the Chinese and the Maya and Inca—has associated lightning and thunder with the occurrence of rain essential for crops and the acts or displeasure of powerful gods. For millennia, lightning was considered an "otherworld" phenomenon, unrelated to earthly elements and forces, although a link between fire and lightning was known.

Leonardo DaVinci (1452-1519) recognized the difference in the speed of sound (thunder) versus lightning, but he imagined that the compression of air and moisture in clouds created steam and fire, "...so it bursts the cloud with devastating lightning and thunder."[2] It was not until the 18th century, when electricity was first isolated and studied, that Franklin postulated that lightning was a form of electricity.

Early Experiments
Benjamin Franklin (1706-1790), the American physicist, philosopher, and statesman, is generally regarded as the first great American scientist. Although he is best known for his

famous kite experiment, he also made fundamental discoveries in fluid dynamics, meteorology, and heat transfer. His practical inventions included the Franklin stove, reading glasses, and the public library. In reality, Franklin's kite was the logical extension of a series of experiments and years of work exploring electrical phenomena. In 1747, at age 41, he began his electrical experiments; four years later, his book *Experiments and Observations on Electricity* was published in Europe and translated into several other languages.[3] During this period, he experimented with Leyden jars (an early form of capacitor) capable of storing electric charge, tested various means of producing static electricity, examined how "electric fire," (as he characterized electricity) could be transmitted, studied the effects of electric shock on animals and humans, and demonstrated that electricity could start fires and melt metal. By various experiments he succeeded in creating large sparks and understood that a high voltage could break down the resistance of air and cause a spark to jump between two objects—more easily if a sharp pointed metal rod was employed. He was the first to truly understand the fluid nature of electricity and explain the workings of a capacitor (how energy could be stored in a nonconducting material now known as a *dielectric*). He demonstrated that charge was conserved, and that like charges repel. He made a giant capacitor, 10-feet tall and 1-foot in diameter, that he covered with gilt foil and suspended from the ceiling by silk threads. After charging this with his electrostatic machine, he was able to draw sparks as long as 2 inches from the cylinder to a grounded individual holding a needle. From this he reasoned that a large electrified cloud could strike the earth at a great distance.

On July 29, 1750, Franklin wrote to Peter Collinson in England, thanking him for the gift of an "electric tube," and reporting on the 30-plus experiments that he had subsequently performed.[4] After discussing his lightning theory, in item 21 of the Collinson letter he proposed an experiment—known to history as the "Sentry Box Experiment"—to verify the theory. In his words:

> "To determine the question, whether the clouds that contain lightning are electrified or not, I would propose an experiment to be try'd where it can be done conveniently. On the top of some high tower or steeple, place a kind of centry-box (sic), big enough to contain a man and an electrical stand. From the middle of the stand let an iron rod rise and pass bending out of the door, and then upright 20 or 30 feet, pointed very sharp at the end. If the electrical stand be kept clean and dry, a man standing on it when such clouds are passing low, might be electrified and afford sparks, the rod drawing fire to him from the cloud. If any danger to the man should be apprehended (tho' I think there would be none), let him stand on the floor of his box, and now and then bring near to the rod, the loop of a wire, that has one end fastened to the leads, he holding it by a wax handle. So the sparks, if the rod is electrified, will strike from the rod to the wire and not affect him." (Note: by "electrical stand," Franklin meant an insulated plate.)

Later in the same letter Franklin describes the use of lightning rods to protect buildings against lightning damage; even though he had not yet done the "centry-box" experiment, he was, on the basis of his experiments, confident of the principles of protection. But Franklin never conducted the experiment, possibly because he was waiting for the completion of a tall church steeple that was under construction nearby.

After Franklin's experiments were published in Europe, his book was translated into French by Jean-Francois D'Alibard. On May 10, 1752, D'Alibard successfully performed the sentry box experiment using an apparatus based on

Franklin's design (Figure 1), and was able to draw sparks from an iron plate connected to a pointed bar of iron 12 meters (40 feet) high. D'Alibard prudently observed Franklin's cautionary note and stood on the floor![5]

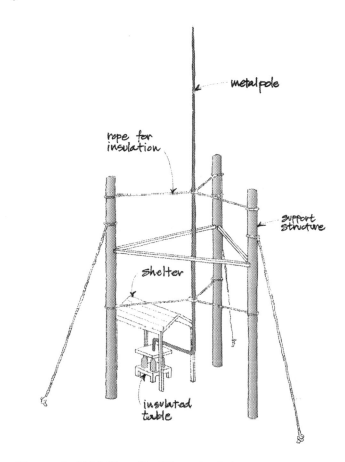

Figure 1: D'Alibard's Electrical Apparatus

Meanwhile, in Philadelphia, Franklin continued to think about the experiment (he was aware of the European results) and decided that a kite would be an improvement over the experiment described to Collinson. He fabricated a silk kite, flew it in a storm, and from a metal key dangling from the kite string, charged a phial (capacitor) with electricity. Writing to Collinson on October 19, 1752, Franklin reported:

"...At this key the phial may be charg'd; and from the electric fire thus obtain'd, spirits may be kindled, and all the other electric experiments be perform'd, which are usually done with the help of a rubbed glass globe or tube, and thereby the sameness of the electric matter with that of lightning completely demonstrated."[6]

Franklin studied the effect of lightning on unprotected buildings. In 1752 he published a description of a lightning strike on two homes, describing how the current preferentially sought out a path through metal. Around this time, the first lightning rods went into operation.[7] While there have been refinements and improvements in the hardware, the basic concept is unchanged from that first described by Franklin in his July letter to Collinson more than 250 years ago.

Franklin correctly surmised that clouds generally hold large negative charges, and that following a breakdown in air, the flash most likely travels from the ground up to the cloud. However, proof of the nature of charge formation in clouds did not occur until 150 years later, when a Scottish physicist, C. T. R. Wilson (1869–1959), made a glass chamber to study weather effects. He found that when air saturated with water vapor is caused to expand rapidly, some of the water condenses. He learned that the process is facilitated by the presence of dust particles, which serve as condensation nuclei. Through further experiments, he discovered that electrically charged ions can also serve as condensation nuclei. What are ions and what is ionization? An *ion* is created when an atom or molecule loses or gains electrons so that it has a net positive or negative charge rather than being neutral. The process of creating ions is called *ionization.* Ionization in gases and liquids is an important factor in many electrical processes.

Based on this research Wilson postulated the electrical charge characteristics of thunderclouds.[8]

Another unique development was the invention of the Tesla Coil, which gave researchers a tool with which to experiment with high voltages. It is named after Nikola Tesla (1856–1943), a Serbian-American who made many fundamental discoveries in the field of alternating currents, including the development of polyphase ac motors. Tesla's developments were essential to the commercial deployment of electrical power.[9] As a child, Tesla had been fascinated by lightning. As he gained experience with alternating currents and developed equipment capable of generating high voltages, he had a vision that it would be possible to transmit large blocks of electrical power by wireless means. His early work led to the development of the *Tesla Coil*, basically an air-core transformer with primary and secondary coils tuned to resonate at a high frequency (Figure 2). This device was capable of transforming a low voltage, high current input into a high voltage, low current output. Over the course of several years in the late 1890s Tesla built ever larger machines, capable of operating at potentials of 3 million volts or higher, and discharging a high energy spark dozens of feet long. During the course of his research he demonstrated how wireless communications were possible, using his coils to send radio frequency signals over distances as great as 25 miles from a boat on the Hudson River to his New York laboratory.[10] During this time he filed several patents that later formed the basis for short wave radio communications. He also developed the concept of radio controlled aircraft and made a number of other fundamental technical developments, several of which he did not bother to patent.

This was perhaps Tesla's greatest failing; he flitted from one discovery to the next, never stopping to follow through to practical demonstration and commercialization of his discoveries. Others, less talented and more opportunistic than Tesla, doggedly pursued the concepts he elucidated and then reaped the financial rewards of commercial success that always seemed to elude Tesla. In hindsight, Tesla made a fundamental error in pursuing his concept of wireless transmission of electrical power rather than recognizing that wireless *communications* would become a major industry, revolutionizing global communications.

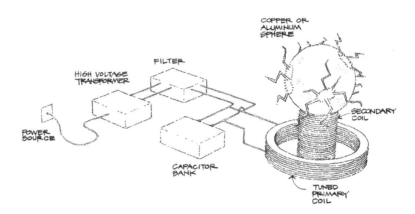

Figure 2: Diagram of a Tesla Coil

The summer of 1899 found Tesla building a new laboratory not far from Colorado Springs. There he con-structed a tower over 200 feet high and produced electrical discharges of 12 million volts and 1,100 amperes.[11] This was the closest anyone had ever come to making artificial lightning. Tesla could observe lightning flashes shooting more than 130 feet from the top of his tower, and reportedly the sound of the thunder it produced was heard in the town of Cripple Creek, 15 miles distant. In his journals he speculated that he had created a resonant effect in the earth's atmosphere and from this could deliver power at any spot in the globe. Unfortunately, his estimates failed to realize that the energy losses that occurred from this propagation method rendered it impractical.

At that time, Tesla was satisfied with his Colorado research. He dismantled his equipment and moved to New York to build a larger version of his equipment to transmit power across the Atlantic. Here success eluded him and he eventually lost funding and had to give up the laboratory. After this, he continued to make contributions in a number of fields, including turbine development, a vertical takeoff aircraft, air conditioning, and specialty lightning rods. In reality, Tesla did little to advance our understanding of lightning. His primary contribution was to pioneer the development of high voltage alternating current equipment.

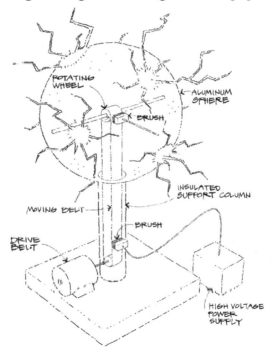

Figure 3: Sketch of a Van de Graaff Generator

In 1929, Robert J. Van de Graaff noticed that an industrial printing press produced sparks as paper passed over high speed rollers when humidity was low. This led him to develop the *Van de Graaff generator*, a device for producing high voltage direct current as shown in Figure 3. Students in physics classes or persons attending science fairs have probably observed sparks flying from a Van de Graaff generator or possibly have experienced their hair standing on end if they were persuaded to touch the machine. While the demonstration machines produce high voltage—as much as 50,000 to 500,000 volts—it is at a very low current and therefore not useful as a lightning test device. Higher powered Van de Graaff generators have been used in high-energy particle accelerators.

The primary lightning simulator, found in all high voltage laboratories, is the Marx Generator, first described by E. Marx in 1924. This device uses the principle of charging capacitors to provide a high voltage direct current discharge. Marx conceived a very clever way to create the high voltage.

A group of capacitors connected in parallel is charged to the level of a supply voltage. Suppose there are 10 stages— 10 capacitor-resistor pairs, each charged to a peak voltage of 10,000 volts in the configuration shown in Figure 4. Now, if we could suddenly connect all of these capacitors in *series* (so they add), the output voltage would be 10 times 10,000 volts or 100,000 volts.

Note that there is a spark gap across each stage. Normally no current flows in this connection because the air in the gap is an insulator. However Marx realized that if he carefully adjusted the length of the gap in the first stage, he could cause the air to break down and a spark to develop just as the first capacitor was fully charged (10,000 volts in this example). When this happens, it is electronically equivalent to throwing a switch to connect the first stage in series with the second, so the second spark gap sees 20,000 volts and of course breaks down immediately, connecting the first two stages in series with the third, and so on down the line. The entire process happens very quickly. For actual high voltage test purposes where the output voltage is millions of volts, the equipment is more complex. The resistors can be replaced by inductors to reduce the resistive power loss. Rather than a spark gap, electronic means can be used to trigger each stage rapidly and simultaneously.

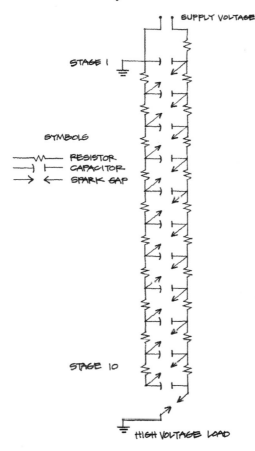

Figure 4: Circuit Diagram of a Marx Generator

Following the invention of the camera it was logical that photographers would capture lightning flashes striking the ground, trees, or buildings. However, it was not until 1926 when a British scientist named Charles V. Boys invented a unique camera capable of resolving the rapid movement of a lightning flash. The Boys' camera has two lenses that rotate at high speed in opposite directions. Using this camera, researchers were able for the first time to see how lightning approaches the earth in a series of jagged steps. (See Figure 8 in Chapter 2.) Modern cameras, called streak cameras, achieve the same result by having the film moved at high speed behind a fixed camera lens.

In the 1930s and 1940s the first use of balloons launched into thunderclouds to measure the structure of the electric charge in clouds occurred. These measurements were of interest because they revealed how the charge varied with elevation and temperature. The measurements showed that there was a positive, then negative, and then another positive charge region as the balloon ascended. The method is not perfect, since in the time it takes for the balloon to rise to the top of the cloud other dynamic effects are taking place within the cloud and there is no guarantee that the balloon's measurements are truly representative of the entire cloud.

The Empire State Building and Other Tall Structures

In 1931 builders completed the 1,454-foot-high Empire State Building in a record-breaking 15 months.[12] Realizing that the building was certain to be struck by lightning, its architects designed it as a giant lightning rod with air terminals on the top connected to the ground through the steel structure and its contents protected by a series of steel cages. In 1935, after the building had been struck a number of times, the General Electric Company installed cameras and current measuring instrumentation and began a 10-year study of lightning, using the building as a test facility. An important finding from the Empire State Building research was that the building itself originated many lightning strikes. At the top of the building the electric field is concentrated and the field strength is high, causing a breakdown of the air resistance to occur. A stepped leader travels from the top of the building upwards and initiates the strike.

Plate 3 shows a lightning strike on the Empire State building in New York City. Look carefully at this remarkable photograph and an airliner can be seen passing overhead at the instant the photograph was taken. It too was struck by the same lightning flash. The Empire State Building is struck by lightning at least 20 or more times per year. On July 28, 1945, the Empire State Building was struck in a very different manner; in dense fog, a B-25 bomber plowed into the side of the building at the level of the 79th and 80th floors. Fourteen people died, but the building survived and was repaired.

Historic ground-based lightning measurements were made by researchers in Switzerland for more than 40 years, using tall steel instrumented towers on Monte San Salvatore, near Lugano. The mountaintop is about 2,100 feet above Lake Lugano. The towers are struck more than 40 times per year on average. These measurements provided a great deal of information concerning the electrical properties of lightning.[13]

Lightning Detection Networks
Scientists have developed systems for detecting lightning on a broad scale. These consist of a network of sensors that detect electromagnetic signals emanating from lightning strikes. Data are transmitted to a central location where there is a network control center. Here the data are analyzed and triangulation of the signals from several sensors enables precise determination of the position of the lightning strike. To see an example of such a display, go to www.lightningstorm.com and follow the links to "lightning explorer free map." The North American Lightning Detection Network is an example. This network covers the United States and Canada; refer to Chapter 8 for details.

Today many countries in areas where lightning frequently occurs operate national detection systems. Examples include Scandinavia (Norway, Sweden, Finland, Denmark), Europe (France, Russia, Austria, Italy, Spain), Asia and the Pacific (Japan, Korea, Taiwan, Australia, South

Africa, Indonesia), and Central and South America (Mexico, Brazil and Colombia).

Aircraft and Rockets
Between 1964 and 1988 there were four major research programs during which instrumented aircraft were deliberately flown into thunderstorms and struck by lightning. Three of these were in the United States and were sponsored by the United States Air Force, the National Aeronautics and Space Administration, and the Federal Aviation Administration. The fourth program took place in France.[14]

During the NASA program—1980 to 1986—an F-106B delta wing jet aircraft made 1,500 passes through various thunderstorms at altitudes ranging from 5,000 to 40,000 feet. The plane was struck by lightning more than 700 times, nearly 10 times as many strikes occurring at altitudes over 20,000 feet compared to the lower altitude flights. The plane was equipped with high speed movie cameras, still cameras, and video cameras, in addition to electronic instrumentation that measured the lightning current and the electric and magnetic fields that were produced. Information from these flights, along with the other research programs mentioned above, provided a fairly complete basis for understanding the interaction between lightning and aircraft in flight.

Rockets have also been used to carry electronic instrumentation into thunderstorms, but in general balloons and aircraft provided a better platform for measurements over a longer period of time. Rockets, like aircraft, can trigger lightning.

Can we create lightning? Greek legends tell of an ancient king of Telis, who imitated thunder by pulling bronze kettles behind his chariot as he hurled flaming torches to simulate lightning, all in the hope of breaking a drought. In the laboratory, high voltage arcs can be manufactured, but with a minute fraction of the total energy in an actual lightning bolt.

Of greater interest is natural lightning that is "triggered" in a manner to cause it to strike a test specimen.

The discovery that rockets can trigger lightning flashes has been used to create lightning strikes in a controlled manner. One approach employs small solid-state rockets that are launched into thunderclouds when ground and atmospheric conditions are appropriate. The rocket is fired up to an elevation of around 1,000 feet trailing a long thin copper wire connected to the earth. Current from the charged earth travels up the wire, vaporizing it and creating a conducting path that triggers a lightning flash back to ground. The return stroke hits a series of lightning rods above the rocket launcher; these are connected to a heavy cable that leads to the system being tested.

Thunderstorms frequently occur in northern Florida during the month of July. I paid a visit to Professor Martin Uman's research facility at the International Center for Lightning Research and Testing at Camp Blanding, Florida. Uman, an internationally recognized lightning expert, gave me a tour of the facility and explained how tests were conducted. Climbing to the top of a tall wooden tower, where the rocket launcher is located, provided an excellent overview of the entire complex. (See Plate 4.) Scattered around the site in various locations are electric field mills used to measure the electric field intensity near the ground as a storm approaches. A rocket is launched when these instruments indicate a cloud charge electric field intensity of 5,000 volts per meter. Also on the ground was a network of 20 electric and magnetic field sensors with frequency response from dc to 20 megahertz along with shielded radiation detectors used by Professor J. R. Dwyer to measure X-ray bursts that accompany lightning strikes.

From the top of the tower a heavy cable extends to a section of distribution line used to study lightning affects on electric utility equipment. Nearby is a strip of pavement lined with airport runway lights, used to determine lightning effects on runway lights for the Federal Aviation Administration. Adjacent to the tower is an experimental house; another cable connects to it. Here experiments concerning lightning effects on building materials, residential electrical installations, and lightning protection systems can be made. The site is underlain by sandy soil, and on several occasions lightning strikes on the soil have created fulgurites. Professor Uman showed several examples of these to me. Plate 2 is an example.

At some distance from the rocket launch tower is a building containing offices and the control and data acquisition instrumentation for the site, including high speed cameras for recording lightning flashes. The building also houses a work-shop for building, repairing, and calibrating equipment and instrumentation. Launch control and other data acquisition equipment are housed in a trailer not far from the tower. All structures are protected by an overhead array of ground wires to prevent lightning from striking the structures. Figure 5 is a site plan for Camp Blanding.

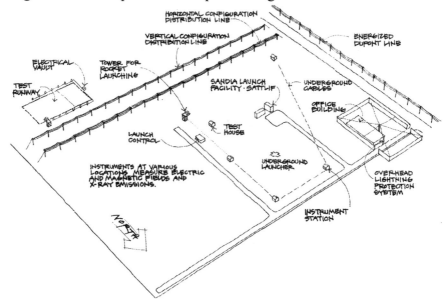

Figure 5: International Center for Lightning Research
and Testing Site Map

In the distance we could hear thunder. A few drops of rain fell—intermittent, but not heavy. The instrumentation included a display that showed the distance to and direction of local storms. It appeared that this storm was going to pass too far south of the site. Time passed slowly in the control building as we waited and watched the instruments. Finally, at 6:30 P.M. we called it quits and shut down the equipment. The electric field instrument readings got as high as 1,500 volts per meter—not high enough to trigger lightning. This particular sequence of tests would have to wait for another day.

When conditions are right, launching the rocket produces a spectacular effect. Almost instantaneously there is a brilliant flash and a crash of thunder. The observer sees only the return stroke; it takes the high speed camera to reveal the wire vaporizing and the other initial processes preceding. Surprisingly, most often the rockets survive and can be re-used. A parachute allows them to float back to earth. Triggered lightning is not the same in all respects as natural lightning. However, the advantages of being able to produce lightning strikes almost at will when natural conditions permit, has enabled Professor Uman and his colleagues to make many important and fundamental discoveries concerning the behavior and properties of lightning.

Satellites and Space Stations
Satellites that orbit the Earth provide a new dimension in lightning detection, making possible better estimates of global lightning activity. Satellites use both optical detection systems and radio frequency detection to determine the frequency of lightning flashes. The detection systems are unable to differentiate between mostly intracloud strikes and cloud-to-ground strikes, however. Yet the satellite data do confirm that lightning strikes occur much more frequently over land than over the oceans. Variations are also found depending on the season. Studies based on satellite data indicate that the global

flash rate is in a range of 40 to 120 flashes per second.[15] This compares favorably with the oft-quoted average value of 100 flashes per second worldwide estimated in 1925.[16]

On another trip to Florida to consult with Professor Uman, I also attended a conference in which astronaut Jerry Linenger spoke of his experiences while stationed aboard the Russian space station *Mir*. I asked him if he had occasion to observe lightning storms during his stay in space. Captain Linenger gave me a fascinating description of an extensive lightning storm he watched as *Mir* passed over the tropics. Far below, the darkness was broken by flickering flashes of light as a vast lightning storm spread from point to point in spider web fashion over thousands of kilometers.[17]

Still, in retrospect, the additional measurements and data obtained in the last two and one-half centuries confirmed and embellished Franklin's original discoveries, made using the crude apparatus available to him in 1750! Franklin is entirely deserving of the epigram coined by the French finance minister Turgot, who met Franklin during his mission to seek French aid during the war for independence: "He snatched lightning from the sky and the scepter from tyrants."[18]

2

That Bolt from the Blue

We have all experienced the discomfort—and sometimes the thrill—of a summer outing interrupted by lightning. My most memorable lightning storm occurred during the summer of 1980 when I was backpacking with my family in California's High Sierra Mountains. We had just climbed to Gardisky Lake, under the peak of Mount Tioga near Yosemite National Park, when it began to rain. We were at an elevation of 10,500 feet, where the few trees were gnarled and stunted from the force of wind and weather. We hurriedly set up our tents in a small depression in the granite rock and tried to cook dinner on our small propane stove while the wind howled and blew. As the rain abated, we were treated to a truly spectacular display of lightning over the mountains in the Minarets Wilderness Area and Yosemite National Park to the south of us. To all appearances we were on the top of the world. The sky was clear, and from our vantage point it seemed as if we could see the whole width of the Sierras. The jagged flashes of lightning illuminated an area 5 to 10 miles across, and the booming, rolling thunder that followed seemed to shake the solid granite of the mountain, where we lay awestruck in our flimsy tents and watched. Plate 5 shows a similar lightning strike in the Southern California desert.

Lightning usually occurs in conjunction with thunderstorms and is the result of the accumulation of a large electric charge in cumulonimbus clouds. However, stratocumulus and other cloud types can potentially cause lightning, as can snowstorms, volcanic emissions, or dust storms.[1]

For lightning to reach the earth, four things have to happen. First, a special type of weather system has to occur. Today we call this weather condition a thunderstorm, after the characteristic noise produced by a lightning strike. Thunderstorms are generally notable for the towering cumulonimbus clouds, called thunder clouds, although other cloud formations can cause lightning. Secondly, within the cloud formation, an electrification process occurs, permitting a large electrical charge to build up. Third, somehow the resistance of the air must be overcome so that the accumulated electrical charge can flow, creating the high-powered electrical current we know as a lightning discharge. Most lightning discharges never reach the earth but move inside the cloud. For the lightning discharge to reach the earth, a fourth condition has to be satisfied: Air resistance has to be overcome so the lightning current can flash to ground.

Ever since Franklin made the fundamental discovery that lightning is electrical in nature, scientists have been studying lightning in order to better understand what causes it and exactly how it is formed. Despite several centuries of research, there is much about lightning that is still unknown. Theories have been put forth that seem to explain some elements of the lightning discharge, but fail to fully account for other aspects.

Thunderstorms

Thunderstorms occur when atmospheric conditions are such that masses of cold, dense air in the upper atmosphere interact with rising columns of warm, moist air, forming thunderclouds. One type of thunderstorm—known as a *convective* thunderstorm—is created when local surface conditions heat the air, causing it to be unstable and buoyant. A second type of thunderstorm—a *frontal* thunderstorm—occurs when there is turbulence following the arrival of a cold front in an area. The dense cold air causes the lighter warm air at the surface of the earth to become unstable and rise.[2]

The billowing white columns of a thundercloud can be seen hovering anywhere from a few miles to as much as 10 miles into the sky. What is not apparent to an observer on the ground is the turbulence taking place in the cloud as the rising warm air mixes with the descending, heavier cold air. There are strong upward currents of warm air carrying considerable water vapor. As the cloud rises, it eventually forms a distinctive "anvil" top. The anvil appearance is caused by the high velocity winds in the upper atmosphere blowing the tops away from the updraft.

In either the convective or frontal case, the rising column of warm air creates a thunderstorm *cell*, a turbulent region of air with one or more strong updrafts. These upward-moving air currents will rise as long as the air is warmer than the surrounding air. As the air column rises, it continues to draw in more warm moist air. The water vapor in this air condenses into water droplets, releasing latent heat and providing more energy to continue and expand the process.

As a cell expands and collects more water content, larger raindrops are formed, and at higher altitudes where the temperature drops below the freezing point, ice crystals are formed. These will continue to rise in the updraft until they become large and heavy enough that gravity causes them to fall. At this point, the cumulonimbus cloud may have reached 6 to 12 miles in height and will have taken on the typical anvil-shaped top described above. In the upper part of the cloud are ice crystals, and as the cloud eventually begins to dissipate, *supercooled* droplets of rain will fall. Supercooled means that the raindrops are still liquid although their temperature is below the normal freezing point.[3] It is during this process that lightning is formed, as will be discussed later.

Thunderstorms normally occur in the late afternoon or evening hours, when the effect of surface heating is at its maximum. Frontal thunderstorms can occur at any time of day or night, although generally they are most common in the late afternoon or early evening and can continue throughout the night. As noted elsewhere, thunderstorms occur most frequently in the lower latitudes. Florida, for example, has areas that may experience 100 thunderstorm days per year, while along the southeastern United States and Gulf Coast, 70 days per year is typical, and the northeastern United States and central region has 30 to 40 days of thunderstorms per year, decreasing to fewer than 5 or 10 on the West Coast. An exception to this trend is the central Rocky Mountains in Colorado and New Mexico, which can have 50 or more thunderstorm days per year.

Thunderstorms occur most frequently during the summer or warm months of the year in both the northern and southern hemispheres. In the northern hemisphere, the exception to this is on the Pacific Coast, where thunderstorms are likely to form in connection with warm and cold fronts that occur during winter storms.

However, it was a summer day in Sequoia National Park—July 30, 2005. Lightning had been flashing in the distance, and a group of Boy Scouts hiking along the John Muir Trail toward Mount Whitney at 10,000 feet elevation observed that it was about to rain. There were seven scouts and five adults. They separated into two groups and began erecting tarp shelters in an open meadow, rather than a safer location. After they had taken shelter, lightning struck one of the tents, killing an assistant scout leader instantly. Another adult and five scouts were injured, one critically. While some scouts administered CPR to the scout with the most serious injuries, others raced back to a ranger's station to summon help. Four helicopters with paramedics evacuated the scouts to safety during the storm, but the critically wounded scout succumbed to his injuries.[4]

I have hiked that area with my family, and upon reflection, it is only about 80 miles south of where we camped at Gardisky Lake as described at the beginning of this chapter. We have spent many pleasant days backpacking in the area between Mount Whitney and the Tioga Pass, and we too have taken to our crude plastic tube tents when storms threatened. Once, in a sudden snowstorm, as we made our way down a mountain trail at a place called Lamarck Col, we were all very tired and cold. We'd made a long hike up from North Lake to the top of the pass at 12,900 feet and then turned back when the weather deteriorated. My singular memory of that day as we trudged along through mist, snow, and rain was of my wife Nancy's hair. She was wearing it in a pony tail and it had frozen stiff, and stuck out from under her hat like a paint brush. Fortunately, we reached shelter before the worst of the storm hit.

Cloud Electrification Theories
How exactly does a huge electrical charge build up within a cumulonimbus cloud? Several theories have been advanced, each of which has some limitations. In the paragraphs that follow I will describe two of the best known theories. But first, a simple analogy may aid in understanding. Consider the situation on days with little humidity, when the friction of walking in leather-soled shoes on a carpet strips away electrons and creates a static electricity charge. What happens when you extend your key to unlock the door under this condition? You receive a shock (and under certain circumstances can see a spark!) as the charge that has built up discharges from your body through the outstretched key to the nearby lock.

The flow of electric current is considered by convention to go from positive potential (as in the positive terminal of the battery in your car) to a negative potential. This convention is another contribution of Benjamin Franklin. However, in reality the electrons that make up the current flow in the opposite direction, since a *positive* potential is in fact the result of an electron deficit. This difference in potential (12.6 volts in the case of the car battery) is measured in *Volts,* a unit named for Count Allesandro Volta (1745–1827), the Italian physicist who invented the battery in 1796. His invention made experimentation with electricity practical and ultimately led to the development of electric circuit theory.

In the early 1900s, scientists taking measurements from the ground and with balloons recognized that neutral clouds became charged during the formation of a thunderstorm. (See Figure 6.) At first it was thought that clouds were dipoles, meaning that one part (the upper portion)

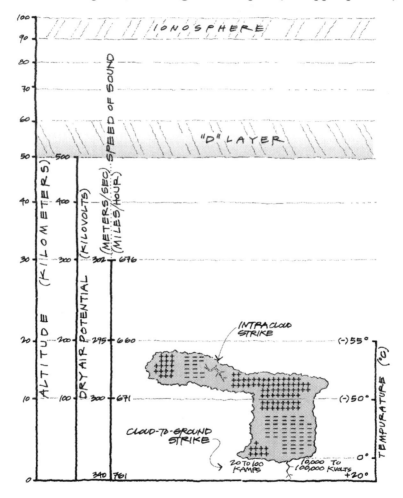

Figure 6: Sketch of a Cloud Showing Charge Distribution.

carried a negative charge, and the lower part held a positive charge. Since electrons are charged negatively, this finding implied that the upper portion of the cloud had an excess of electrons, while the lower portion had an electron deficit. Subsequent research showed that clouds are generally tripolar—a positive charge at the top, the main negative charge at midlevel in a cold part of the cloud where the temperature is in the range of +14 to -13 degrees Fahrenheit (-10 to -25 degrees Celsius), and a region of smaller positive charges at lower levels.[5]

The first widely accepted theory of cloud electrification is called the *inductive mechanism* theory.[6] In this theory, a water drop falling in an electric field has opposite charges on its top (negative) and bottom (positive). In this violent region of swirling air and water vapor, the turbulent flow of moist air rising in the cloud carries smaller droplets upwards, impacting larger drops that are falling, and sweeping some of the positive charge to the top of the cloud. The same theory applies when hailstones are falling and lighter ice crystals are swept upwards. Some problems with this theory occur when experimenters try to duplicate the process in the laboratory. Droplets are far more likely to coalesce than bounce off, and the charge transfer appears to be greater than is possible using this theory.

In a variation on the inductive mechanism theory, consider instead that *graupel* (soft hail or small snow pellets with a fragile crust) falls through a fine mist of super-cooled water droplets and ice crystals. During collisions with the ice crystals, positive charge is removed, causing the graupel to carry negative charge downward. In lower, warmer regions of the cloud, the opposite process occurs, and the graupel becomes positively charged. There is a critical temperature—believed to be between 14° F and minus -4° F—where this charge reversal occurs. This theory seemingly can account for the tripolar nature of cloud electrification. A number of ingenious laboratory experiments have been performed to validate theory, but only with partial success. Still, the graupel-ice mechanism is gaining favor as a key mechanism for cloud electrification.[7]

It has been known for some time that friction between the liquid and solid forms of a substance can produce an electric charge. In the case of ice and water, the ice becomes positively charged.[8] In one experiment researchers blew particles of snow against a block of snow, and determined that the block became negatively charged as small particles of snow carried away a positive charge. Other researchers poured snow through an ice-coated funnel and collected the snow fragments in a metal can connected to an electrometer. What they found was that the snow acquired a negative charge. In still another experiment, researchers blew snow with air that was either warmer or colder than the snow. The snow was blown from an electrometer plate and collected in a vessel. When the air was warmer, the blown snow carried small positive charges; when the air was colder, the snow fragments carried fairly high negative charges. These examples illustrate that a complex process is taking place; however, the evidence seems to point to small snow or ice particles acquiring negative charge during thunderstorms.[9]

The second general theory is called the *convective theory* and postulates that electric charges come from external sources—either cosmic rays at high altitudes or space charge and corona discharge at the ground. Negative charge is carried downwards near the edges of the cloud and causes more corona (positive discharge) to occur near the ground. Warm updrafts then convey this positive charge up into the center of the cloud.[10] The positive charges attract small negative ions to the top of the cloud. These in turn will attach to raindrops or ice particles and will fall at the perimeter of the cloud or wherever there are downdrafts to transport them to the lower part of the cloud. The presence of a negative charge causes more positive ions to be produced, thus causing more negative ions to be attracted, et cetera. One problem with this theory is that measurements show that there are too few ions present around thunder clouds to account for the growth of charge in the cloud.

Another theory suggests that drops can break up, one half carrying a positive charge, the other half a negative charge, and the two halves subsequently being carried to different parts of the cloud. Experiments show that melting ice acquires a positive charge; apparently when ice melts, tiny bubbles of water separate away, carrying with them a negative charge. Still another theory notes that the mobility of positive (H+) ions in ice is much greater than negative (OH-) ions, and the mobility of both types increases with temperature. This suggests that the warmer part of an ice particle would develop a negative charge as the positive ions migrated away.[11]

The positive-negative-positive charge distribution described above may be the most common one associated with lightning, but it is not the only possibility. The cloud could have several positively and negatively charged areas at once, depending on its size and state of formation. No doubt the charged regions are not static; they must change and move in the turbulent chaotic motion taking place in the cloud, and are certainly modified by the lightning discharge itself.

There are still more theories, but it would take many pages to discuss the pros and cons of each. I cite these brief examples to illustrate the difficulties. In summary, there are many theories, but basically none explain all of the phenomena known to occur, so we really don't know what causes the electrification of clouds—what creates the enormous charge of electrical energy that can send not just one but multiple bolts of lightning crashing through the heavens. However, it seems certain that freezing temperatures, ice particles, and super-cooled water are critical components of the complex process by which lightning is produced.

Breakdown in a Sea of Electricity
The third step in the process of generating a lightning flash is the actual breakdown of the air itself to allow an electric

current to flow. Under the usual conditions near sea level air is a *dielectric*, meaning that it does not conduct electricity. However, under certain conditions the natural resistance of air is overcome and in 20 to 50 millionths of a second, lightning flashes to another part of the cloud, to another cloud, or to the ground. Why is this?

As astonishing as it seems, we live in a sea of electricity. But because of the insulating qualities of dry air at sea level, we are unaware of it. Near sea level, in fair weather, the earth's electric field strength is around 150 volts per meter, meaning that at head height (6 feet, or 2 meters), the potential is 300 volts. Compare this to the voltage supplied to the contemporary home, which is a little more than 200 volts. Since our bodies have much less resistance than dry air, we remain at the same potential as the earth, and are unaffected by the earth's electric field under normal conditions.

During thunderstorms, the electric field can rise to as much as 50,000 volts per meter beneath the clouds. Likewise the electric field intensity near the ground increases as conditions shift to those favorable to lightning. The near-ground field intensity can be 5,000 volts per meter or higher. It is under conditions such as this that your hair stands on end and you might experience other sensations of a static electricity discharge. This is a warning that you are in significant danger, by the way.

The electrical conductivity of the atmosphere increases rapidly with altitude, so at an altitude of 115,000 feet, it is about one thousand times greater than at sea level.[12] At an altitude of around 165,000 feet, there is a lightly charged area below the ionosphere called the "D layer", where the potential has risen to 300,000 to 500,000 volts. Despite the tremendous voltage, we are unaffected by the sea of electricity, just as a crow can perch on a high-voltage wire without risk, because no current flows through its body. However, even in the absence of lightning, there is some *ionization* in the air caused by cosmic rays.

The earth's surface—whether soil, rock, or ocean— conducts electricity. At an altitude of 30 to 220 miles above the earth there is that highly conductive region known as the ionosphere. Hence the earth and its atmosphere may be thought of as two conductive spherical surfaces separated by air, which is nominally a dielectric or insulator. The natural ionization in air is sufficient to cause extremely small currents—measurable only with the most sensitive of instruments—to flow between these conducting surfaces. The ground has a surplus of electrons and it is these that constantly leak into the atmosphere from leaves on trees, blades of grass, and other objects.

As small as these leakage currents are, the total electron flow from the entire earth's surface is huge, such that physicists estimate that the earth could be "discharged" in an hour—just as leaving a car's headlights on overnight will discharge the battery. The average global air-earth current is 1,000 to 1,500 amperes; since the potential difference between the atmosphere and the earth's surface is 300 kilovolts on average, by Ohm's law the equivalent resistance of the atmosphere is 200 to 300 ohms.[13] It is these thousands of thunderstorms occurring at any one time—all over the planet—that recharge the earth. Thus the slow, minute transfer of electrons to the atmosphere is compensated for by a series of violent lightning strikes that return, on average, one hundred septillion (one followed by 26 zeroes) times more electrons in an instant than is lost by one of the small leakage currents.

As an example of one of those violent lightning strikes, in May 2007 a sudden thunderstorm came up in West Bengal state of India. Five elephants—three adults and two calves— were found dead in a sitting position. An autopsy confirmed that they had been killed by lightning.[14]

What would happen without lightning to recharge the earth? No one knows for certain. Probably many of the technologies we take for granted—radio communication, among others—would be affected. Navigations systems that depend on the earth's magnetic field might shift.

Air is a good insulator, as reflected by the fact that high-voltage electric distribution lines are placed up in the air and spaced apart to avoid short circuits. But air is not a perfect insulator. As the potential difference between two conductors is gradually increased, at some point the resistance of the air breaks down and an electric current can flow. This point is referred to as the *dielectric strength,* measured in volts per meter. Breakdown occurs because the *electric field* that is created between conductors accelerates electrons and causes a current to flow when the electric field is sufficiently intense. The ordinary spark plug in an automobile engine is an example; when the potential of the car battery is increased by the ignition system to around 8,000 volts (8 kilovolts), the fuel-air mixture in the gap between the spark plug electrodes breaks down and current flows. At sea level in air at standard temperature and pressure it takes a potential of 30,000 to 70,000 volts to jump a gap of 1 inch.[15] When this happens, the air is said to be *ionized.* Once an arc is struck, about 50 volts per inch is all that is needed to maintain the arc. A good example or illustration of this is an arc welder, where once the arc is struck only 40 volts can maintain an arc for a distance of about 1 inch. Of course, this is due to the lower resistance of the ionized path of the arc compared to dry air. The potential required to cause breakdown in air depends on distance, temperature, and pressure; since the distance in clouds is on the order of miles, very high voltages are required. At high altitudes, where the air pressure is less and the temperature below freezing, breakdown occurs at field strengths that are only 25 percent to 50 percent of the sea level value, whereas in the hot, pressurized environment of a car engine, the breakdown voltage is higher. As negative charge accumulates in the lower sections and the top of the thundercloud becomes positively charged, the potential difference between parts of the cloud becomes dramatically different—building to millions of volts or more, setting the stage for a lightning discharge.

The charge buildup in clouds is on the order of 10 to 100 *Coulombs*—named after Charles Augustin Coulomb (1736–1806), a French physicist who conducted early studies on electricity. An enormous number of electrons—six million trillion, or six followed by 18 zeros—is needed to make one coulomb of charge. In effect, this buildup of charge represents the conversion of the mechanical energy of the cloud movement—millions of kilograms of air being violently tumbled about—into electrical energy. When the charge differential is sufficiently high, air in the cloud ionizes, and a large electric current flows—either to another part of the cloud or to the ground below—traveling at a speed of 360,000 miles per hour or more. Electric current flow is measured in *Amperes:* One ampere is the flow of one coulomb of charge per second. Andre-Marie Ampere (1775-1836) performed pioneering work in the field of electromagnetics, including developing the concept of an electric current and methods for measuring current.

When a nonconducting gas is ionized, it will conduct an electric current. Television is a familiar application; ionization in the picture tube enables a beam of electrons, flashing across a screen of phosphors, to create the television picture. Cosmic rays from outer space entering the atmosphere create a small amount of ionization. Besides being radioactive themselves, collisions between cosmic rays and air molecules also generate radiation. (The higher levels of radiation experienced in orbiting satellites, the space shuttle, rockets, and space flight—and even in commercial airliners flying at 30,000 feet—is due to cosmic radiation.)

For the moment, let us suppose that cosmic rays interact with air molecules to eject electrons. If these electrons are very energetic, they can collide with other air molecules, producing still more electrons, and creating a chain reaction— called an *avalanche* of electrons. These electrons could produce an ionized path enabling the high potential existing between different parts of a cloud to break down the intervening air and allow an electric current to flow. Another feature of such electron/molecule collisions is that X-rays are emitted. Guess what! Recently, Professor J. R. Dwyer and other researchers have discovered that lightning strikes are accompanied by bursts of X-rays. Also at higher levels in the atmosphere, gamma rays have been detected—further evidence of collisions between high-energy electrons and air molecules.

There is still scientific debate and uncertainty concerning exactly how clouds are ionized. For our purposes, it is sufficient to recognize that somehow ionization occurs.

Once an ionized path has been created, the resistance of air along the path breaks down and a lightning flash can occur. The most common occurrence is that breakdown takes place in one part of a cloud and lightning flashes to another section of the cloud that carries an opposite charge. The flash might illuminate the cloud for up to 500 milliseconds. Based on data obtained with instrumented aircraft, a typical cloud flash has a current of several thousand amperes. On rare occasions it travels outside the cloud and terminates in the surrounding air. About two-thirds of all lightning strikes are cloud flashes and never reach the earth. However, it is the remaining one-third—the ground flashes—that most concern us.

The Ground Flash

Scientists have identified four types of lightning discharges to the ground. (Figures 7A-7D.) The most common—accounting for around 90 percent of strikes involving the ground—is that described above when the bottom of the cloud is charged negatively and the lightning strike delivers tens of coulombs of electrons to the ground. The next most common strike delivers positive charge to the ground; this accounts for around 10 percent of the lightning strikes. The remaining two other types are ground-to-cloud, delivering either positive or negative charges upwards to a cloud bearing the opposite charge. Upwardly directed discharges are not common and occur from the tops of tall buildings or mountains.

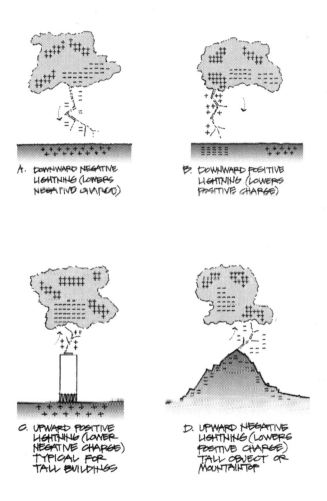

Figure 7: Various Types of Cloud-to-Ground Flashes

Around 1900, Sir Charles V. Boys invented a camera featuring two counter-rotating lenses that turned at high speed.

Although it took several decades to perfect this camera, Boys finally succeeded in taking the first photograph that revealed the true nature of a lightning flash.[16] An improvement on the Boys' camera is the *streak* camera, which moves the film at high speed behind a fixed lens. Researchers using these cameras were able to view the initial phase of a lightning strike. The photographs show that an initial discharge shoots out from the bottom of the cloud. The initial breakdown is thought to be a discharge between the negatively charged center region and the positively charged bottom region of the cloud. This discharge travels a short distance, pauses, branches to another direction, pauses, changes direction, and continues downward in a series of steps, each about 150 feet long. This jagged flash, shown in Figure 8, is called a *stepped leader*.

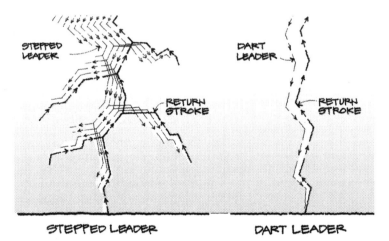

Figure 8: The Stepped Leader, Dart Leader, and Return Stroke

The stepped leader current is typically between 100 and 1,000 amperes, with the voltage at its tip (with respect to ground) about 10 million volts. As the stepped leader approaches the positively charged earth it follows a path of least resistance to a point where there is a strong electric field—possibly a tree or other tall object—such that a rising current or upward leader can occur. When the stepped leader descending from above connects with an upward leader from the ground, a circuit is completed between the stepped leader and the ground. This is called the *attachment process*—and the stage is set for a *return stroke.*

The stepped leader creates a low resistance ionized path—the resulting channel has excellent electrical conductivity—about equal to carbon![17] When the stepped leader is "connected" to the earth by the attachment process, it is analogous to a short circuit between earth and cloud—you could think of the ionized path created by the stepped leader as a copper cable leading to the heavens. The return stroke carries charge upward along this path to neutralize the charge in the cloud.

With the stepped leader, the amount of charge transferred is small. The return stroke, however, carries a greater amount of charge—currents average 30,000 amperes but could be as great as 100,000 amperes or more. To avoid confusion, remember that in accordance with the convention first established by Benjamin Franklin, an electric current flows in the opposite direction as electrons flow. Thus if electrons (negative charge) flow from cloud to ground, the current is said to flow in the opposite direction. The wave of light moves upwards as does the current front, hence the term "return stroke."

From photographic studies scientists have determined that the luminous diameter of the return stroke channel is around 2 to 4 inches while the portion carrying electrical current is about one-half inch in diameter. Professor Uman determined that the conductivity of the channel is about 18,000 siemens per meter.[18] The high current in this confined volume heats the air to temperatures in the range of 25 to 30,000°K, producing the luminous flash we know as lightning. At the same instant, the hot air around the lightning channel expands outward, creating a shock wave that produces the explosive noise we know as thunder.

If the return stroke fully discharges the cloud, there may be just a single flash. In the typical case there are three or four return strokes, but there can be as many as 25 or more. Following the first return stroke, the charge distribution in the cloud will be somewhat altered. It takes a few milliseconds, but eventually a second discharge leaves the cloud. Since there is a residual ionized path, this new leader does not undergo the stepping process, but darts directly to the earth. For this reason, it is called a *dart leader*.

As the dart leader approaches earth, there is a new attachment process (often at a different location), followed by a second return stroke. The next return stroke current rises to 10,000 to 15,000 amperes. This process will repeat three or four times. Following the last return stroke a continuous current of 10 to 100 amperes may flow for as long as one-tenth of a minute.

While the power generated in a typical lightning flash is tremendous—equal to the electrical output of ten or more 1,000-megawatt nuclear power plants—this power is produced for such a short duration that the total energy released is only a few hundred to a few thousand kilowatt-hours. This is about the same amount of energy that would be released by burning one barrel of crude oil.[19] Lightning energy is radiated as light, radiofrequency power, thunder, and heat deposited in the atmosphere and earth. Due to the extremely short duration of this high-energy pulse, there is no apparent method whereby lightning energy could be captured or stored to perform useful work.

Sheets, Ribbons, Beads, and Balls
Occasionally, one reads or hears reference made to other types of lightning. So-called sheet lightning is actually an intracloud or cloud-to-cloud discharge. The flash is partially veiled by the cloud and gives the appearance that it is very broad, but in

reality it is just that the flash lit up a large area of the cloud. This is sometimes called heat or dry lightning because it is observed in locations where there is no rain. This is because it is being seen at a distance and the rain is falling somewhere else.

Sometimes photographs reveal a wide lightning channel that resembles a luminous ribbon. It occurs when there are multiple return strokes and strong winds. The wind moves the charged cloud a short distance between strokes so to the eye (or through a camera lens) the lightning channel appears to broaden. High speed photography reveals that ribbon lightning consists of multiple parallel strokes that are close together.

Bead lightning has been reported to resemble a string of luminous beads connected by a luminous strand. Usually bead lightning is seen only in heavy rain. It is thought that this phenomenon is actually ordinary lightning but that parts of the flash are obscured. Consider a jagged, zigzag flash with a vertical segment that "zigs" downward at a slant (the eye could perceive this as a long "bead") followed by the next segment that "zags" horizontally toward or away from the observer. Looking end-on at this segment, the observer might see nothing—or only a faint luminosity—until the next zig occurs. Another theory postulates that rain might mask portions of the lightning channel.

Ball lightning is an unusual lightning phenomenon about which entire books have been written, but as yet there is no good physical explanation. There have even been international conferences dedicated solely to the topic of ball lightning, but it still remains pretty much of a mystery. The earliest attempts at studying and reporting ball lightning date to the early 1800s and even to ancient times. According to thousands of eyewitness accounts ball lightning takes the form of luminous balls ranging from 4 to as much as 12 inches in diameter—that move through the air and exist for periods of seconds to perhaps as long as a minute. They usually appear near the ground during a thunderstorm and are white, yellow, red, orange, or and occasionally blue in color. The balls travel horizontally at a few yards per second. Most observations occur outdoors, but a number of sightings have taken place from inside buildings or even aircraft. They have been observed to pass through doors and windows, fly into houses, start fires, hit a tea kettle and boil water, injure people, and even fly up chimneys. Sometimes a hissing sound is associated with them. At the end of their brief life, the balls collapse and silently disappear, although in a number of cases they decay explosively with a loud noise.[20]

There are many ball lightning incidents in the literature. A typical example is what happened to a group of young people who took refuge in a house during a sudden storm in Ural'sk, western Kazakhstan, in May 1901. Following a loud blast of thunder, a bright ball of fire descended toward the door of the house, entered the room, and touched on the head of a 17-year-old girl seated at the threshold. She bowed down at once; meanwhile the fireball fell to the floor, passed through the room where others were present, and then continued into an adjoining room occupied by the owner of the house. It touched and singed his boots, went through a wall into an adjoining room, smashed the stove, and finally exited through a broken window.

The girl at the doorway, who had not moved during the incident, appeared to be asleep but was found to be dead; there were burn marks on the nape of her neck, back, and one hand. One of her shoes had been torn off, and there was a hole in one of her stockings. The other witnesses survived.[21]

More recently, in the summer of 1974, Randi Boyd was in her backyard in Colorado Springs, Colorado, watering strawberries in her garden while her two young daughters and the family dog played nearby. Lightning apparently hit a power pole a half a block away, then jumped to a chain link fence that went along one side of the yard. Boyd was only aware of a simultaneous flash and a deafening crash of thunder—so intense, she said, that there are no words to describe it. She found herself knocked to the ground, actually rolling up the hill backwards, the water hose chasing her, coiling upwards like a green snake spouting water. Her daughters later said that a ball of lightning hit the hose. In a second, Boyd recovered enough to jump to her feet and run to the front yard, where neighbors had already gathered due to the loud noise and nearness of the strike. Then she remembered her two daughters, abandoned on the patio. Fortunately, they were not injured.

In the aftermath of the strike, the entire left side of Boyd's body went numb for about 20 minutes. The fillings in her teeth became sensitive; her teeth and jaws ached, along with numbness of the left side of her face. Over time she experienced fatigue, aches, stiffness, headaches—classic symptoms of a lightning strike, although doctors considered her a hypochondriac because there were no outward physical symptoms. Thanks to an encounter with other lightning strike survivors through the *Lightning Strike and Electrical Shock Survivors International* organization, Boyd finally learned that her symptoms were typical and she was able to reach closure on the root cause of her health problems and get on with her life.[22]

Even more interesting are the accounts of ball lightning entering the cockpit of airplanes through the windshield, flying past the pilot, flying out of the cockpit, passing down the aisle, and exiting the rear of the aircraft. These cases are unique because the initial observation by pilots or navigators should be reliable by virtue of the training they have received; in addition, there are multiple witnesses (such as passengers and flight attendants) who saw the luminous ball pass through the cabin and exit the rear of the aircraft. No injuries resulted and the planes continued their flights. At least eight such incidents have been reported, the earliest in 1938. What is striking about these incidents is how similar the descriptions are; there is a remarkable degree of consistency despite the fact that they took place in different countries and involved different types of aircraft.[23]

To date no satisfactory explanation of what causes ball lightning has been made, and no theory has been found that would explain its behavior.

Saint Elmo's Fire

Some reports of ball lightning have been found instead to be Saint Elmo's fire, and some are cases where real lightning occurred. Saint Elmo's fire is not actually lightning, but a corona discharge. A corona arises when the electric field is strong enough to ionize air but not strong enough to cause a spark. While ball lightning can move, Saint Elmo's fire remains attached to its point of origin. When early mariners saw this discharge near the top of their masts (usually during storms) it seemed to them to be a heavenly glow protecting their vessels. (Saint Pedro Gonzalez, later Saint Elmo, was the patron saint of Mediterranean sailors.) There are early references to St. Elmo's fire in the literature, going back to the earliest days of sailing ships. When Magellan sailed south from the Canary Islands on his historic voyage of discovery, his fleet of five vessels encountered storms that persisted for weeks. Morale plummeted, until one day several hissing, luminous balls appeared near mast-top on Magellan's flagship *Trinidad*. So strong was the sailors' belief that they gave praise to this "holy light," for it convinced them that God had blessed Magellan and was watching over him.[24]

New Insights into Lightning Formation

The exact process by which stepped leaders are formed is still a puzzle to scientists. One theory is that at each step the leader stalls, but nearby a high electric field creates a new ionized channel that attaches to the old leader and permits it to take the next step. As mentioned earlier, new research by Professor J. R. Dwyer at the Florida Institute of Technology has shown that bursts of X-rays accompany each of the discrete steps taken by the stepped leader.[25] This discovery is significant since radiation can be produced only if the electrons—and thus the electric fields in the stepped leader—are much more energetic than previously believed. Even more interesting are satellite and ground measurements that show that high-energy gamma rays—ten times the X-ray energy—may be emitted during thunderstorms, from where is not known.

These new discoveries that lightning flashes are accompanied by bursts of radiation—low-energy X-ray pulses at low elevations and high-energy gamma rays at high elevations—have provided new insights into the mechanisms of lightning formation and have also prompted new speculation about the cause of lightning. Since much of the basic research is being done by Dr. Martin Uman and his colleagues at Camp Blanding Florida, I decided that I had better pay Professor Uman another visit and get his opinion on these new developments.

A visit to Martin Uman's home in northwest Florida is always interesting. This meeting was conducted as we drifted down the Santa Fe River in kayaks. The weather was perfect, no lightning threatened, no alligators appeared, and we were able to enjoy the spectacular scenery, including shy turtles that slipped off rocks into the stream and blue herons that stood motionless as we floated past.

Professor J. R. Dwyer is a colleague of Uman's and the principal investigator for the radiation measurements. During my first visit to Camp Blanding, I saw Dwyer's radiation detectors—carefully shielded against electronic noise in heavy aluminum boxes. These detectors have measured X-rays during triggered lightning and also during natural lightning strikes.

This gave Dwyer and his colleagues an idea. Under certain conditions a phenomenon known as runaway break-down can occur. This phenomenon has been observed in solids and semiconductors and results when a strong electric field causes an avalanche of electrons to be emitted. They wondered if this could be happening in the cloud. Could there be an avalanche of runaway electrons with sufficiently high energy to punch through a highly charged cloud? Moreover, as electrons traverse the initial ionized path used by the stepped leader, could they possibly pile up or accumulate at the tip of the leader, initiating the next step, undergoing further acceleration, and gaining enough energy to give rise to the bursts of radiation seen by Dwyer and his associates?

It is a well-known law of physics that high energy electrons interacting with matter (in this case the oxygen and nitrogen molecules in air) will produce X-rays. (This is also how an X-ray machine works, although in that application the electrons interact with a metal target.) Part of the energy of the electron is converted into X-rays. The loss of energy causes the electron to slow down, so the X-ray radiation is referred to by the German name *bremsstrahlung*—which literally means "braking or slowing down" radiation. For runaway breakdown, the catch is that upon hitting a molecule, the electrons must have enough energy after the interaction to knock out another electron. Previously it was thought that the electric fields in air—even during a highly charged lightning storm—were not intense enough to accelerate electrons to the point at which an avalanche would occur. Yet, indisputably, bursts of X-rays were being detected.

While more work remains to be done, the potential implications of this discovery are significant. It may ultimately shed considerable light on the actual mechanism of lightning formation, or it might provide a means for improved lightning warning systems, since the X-ray bursts are detected before the lightning return stroke occurs.

Long-Range Effects of Lightning
Anyone who happens to be listening to a radio during a lightning storm has likely heard a crackle and hiss when lightning flashed. I'm a licensed radio amateur and at my home have HF and VHF transmitters and receivers. Using HF,

I've contacted other radio amateurs in New Zealand, Europe, South America, and throughout the United States. Lightning-produced electrical noise is one of the interfering signals that can disrupt communications over long distances. In addition, the long-range propagation of lightning provides a tool with which to study properties of the Earth's atmosphere.

As noted in the description of the North American Lightning Detection Network in Chapter 1, radio-frequency signals from lightning are used to locate the point of impact of the strike. In the near distance region—say, 30 miles—the dominant radio-frequency signals produced by lightning are in the range of 5 to 10 kilohertz.[26] Signals are also emitted at higher frequencies, but with decreasing amplitudes in the HF band at 3 to 30 megahertz. The electronic signals received by the detection stations are filtered to ensure that only lightning is being detected and signals from several stations are triangulated to find the actual location of the strike. At distances of a few hundred miles or less, radio signals from lightning travel in much the same manner as other high-frequency signals—by means of a *ground wave* or by a direct line-of-sight *sky wave*.

The ground wave induces charges in the earth's surface as it propagates along the surface. The earth, acting as a leaky capacitor, absorbs some energy and attenuates the ground wave; the amount of attenuation depends on the soil conductivity and dielectric constant. In other words, as the radio wave travels along the earth's surface, part of its energy leaks into the soil. Low-frequency components travel farther—perhaps as far as 600 miles—while high-frequency ground waves lose energy more quickly and might travel only 60 miles. The ground wave can also be reflected from the earth's surface.[27]

In addition to these signals, lightning produces very-low-frequency signals—in the so-called extremely low-frequency and very-low-frequency bands (denoted as ELF and

VLF bands) as well as signals in the high-frequency and very high-frequency (HF and VHF) bands.

The latter signals—HF and VHF—are familiar to us as the frequencies used by radio broadcasts, shortwave radio, and television stations. Propagation in the HF frequency bands occurs when a signal is sent from a transmitter at location "A" through the atmosphere to the level of the ionosphere. The signal is reflected back to earth by the ionosphere, reaching location "B" 300 to 600 miles distant. It is also possible to have two or more "hops" in the transmission path—that is, the signal skips from the ground at location "B" back to the ionosphere and then reaches station "C" that might be halfway around the world. How does this occur?

Ionization of the ionosphere is caused by the absorption of energy from the sun—which creates some free electrons and positive and negative ions—and by such other events as thunderstorms, meteors, and cosmic rays. The ionized region extends between 30 and 220 miles above the surface of the earth and is divided into several distinct regions, named for the levels where the electron density is at a maximum. The lowest region, called the D layer, lies between 30 and 55 miles. It exists during the day and disappears at night. Above that, one finds the E layer with a height relatively constant at around 68 miles and the F1 layer at an elevation of 135 miles. Above the F1 layer is the F2 layer with typical height in a range of 155 to 220 miles. At night the F1 and F2 layers coalesce to form a single night time F2 layer as illustrated in Figure 9.[28]

Important descriptors of the ionosphere are its virtual height and critical frequency, the latter being the highest frequency that is returned by a layer. (Frequencies higher than the critical frequency are not reflected back to earth but continue out into space.) Critical frequencies follow a diurnal cycle, being maximum at noon, tapering off at other times, and decreasing at night. The critical frequencies are also affected by sunspot activity, increasing in years where there is more sunspot activity. This fact suggests that increased solar activity may lead to increased lightning.

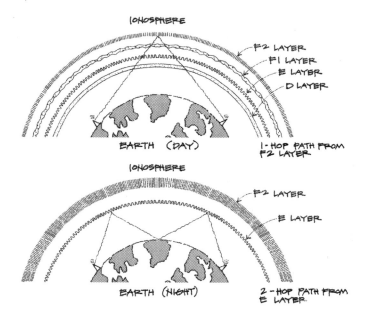

Figure 9: Sketch of Atmosphere Showing Ionized Regions and Hop Transmission Paths

Whistlers and Sferics
Of special interest are the ELF and VLF modes of lightning propagation. The majority of energy in the VLF band comes from radiation due to lightning and peaks near 10 kilohertz.[29] These low-frequency signals travel in a different mode than the HF signals described above. While communications engineers and radio astronomers differentiate between many different types of such signals, I'll mention only two general types here as being of interest in relationship to lightning.[30]

- Whistlers
- Atmospherics, usually called by a shorthand name of *sferics*

My intimate acquaintance with whistlers stems from my undergraduate days at Stanford University. Barely able to make ends meet on an engineering scholarship, I sought out a series of part-time jobs. One was as a student assistant to Professor R. A. Helliwell in the electrical engineering department. Helliwell was engaged in a pioneering study of whistlers at that time and my task was to take strip chart records of whistlers and compile data on their characteristics. The tools used to perform this work in the late 1950s were a hand-cranked Marchant calculator and a ruler. I spent hours in a tiny attic garret in the old physics building performing this work for a few dollars per hour.[31]

Whistlers get their name from the earliest researchers who heard strange signals on the radio receivers. The sound resembles a whistle, starting out at a high frequency and then rapidly decreasing in tone and disappearing. The sound persists for about a second. (Imagine the sound of a bomb falling in an old World War II movie and you get the idea.)

Whistlers are signals in the ELF and VLF bands that travel out through the ionosphere along lines in the earth's magnetic field that are called ducts and then re-enter the ionosphere at a distant point—called a conjugate point—in the opposite hemisphere, traversing a path that may be as long as 19,000 to 31,000 miles.[32]

Sferics occur in the frequency range of from a few kilohertz to a few hundred kilohertz, and can travel for a thousand miles from a lightning strike. They travel by multiple reflections between the earth's surface and the ionosphere. The spherical annulus between the earth and the lower surface of the ionosphere can be considered a cavity or *waveguide* for the signals. Waveguide is the name of metal tubes used to conduct such high-frequency signals as radar. In effect, the conducting surfaces of the earth and the ionosphere function in the same manner as the metal wall of the waveguide, but on a much larger scale.

Both sferic signals and whistlers are partially attenuated by their travel through the atmosphere; some frequencies are absorbed or dissipated in the ionosphere. In addition to yielding information about lightning, these signals have been used to research the properties of the ionosphere.

Upper Atmosphere Fireworks
Commercial jet airliners typically fly at altitudes of from 30,000 feet to 40,000 feet (5.7 to 7.5 miles) —high enough to fly above the weather in many situations, but not so high as to fly above the highest thunderclouds, which can reach up to 12 miles or higher. This altitude marks the upper limit of the troposphere—that part of the earth's atmosphere that is densest and closest to the earth's surface. Above the troposphere is the stratosphere, extending upward to around 30 miles and above that the lower portions of the ionosphere are encountered at altitudes of around 56 to 62 miles.

High-flying aircraft have observed lightning flashing upward from the tops of thunderclouds, but in the early 1990s, some remarkable strangely colored discharges were first observed.

Blue jets originate from the top of thunderclouds at an altitude of around 11 to 12 miles and flash upward a distance of 10 to 12 miles higher. (Smaller flashes, called *blue starters*, have also been observed, but there seems to be no significant difference between them and blue jets.)

The blue jet is a cone-shaped luminous blue discharge that shoots vertically upward at an angle from the top of a thundercloud. It has been described as "trumpet shaped" because there is a flare-out at the end of the cone where individual streamers can be seen.[33] The phenomenon lasts for a fraction of a second and then fades away. The blue light color may be due in part to doubly ionized nitrogen and singly ionized oxygen, but the mechanism by which a blue jet is created is not yet understood.[34]

Next in the trilogy of atmospheric fireworks are *sprites*—reddish discharges that occur at altitudes of from 25 to 55 miles above large thunderstorm systems.[35] They occur primarily in conjunction with positive cloud-to-ground strikes. Sprites are transient discharges that take on a variety of characteristic shapes. They "hang" in the atmosphere as a cluster of vertical columns for a fraction of a second before fading. Some typical forms are the *Carrot Sprite*, which is characterized by a bright red upper or head region of red color with a wispy red fringe on top, and the *Angel Sprite*, which also has tendrils, but the "head" is surrounded with a glowing halo of light. Sprites typically occur at altitudes in the range of from 25 to 55 miles. Some have blue tendrils that extend below the head to as low as 25 miles above the earth's surface.

The final player in the upper atmosphere fireworks show is, of all things, an "elf." Not a dancing display of lights, as the name suggests, but rather a very brief (around $1,000^{th}$ of a second), expanding, doughnut-shaped ring of luminosity. These are actually called *elves* (an acronym for "emissions of light and VLF perturbations due to electromagnetic pulse sources.") Elves were observed from the space shuttle on a 1992 flight over a tropical ocean thunderstorm. Elves are 6 to 12 miles thick, occur at elevations of around 56 miles, and may extend across the horizon for as far as 125 to 430 miles. Given that elves occur at the lower level of the ionosphere, it is possible that transient radiation fields from lightning strikes accelerate electrons in the ionosphere, giving them sufficient energy to undergo collisions with molecules that results in the release of energy with wavelengths in the visible range.

Extraterrestrial Lightning

Given the significant differences between the atmospheres of the other planets in our solar system in comparison to that of earth, we should not discount the possibility that lightning, if it exists on other planets, takes on a different form from what we know on earth.[36] Scientists have observed luminous discharges resembling lightning on some of the planets in our solar system. The evidence comes from deep space satellites that either probed or in some cases orbited planets and relayed observations back to Earth. In addition, there is some indirect evidence, such as various types of radio emissions including whistlers. Are these displays indications of lightning?

For lightning to occur on other planets, a process for electrical charge buildup in their atmospheres is required. None of the nine planets in our solar system have atmospheres identical to that of earth, so it is possible that lightning, if it occurs, is caused by a different process entirely. The best evidence for extraterrestrial lightning comes from Jupiter. Six spacecraft have collected data from the planet as they passed by; and the Galileo spacecraft sent a probe into Jupiter's atmosphere while on its way to orbit the planet.[37]

Jupiter is thought to have a solid core (roughly 10 to 15 times the mass of the earth) that is surrounded by an extremely deep "ocean" of liquid and gaseous hydrogen and helium. Above this there appear to be layers of ammonia-water solution, water or water vapor, ammonia gas, and ammonium hydrosulfide. The total mass of Jupiter is more than 300 times heavier than the earth. The Jovian atmosphere is also characterized by winds, strong updrafts, and clouds containing water and ammonia ice crystals. Given what is known about Jupiter and its atmosphere, along with optical and radio-frequency data gathered by satellites, is highly likely that lightning occurs on Jupiter.

Venus is the planet closest to earth and therefore one of the most studied of all the planets.[38] The Venusian atmosphere is around 97 percent carbon dioxide and 3 percent nitrogen. Venus has a dense cloud cover. Optical and radio-frequency signals indicative of lightning have been recorded; a number of these have been attributed to Venusian lightning. Overall, however, the data are ambiguous, so at present the existence of lightning on Venus is still a matter of scientific debate.[39]

Of the remaining planets and moons, lightning is not likely on Mercury or Mars due to their weak atmospheres. Beyond Jupiter lie the planets Saturn, Uranus, Neptune, and Pluto. Pluto is an unknown, but Saturn (and its moons), Uranus, and Neptune are possible candidates. Bursts of radio-frequency energy have been observed on Saturn, but without any optical confirmation that they are from lightning or at least from lightning as we know it. Uranus and Neptune are believed to have atmospheres composed of hydrogen, helium and methane. The evidence for lightning on these planets is very sparse and is limited to whistlers and other radio emissions (some similar to those emanating from Saturn). Thus we cannot say with certainty that Uranus or Neptune have lightning. Future space exploration will hopefully shed more light on this question.

Earlier in this chapter, I stated that "we live in a sea of electricity." This is not quite correct; perhaps it would be more accurate to say that we live at the interface between strong and weak electric and magnetic fields. James Clerk Maxwell (1831-1879) was a Scottish physicist who conducted pioneering work in electromagnetics and the theory of gases. Maxwell's equations—four linear partial differential equations—summarized the classical properties of electrical and magnetic field intensities, magnetic induction, and electric current and charge densities. Maxwell first showed the duality of electric and magnetic fields, and from his work we note how electricity can be used to create magnetic forces and magnetic fields can in turn produce electricity, so it is perhaps more accurate to characterize the atmosphere above us as a swirling, changeable vortex of interacting electric and magnetic fields. We look up into the blue sky during the daytime, or into the black sky at night, and see none of this. Our senses are tuned to other stimuli. But other species are more aware than we; homing pigeons and migrating birds make use of the earth's magnetic field to navigate unerringly over long distances.

Thus, while we see dramatic illustrations of the power and energy present in the earth's atmosphere when its magnetic and electric fields are disturbed, we still have a long way to go before a complete understanding of these complex processes is achieved.

Finally, as interesting as the notion of extraterrestrial lightning might be, it is the lightning that falls to earth that is our most pressing concern. In the following chapter we will examine how frequent lightning strikes are, in order to better understand the societal risk posed by lightning.

3

When Lightning Strikes Twice

Can lightning strike the same place twice? Absolutely. As noted in Chapter 1, tall buildings may be struck repeatedly. Sometimes the capriciousness of lightning seems almost malicious. On August 8, 1937, crowds of people thronged the beach at Jacob Riis Park in New York. The park—not far from Breezy Point, and with Jamaica Bay on one side and the Atlantic Ocean on the other—was hot and sultry and anything but breezy that day. Suddenly lightning flashed and three people were killed. One year later—on August 7, 1938—lightning struck again at the same beach and killed three more people.[1]

How Often Does Lightning Strike?

On the basis of measurements made with weather satellites, lightning strikes about 100 times every second somewhere around the globe.[2] A rate of 100 flashes per second translates to 3.15 billion flashes per year. Given that the surface area of the earth is 197 million square miles, on average, we can expect about 16 flashes per square mile per year. Not all reach the earth; many are intracloud strikes and never reach the ground, while others occur over the oceans.

Despite the proverbial "lightning never strikes twice," in fact on average only about 15 to 25 percent of lightning flashes consist of a single stroke. In most cases there are 3 to 5 strokes in a given lightning flash, and in some cases as many as 25 strokes. Due to cloud movement in a typical thunder storm, the next strike may be a few hundred feet away or a mile or more, but it could also hit the exact same spot. Measurements in various storms show that the average distance between successive flashes ranged from 2 to 3 miles and the maximum distance was 6 to 7 miles.[3] In an area where there are frequent thunderstorms, if lightning strikes a particular tree that stands alone on the top of a hill, there is a good likelihood that the same tree will be struck again the next time there is a storm in the neighborhood, because it probably has characteristics that favor a strike.

Intracloud and Other Cloud Flashes versus Cloud-to-Ground Flashes

Lightning strikes within or between clouds occur more frequently than flashes that reach the ground. Of course, for our purposes, the important thing is the number of lightning strikes that reach the earth and represent a hazard to humans, animals, and infrastructure. A number of studies have been conducted to determine the ratio of cloud flashes to cloud-to-ground strikes. A rough average for this ratio is three cloud strikes for every cloud-to-ground strike.[4] However, measurements indicate that there is a rather broad range to this ratio. The ratio may be affected by the intensity of the thunderstorm or by the phase of the storm. There is some evidence to indicate that more ground flashes occur during the intermediate stage of the storm, when activity is most intense, compared to the early or late periods when the storm is building or dissipating.

The Effect of Height

As noted in Chapter 2, the vast majority of ground strikes lower charge to the ground. However, a small fraction of strikes are upwardly directed. Upward flashes depend on the presence of a tall object—such as a tall building or tower—that creates the proper electric field conditions to initiate the flash. Tall grounded structures (such as high-rise buildings) increase the electric field gradient near their uppermost point. Plate 6 shows lightning striking the Eiffel Tower in Paris. This historic photo is one of the earliest to capture a lightning strike. On the date this photograph was taken (June 3, 1902), the tower was 1,023 feet tall.

As a rule of thumb, objects less than 330 feet high will be struck only by downward lightning, those more than 1,640 feet in height predominantly will be struck by upward flashes, and those with heights between these two extremes will experience a mixture of upward and downward flashes.[5] In determining the effective height of a structure, the nature of the terrain must be taken into account. Thus a 200-foot-high structure on a hill with an elevation of 1,000 feet above the surrounding area would have an *effective* height greater than 200 feet (but not necessarily 1,200 feet).

Grand Teton National Park in Wyoming publishes useful information for visitors on its Web site. It describes hiking and bicycle trails, camping sites, how to behave in the presence of bears, and most importantly, the weather. Afternoon thunderstorms arise suddenly and frequently in July and August. With respect to mountaineering, risks are said to include rock falls, avalanches, extreme weather conditions, and lightning.

In July 2003, a party of 13 mountain climbers began an ascent of Grand Teton peak.[6] The group had spent the night in tents pitched on a rocky ledge at 10,800 feet, and faced a climb of 3,000 feet to reach the summit. The last third of the climb was a difficult one. The climbers had to ascend a shear wall known as Friction Pitch—using steel anchors driven in the rock—and from there make the final push to the peak. All of the climbers wore harnesses and were roped together in groups, one person belaying the group for this part of the ascent.

At dawn the weather was perfect and the four groups of climbers made good progress up to a flat ridge at 12,000 feet known as Wall Street. As they climbed, they enjoyed the spectacular view of the Tetons and, far below them, scattered lakes. At this point the climbers were delayed by another group preparing to make the ascent ahead of them. Minutes stretched into hours as they waited for the trail to clear. Meanwhile, the weather began to shift ominously. It was summer and as the day wore on hot air from the stifling heat in the valleys below rose, producing wispy white clouds that piled into larger clouds as they waited.

They did not approach Friction Pitch until 2:30. By now dark thunder clouds ranged above them and rain started to fall. The leaders decided to abandon the attempt to reach the summit. Instead, they would climb Friction Pitch, and from the top of it they would work their way around to a ledge where they could rappel back down about 150 feet to an easier route back, and be off the mountain to safety in an hour or two at most. As the group reached the top of Friction Pitch, one of the leaders made his way around the side to prepare for the descent. At this moment he heard a loud humming or buzzing sound; next there was a horrific crash and flash as lightning struck the area where most of the team clung to a narrow shelf of stone above the straight drop-off they had just ascended. Lightning had made a direct strike on Erica Summers and injured her husband Clinton Summers who had been seated nearby. Erica's clothes were shredded, her lips and throat blackened, her hair matted with blood, her ears leaking fluid, and she had no pulse. Clinton was conscious but seriously injured; his pants were shredded and he had a bad burn on his leg. Despite his own injuries, Clinton and another member of the party frantically applied CPR to Erica.

Another climber drifted in and out of consciousness— unable to speak or move his left arm or left leg, his back in agony. During a moment of consciousness, he suddenly realized that he was no longer with the group, but was swinging in midair over the vast chasm of the mountain, secured only by his harness and a slender strand of rope attached to the rock face above him. Three other climbers had been jarred off the mountain and had rolled and tumbled down the mountainside to land on rocky ledges, injured, but miraculously still alive.

The climb leaders had come prepared with radios and were able to summon help. Given the poor weather conditions, the helicopter was unable to reach the victims for several hours. Finally there was a break in the weather and at 6:00 P.M. the helicopter was able to lower a ranger to assist. The hanging climber was placed in a litter and evacuated. He spent 43 days in a hospital recovering from burns, kidney damage, and other injuries. Those who fell suffered broken bones, contusions, and burns. A total of 7 of the 13 climbers were injured; Erica was the only fatality. Fortunately, this was an occasion when lightning did not strike twice; had it done so, the death toll could have been much greater.

Other climbers have not been so fortunate. A party of 41 students and 5 teachers was returning from a mountain climbing trip in the Japanese Alps when they were caught in a sudden thunderstorm. As they hiked close-ranked in single file over a narrow ridge, lightning struck roughly in the center of the line as the hikers descended from the top of the ridge. Eleven boys died from the lightning strike and 14 were injured—most suffering burns—but 4 of them also tumbled off the ridge and suffered other injuries. There were 19 hikers at the end of the file, ascending a slope to the peak. On the down hill side was a middle group of 26 hikers, spaced over a distance of about 87 feet, or roughly 3 feet apart (some were closer together). At the front end of the line ascending another rise—were 11 more. What is remarkable is that the entire middle group was affected by the strike. Considering the cluster of six fatalities, it seems that the initial strike occurred at the beginning of the middle group (near the crest). Whether or not there was more than one strike is not known. But there were three additional fatalities in the center of the middle group, and at the very end—say, 70 feet away—one more fatality occurred. In between, four hikers were knocked off the ridge. In retrospect it seems likely that the fatalities and injuries resulted from lightning side-flashing (jumping) from one individual to another where they were close together, and possibly from a step voltage to those walking down the ridge as the lightning current coursed through the ground toward them.[7]

Global Patterns

There are fewer lightning flashes over the ocean—by as much as a factor of ten—when compared with the land-based thunderstorms. This is thought to be due to the fact that storms over oceans have weaker updrafts than the minimum required for the graupel-ice mechanism of cloud electrification.[8]

Satellites have made possible some very interesting lightning measurements. When data collected over the period of an entire year are plotted against a map of the world, they show the continents blanketed with lightning flashes and relatively fewer flashes over the oceans. If the same data are replotted using only the northern hemisphere summer months of June, July, and August, you can see that the bulk of the lightning strikes occur in the northern hemisphere north of the equator up to approximately 40° north latitude. Conversely, when the data for the southern hemisphere summer (December, January, and February) are plotted, you can see considerable lightning activity south of the equator down to 40° south latitude, and only a sprinkling of data in the northern hemisphere.[9] If the total number of lightning strikes is determined, for any given year the northern hemisphere summer has about 40 percent more strikes than the southern hemisphere summer. This could be due to a northerly shift of the intertropical convergence zone (a boundary near the equator where warm air rises as part of the pattern of global atmospheric circulation), which rather than lying along the equator actually is north of the equator. Because of the lower temperatures in Antarctica, the northern hemisphere on average has warmer air and water than the southern hemisphere. The overall incidence of lightning in a given region appears to be somewhat sensitive to global surface temperatures.

Satellite measurements now show that two out of three lightning flashes occur in tropical regions worldwide.[10] (Strictly defined, the *tropics* are the regions that lie between 23 degrees 26 minutes north and south latitudes. (As will be noted later, for the purposes of this book I included the region from 30 degrees south of the equator to 30 degrees north of the equator.) Unlike higher latitudes, there are regions in the tropics where thunderstorms are a daily occurrence. This activity poses a significant risk for the nearly two-thirds of the world population living in this region, as will be noted later in this chapter. Lightning is virtually nonexistent in the Arctic and Antarctic regions beyond 60° north or south latitude.

Some scientists are predicting that global warming will increase the number of lightning strikes we experience. Several studies have been made by various scientists, whose predictions range from an increase of 5 percent to as much as 40 percent more lightning strikes per degree Celsius of increase in air temperature. The predictions for global warming are that it might increase the temperature of the atmosphere by 2.7 to as much as 8 degrees Fahrenheit (1.5 to 4.5° Celsius) by the middle of the 21st century. If this were to occur, and if the predictions regarding the increase in lightning activity are accurate, we could see anywhere from a 25 percent to 200 percent increase in lightning activity.[11]

Lightning in Hurricanes and Other Severe Storms[12]
Researchers have determined that the frequency of lightning flashes increases with storm severity. Severe storms—that is, those characterized by large sized hail, strong winds, and the occurrence of tornadoes—are accompanied by more frequent lightning flashes than are found in milder storms. Another interesting comparison is that the frequency of lightning flashes increases with the heights of thunderclouds. The number of flashes per minute could be 10 to 100 times greater for clouds that are 6 to 12 miles high, as opposed to those that are around 5 miles high.

Hurricanes consist of a central eye, an eye wall, and outer cyclonic regions of intense wind and rainfall. Lightning occurs to some extent in the eye wall—with very little in the intermediate region of 25 to 60 miles from the center—and heavy lightning flashes occur in the outer rain bands or areas with intense rainfall.

In 1993, one of the worst blizzards in recent history struck the southeastern and eastern United States. In addition to setting records for snowfall and creating havoc over several days as it moved from Texas through the Southeast and East and up to Canada, the storm produced nearly 60,000 cloud-to-ground lightning flashes. This cold season storm produced more than 5,000 flashes in a single hour at its peak!

It was not a blizzard—just a slight drizzle—on Saturday, July 17, 2005. Up to this point it had been a warm, pleasant day for the more than 100 relatives who had gathered to attend a family reunion on a farm about 70 miles north of Pittsburgh, Pennsylvania. The rain was only an inconvenience, coming as it did in the midst of a talent show put on by family members. People gathered under trees on the property to avoid the rain. Then lightning struck.

A pine tree was hit and took the brunt of the blow—no one died. But 30 people were injured—some suffering minor injuries, some knocked to the ground, some burned. David Rogan, an 11-year-old boy standing next to the tree, sustained the gravest injuries. He was knocked unconscious and probably saved by relatives who performed CPR on him until paramedics arrived and he was taken to the hospital in critical condition. The other injured were also taken to local hospitals. One moment a happy gathering—everyone enjoying themselves—the next moment, chaos, people on the ground, some stunned, some praying, others struggling to their feet to help the injured. It was a reunion no one will ever forget.[13]

In the sequel—probably the best part of the story— David was released from the hospital after 20 days, many of them spent in a coma. His next challenge was rehabilitation in

Pittsburgh's Children's Institute, a center for pediatric rehabilitation. On September 23—more than 2 months after the strike—he was released from the Institute. Back in school, his was a story of a summer adventure that none of his classmates will be able to equal.

Thunderstorm Days

Historically, *thunderstorm days* is the measure used to compare lightning activity from region to region. Weather offices throughout the world have traditionally kept track of thunderstorm days. In some cases records may go back for a hundred years or more. The number of thunderstorm days per year varies from zero in the Arctic and Antarctic regions to as many as 150 to 200 thunderstorm days per year in north Brazil and central Africa. Within the United States, the data range from an average of 5 annual thunderstorm days along the West Coast to around 130 thunderstorm days per year in north-central Florida, the highest exposure.

Maps showing the frequency of thunderstorms (called "thunderstorm day maps") have been compiled for the world, the United States, and other countries where lightning is a significant hazard. Figure 10 is an example of a thunderstorm day map for the United States.

A thunderstorm day is defined as a day in which thunder is heard. This measure has the advantage of simplicity. However, it also has obvious limitations. There is no way of determining whether the observers heard thunder a single time during the day, or whether there were a hundred occurrences of thunder. In addition, given that thunder is generally not audible over a distance much greater than 15 miles, observers at a given location will be able to record only a fraction of the events occurring nearby. Despite these limitations, researchers have attempted to correlate the frequency of lightning flashes with thunderstorm data by using

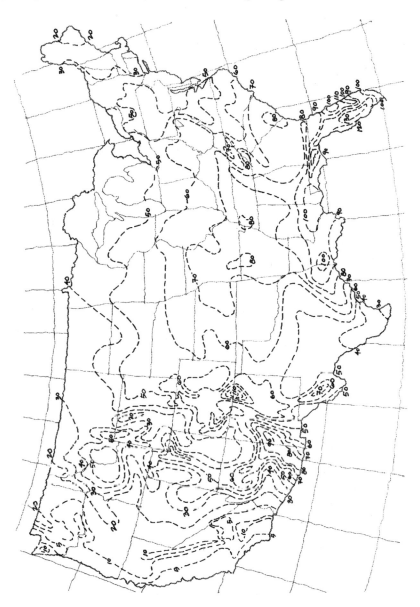

Figure 10: Thunderstorm Day Map of the United States
(Numbers show thunderstorm days per year)

specially instrumented sites where flash frequency can be measured. The results are at best approximate, but indicate that you would expect about one flash per square mile for an area that experiences 28 thunderstorm days per year.[14]

Thunderstorm Hours

Although the thunderstorm day approach has the appeal of simplicity, it must be emphasized that it is very approximate for the reasons cited above. A more useful parameter is defined as a *thunderstorm hour*, or the number of hours per year that thunder is heard at a given location. The thunderstorm hour avoids some of the difficulties of the thunderstorm day measure in that it keeps track of the approximate time of thunderstorm activity—that activity being closely related to the actual production of lightning strikes. Even so, thunderstorm hours are subject to some interpretation by the observer as well. Normal practice is to consider that thunderstorm activity ceases around 15 minutes after the last thunder is heard. The observer is faced with the question of how to handle time records if another burst of thunder is heard near the end of this period of time. Does this mark the start of a new recording period, or should it be added to the end of the previous recording period?

Researchers have attempted to correlate lightning flash density with thunderstorm hours, as was the case with lightning flash density and thunderstorm days. There is a broad range in the data, but typically you might see 10 to 13 ground flashes per square mile per year in a region having 100 thunder hours per year.[15]

Ground Flash Measurements and Data

By far the most useful information is the actual ground flash density, or information concerning the actual frequency of lightning striking the ground. This requires specialized instrumentation, either lightning flash counters, or lightning detection systems such as the North American Lightning Detection

Network described in Chapter 1. The lightning flash counter is an electronic device that detects radio frequency energy pulses produced by lightning and determines the number of lightning events in a given area. These instruments detect both cloud and ground strikes, and therefore a correction factor is applied to eliminate the cloud discharges. Intracloud flashes are more frequent and sometimes produce spectacular effects. On occasion they spread across the sky creating a network known as a *spider flash* as shown in Plate 7.

Another correction must be applied to properly register near and far and small and large events. Lightning detection networks eliminate some of these problems, but still must adjust the data to correct for the occurrence of cloud flashes. Typical ground flash incidence rates are shown in Table 1. The effective range of a lightning flash counter is around 10 to 15 miles.[16]

Table 1: Typical Ground Flash Incidence Rates

Location	Ground Flashes per Square Mile per Year[17]
• Scandinavia (Norway, Sweden, Finland)	0.5 – 7.8
• Australia	3.1 – 25
• South Africa	0.26 – 31
• Canada	4.1-6.2
• United States	6.7-8
• Florida	18-36+
• Gulf Coast (SE U.S.)	21-31
• Rocky Mountains U.S.	2.6-10
• U.S. Pacific Coast	0.26

Today the North American Lightning Detection Network monitors lightning strikes in the United States and Canada. A number of other countries have similar systems. On the basis of the data being acquired by this system, we know that lightning hits the ground in the United States 25-30 million times per year.[18] The incidence of lightning can vary widely due to topography and local microclimates. In Florida, the typical range is from 18 to 36 flashes per square mile per year, but can range to more than 100 flashes per square mile per year in localized areas.[19] Plate 8 is an example of a lightning flash density chart.

Seasonal, Geographical, and Long-Term Variations in Lightning Frequency
There is a marked seasonality to lightning strikes, most (80 percent) occurring during the months of June, July, August, and September in the northern hemisphere, and during November, December, January, and February in the southern hemisphere.[20] However, there is also an increased incidence of lightning during winter storms on the West Coast of the United States. As one might expect, the frequency of lightning in any location varies from year to year, depending on weather patterns and storm activity. When long-term thunderstorm day records are reviewed, we see significant variations over a 5-to-10-year period of time. There is no clear trend: At some locations the number of thunderstorm days decreases over time, and then increases again; at other locations it simply decreases; and in still other locations the trend is toward a growing number of thunderstorm days. While it appears that more than one factor is responsible for these variations in lightning frequency, a number of things point to changes in air temperature as being one of the significant variables. Beyond that, about all that can be said is that the frequency of lightning strikes changes from year to year.

There is a wide variation in the seasonality and timing of lightning events; no single factor seems to be the dominant cause. Within the United States the peak in thunderstorm activity in the central part of the country can occur at any time and is related to cold frontal activity. In the southwestern United States, the peak in lightning activity coincides with the summer monsoon season, when moist tropical Pacific air moves north. In Florida, where the peak activity occurs in the summer and fall, it appears to be related to localized heating effects, as well as to the sea breeze convergence over the Florida peninsula where the Atlantic Ocean is on one side and the Gulf of Mexico is on the other side.

As noted earlier in this chapter, lightning strikes more frequently in high mountains as compared to lower elevations. In the Rocky Mountains, lightning is more likely to strike in the early afternoon—and later at lower elevations—due to the timing differences for warm air updrafts. A more recent phenomenon is the association of increased lightning activity over such major cities as Houston. It appears that the urban heat island effect may increase the frequency of lightning strikes over the city.[21]

Lightning Casualty Rates

At first glance, lightning fatalities are not high on the human risk scale. Recent (2003) statistics for the United States show that more than 2,000 persons per million die every year from heart disease, around 1,900 per million die from various forms of cancer, 150 per million die in motor vehicle accidents, and only 1 to 2 per million population (depending on location) die from lightning strikes. For every death, there are a number of injuries; within a few years a number of the injured also die of the lingering effects of the lightning strike, but their deaths go unnoticed by the lightning statisticians. More about this later. When I saw that the actual number of deaths and injuries was much higher than indicated by the dry statistics, and as I became familiar with the heartbreaking experiences of many of the survivors, I became convinced that this was a global problem worthy of greater attention.

World data on lightning fatalities and injuries are unreliable. There is no adequate comprehensive source of data for worldwide lightning fatalities and injuries. Some countries have no reporting systems whatsoever, and the data that some do report include uncertainties.

On the basis of the information available, death rates due to lightning strikes span nearly two orders of magnitude, from about 0.03 deaths per year per million population (England and Wales) to 2.0 deaths per year per million population (Wyoming, 1990-2003 averaged data). Generally the trend has been downward, possibly as the result of fewer thunderstorms, improved understanding of risk prevention, or increased urbanization.[22] Some typical casualty rates illustrating this trend are shown in Table 2. The data are averaged over 5 or 10 year periods.

Table 2: Lightning Casualty Rates, 1930s vs. 1970s, in Deaths per Million Population[23]

	1920-30s Rate	1960-70s Rate
Singapore	2.6	1.7
Australia	1.3	0.35
United States	1.5	0.5
W. Germany	--	0.8
S. Africa	--	1.5
Austria	--	1.3
England and Wales	0.3	0.03

In the United States, Florida had twice as many deaths as any other state from 1959 to 1994. The states with the highest death rates per million population were New Mexico, Wyoming, Arkansas, Florida, Mississippi, and Colorado—all with more than one death per million population.

Geographically, the high-risk zone lies in the tropics. Around 4 billion persons live in the tropical zone between 30 degrees north and south latitude. (This was 61.5 percent of the world's population in 2005.) Assuming an average death rate of 3 persons per million population per year for this region, the death toll due to lightning would be 12,000 persons. This is only a rough guess, since many countries do not keep records of deaths caused by lightning strikes. However, the number is large enough to justify greater efforts to educate people, particularly rural populations. Many deaths could be avoided by the application of simple commonsense rules. For the balance of the global population—2.5 billion persons— assume 1 death per million population for a total of 2,500 deaths per year yielding an estimated worldwide total of 14,500 deaths per year. I suspect that the actual number is higher. Thanks to improvements in communication and public awareness, lightning has come to the forefront as a health and economic problem in many countries. As an example, in December 2004, the physics department of Jahangirnagar University, Savar, Bangladesh, sponsored a workshop on lightning awareness and protection. Experts there estimated that 500 persons per year in the region die from lightning strikes and thousands more are injured. Economic losses reach hundreds of millions of dollars per year.[24] In 2005, the China International Lightning Protection Forum issued a report estimating that China suffers 3,000 lightning casualties per year and economic losses of a billion dollars or more per year.

In the first half of the 20th century the records for the United States indicate that nearly 500 persons per year were killed by lightning.[25] In the 1940s the number ranged from a low of 231 to a high of 419 deaths (in 1944). In all likelihood, the actual numbers were higher, simply because not all states kept records—and there is reason to question how complete the existing records were.

In the last half of the century, the *reported* number of fatalities showed a steady decline to the current value of around 50 per year. The likely explanation of this change is the shift of population from rural to urban settings, and to a lesser extent, to improved education. However, there is reason to question the accuracy of these numbers, which are apparently collected by scanning news reports.

In the United States, the authoritative national publication is *Storm Data*, produced by the National Oceanic and Atmospheric Administration (NOAA).[26] This publication compiles fatalities reported for the major weather-related natural disasters, including hurricanes, tornadoes, floods, and lightning. Of these four categories, floods have caused the greatest number of fatalities in the last three decades. From 1975 to 2004, floods caused an average of 107 deaths per year; within that same period lightning was the second-most lethal weather phenomenon, causing an average of 66 deaths per year.[27]

Several researchers have compiled local records (state public health records and other sources) and have found discrepancies between local data and the national data. Without going into detail, there is a general consensus that the United States national statistics understate the actual fatality and injury rate by between 15 and 30 percent. For this reason, an annual fatality rate of 75 to 150 persons and an injury rate of about 300 or 400 per year to as many as 1,000 or more injured each year is probably more realistic. The odds of being struck in the United States are around 1 in 240,000 on average, and as stated before, higher for those living in Florida, Wyoming, New Mexico, and other areas where lightning strikes more frequently. In these states the death rates are 1.5 to almost 2.0 per million population and the injury rate is between 4 and 7 times greater.[28]

For example, one researcher compiled all the United States lightning deaths during a single month—August 1977. In just that one month, 30 people died.[29] Most were outdoors; a number had taken shelter under trees. Even more informative is to examine Web sites that list lightning incidents. I found one that posted nearly 3,000 lightning news report headlines for the six-year period from July 2002 to April 2006. Some of these are duplications—two reports describe the same incident—and not all describe fatalities. Some report injuries, some report fires and other incidents caused by lightning. Still, what is impressive is the sheer number of events—500 or so per year—from all around the world. Just to list these one-line headlines took 60 single-spaced pages. And, these are only the incidents that made headlines![30]

Not all lightning strikes result in death; the injury rate is many times higher than the death rate, meaning that many survive the strike. However, a number of these survivors subsequently die as a result of hidden or delayed effects of lightning damage to critical tissue, the nervous system, and such vital organs as the heart. The percentage is not known with any accuracy since subsequent deaths are reported as "stroke," "congestive heart failure," and other causes and are not attributed to lightning. A follow-up study for five years on lightning-strike victim mortality would be of considerable value in helping better define this problem and to define guidelines for long-term care.

Who, When, Where[31]
The available statistics indicate that men are 4.6 times more likely to be killed or injured by lightning than women. About 84 percent of the fatalities are men and 16 percent are women in the United States; in Singapore, the numbers are 83 percent men and 17 percent women; in Australia, the percentage of men is even higher—88 percent versus 12 percent for women.

Persons 20 to 29 years of age have the highest death rate due to lightning strikes—about twice the rate of the general population. Interestingly, some of the data show a second peak in the 40 to 49 and 50 to 59-year-old age brackets. If we suppose the 20 to 29-year-old rate occurs because this group is more active outdoors, could it be that the second peak occurs when people have more leisure time for golf? The very young and the elderly have the lowest death rates.

Most deaths occur in the afternoon, when thunderstorm activity peaks. Data for the United States and Australia show that around 11 percent of fatalities occur between midnight and noon; 70 to 85 percent occur between the hours of noon and 4 P.M.; and the balance occurs between 4 P.M. and midnight. Considering the total casualty rate (both fatalities and injuries), two-thirds occur between noon and 6:00 P.M. in the United States.

Deaths occur at all hours, every day of the week. However, the day of the week with the greatest number of deaths—24 percent more than the next highest day—is Sunday. Readers with strong religious convictions might take heed—perhaps it is better to be in church on Sunday than on the golf course! Churches are by no means exempt from lightning strikes, however. Before lightning arrestors came into use, bell towers were struck frequently. This trend has continued to recent times.[32] The next deadliest day is Saturday, followed by Wednesday. I have no good explanation for Wednesday, other than to note that it happens to be the day my dentist takes off to play golf.

Water and trees are places to avoid in a thunderstorm. An Australian woman attended a lakeside picnic with her children. Two children were swimming as storm clouds gathered and the wind began to gust. The woman sent one child to tell the other two to come out of the water and then retreated under the tree where she sat on a couple of towels placed on the tree root. As rain began to fall she picked up a wooden umbrella and opened it. There was a loud noise and a flash and she was flung to one side. Her daughter returned to find her lying face down on the ground, screaming. She had a burning sensation in her buttocks, her legs were numb, and she experienced difficulty breathing. Clothing and towels under the tree were torn or burnt. She was driven to a nearby hospital, where she was given oxygen and treated for burns. She was discharged after two days. She was very lucky.[33]

Outdoor locations are clearly more deadly than indoor locations; the majority of deaths and injuries occur outdoors. Deaths associated with recreation are on the rise, perhaps reflecting a global trend toward increased leisure activities. Some locations are more dangerous than others; many fatalities and injuries occur when people take shelter under trees during rainstorms, are in boats or in or near open water, are engaged in farming or agricultural activities, or playing golf or other outdoor sports. The data vary somewhat depending on the time period chosen, but for the 35-year period from 1959 to 1994 in the United States, the breakdown for casualties (combined fatalities and injuries) was as follows:[34]

Open fields and recreation except golf	27%
Under trees	14
Water related (boats, swimming, fishing)	8
Golf	5
Operating heavy equipment or machinery	3
Using a telephone	2.4
Using radios, transmitters, or near antennas	0.7
Location/activity unknown	40

Golf courses are prime targets for lightning, and account for a disproportionate number of injuries and fatalities. Why? Open spaces; exposed trees; frequented in the afternoons by sportsmen who will follow their sport in any weather or walk around with a bag of little metal and graphite lightning rods, or who stand and hold one at the 13th hole! In August 1998, a British golfer was struck and killed at Chigwell, Essex, even though British golfers are normally warned by a loud klaxon horn when thunderstorm conditions arise. Retief Goosen, the South African two-time winner of the U.S. Open Championship, was struck while playing when he was 17 years old, resulting in partial deafness and a heart flutter.

However, the classic case is Lee Trevino, the witty, popular American golfer who twice won each of the U.S. Open, the British Open, and the PGA Championships, before retiring in 1985. Trevino's fans, known as "Lee's Fleas," were present when he was hit by lightning on June 27, 1975 at the Western Open, near Chicago. The blast lifted him completely off the ground and caused some lasting damage to his spine and back.[35] He recovered, at least enough to win his second PGA Championship in 1984. With his characteristic sense of humor, Trevino is quoted as saying "If you are caught on a golf course during a storm and are afraid of lightning, hold up a 1-Iron. Not even God can hit a 1-Iron."

We know that lightning is capricious, but fortunately in most cases it selects a single victim for a fatal blow. Not in every case, however; in the 1959-1994 United States *Storm Data* database there are instances of lightning killing as many as eight individuals with a single flash. In 91 percent of the cases there is a single fatality. These numbers exclude an incident in 1963, when lightning caused an airplane to crash, killing 81 passengers and crew. (See Chapter 6).

There are many instances in which two or more individuals have been struck and some survive. The *Storm Data* database includes 275 incidents in which the number of injured victims ranged from 5 to as many as 20 persons. In one such case—in August 1975—eight people were injured when lightning struck near the center of a campground at Leslie, Michigan. In a few incidents, even more have been injured, as occurred in June 1979, at a National Guard camp in Michigan, when 45 soldiers were injured after lightning struck the camp.[36]

Given the data presented above, it is hard to imagine a more dangerous situation than a Sunday in July in Florida. Nonetheless, in Florida on the Fourth of July 1996 (which was a Thursday), a group of spectators were picnicking and watching fireworks in a park when lightning struck. One person was killed and 27 were injured.[37]

As mentioned early in this chapter, most deaths occur in the summer months, as shown in Figure 11. In the United States, 80 percent of fatalities occurred during June to September, inclusive; while for Australia, 80 percent of fatalities occur between October and February (the southern

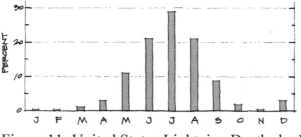

Figure 11: United States Lightning Deaths by Month, 1959-1994

hemisphere summer), with January being the most dangerous month. By far the most lethal month in the United States is July. It also has the most injuries. Cancers and Leos beware!

4

Crabs and Lions Beware: Health Impacts of Lightning

If you were born under the sign of Cancer or Leo and live in Florida, should you avoid participating in a backyard party for your 25th birthday? Quite possibly, since we've seen that July is the month in the United States when the greatest number of lightning-caused injuries occur. As a male, age 20 to 29, you might be at even greater risk. But, risk of what? What happens when electric currents pass through the human body?

Electricity Danger Levels
First, consider a 100-watt household light bulb. In the United States, it requires 833 milliamperes to operate the lamp (half this value in Europe and countries where the nominal voltage is 220 volts). Recall that 1 milliampere is 0.001 amperes or one-thousandth of an ampere. Experiments have been performed to determine the response of humans to electricity; typical results are listed in Table 3. I have "experimentally" verified a few of these numbers, but most assuredly it was by accident and not something I would want to repeat or to recommend that any one else try.

Many years ago it was necessary to add another fluorescent lamp fixture to a long row of lamps in a laboratory high bay and I volunteered to do it. After throwing a circuit breaker to disconnect the power, I climbed an aluminum ladder and hung the new fixture from the ceiling. As I made the electrical connections to the new lamp, I noticed the lamps in the last half of the row of fixtures suddenly blink on. In a split second my mind processed what was happening. The only way those lights could be turning on was if the electric current was passing through me. Yowwweee! Fortunately I was able to let go and did not fall off the ladder. Later, I realized that there were two circuits running the length of the row of fixtures—half of the lamps on one circuit, half on the other. I had disconnected only one of the two circuits.

Table 3: Effects of Electric Current on Humans[1]

Current (milliamperes)	Response
0.5	Will startle a person.
5-10	Causes muscle spasms that make it hard to "let go" of a live wire. Slightly higher values (30-40 milliamperes) can paralyze muscle.
50-100	This current, flowing for 2 seconds or more, can stop the heart through ventricular fibrillation.
833	Current in a 100-watt light bulb.
5,000 to 5,000,000	Typical lightning current in struck individual.

Electrocution depends not only on the voltage and current but on the duration of the shock as well. As noted in the table, if a high-voltage current of 100 to 200 milliamperes flows for as much as two seconds there is a strong possibility of death; however, it is possible to survive 1,000 milliamperes for very brief intervals of less than 0.01 seconds. Survival also depends on where in the heartbeat cycle the strike occurs.

Electrical building codes require the installation of ground fault interrupters (GFIs) in areas in which individuals using electric tools or appliances might be shocked. GFIs are electrical devices that sense a current flow to ground, the indication that something is wrong. They are quite sensitive and are set to trip and disconnect the power if they detect a leakage current greater than 0.5 milliamperes. This value has been selected on the basis of the threshold voltage during which the "can't let go" reaction takes place.

The current due to a lightning strike is 100 to 100,000 times greater than the amount needed to stop the heart. Given this huge flow of current, how is it that anyone survives a lightning strike?

To answer this question, I have to introduce the concept of electrical resistance, which is measured in *Ohms*. The ohm is named after Georg S. Ohm (1787-1854), a German physicist who discovered that current will flow through a wire in direct proportion to the voltage potential applied to the conductor. The constant of proportionality he defined as *resistance*; later the unit of resistance was called the ohm in his honor. Ohm's work used direct current; later, Ohm's law was extended to alternating current. With respect to alternating current, the constant of proportionality is called *impedance* and has the same unit as resistance, ohms. Ohm's law states that voltage equals current times resistance. To understand resistance (or impedance), think of a pipe containing flowing water that is under pressure. For a given pressure (analogous to voltage), more water (current) will flow the larger the pipe is—that is, the less resistance the pipe has, the greater the current that can flow. Double the voltage and the current doubles and so on. Because Ohm's law is fundamental to understanding the effects of lightning on humans, I will restate it here:

Voltage (volts) equals current (amperes) multiplied by resistance (ohms).

The resistance of a length of wire, for example, is determined by the *resistivity* of the wire material, measured in ohm-meters. Resistivity is a fundamental property of any substance that conducts electricity. Some metals—such as aluminum, copper, gold, and silver—have very low resistivities, around 0.02 microhm-meters; iron and steel have 10 to 40 times greater resistivity, carbon, a thousand times higher, wood, ten million times greater, and limestone, a billion times greater. *Conductivity* is a measure of how easily electricity flows in a material and is the reciprocal of resistivity.

In constructing electronic circuits, special devices called *resistors* are used. They are designed to have a specified value of resistance—say, 49 ohms, 33,000 ohms, or higher. If you have ever looked inside your computer at one of the printed circuit boards, or looked inside a transistor radio, you've no doubt seen some resistors. They are brightly colored and resemble small firecrackers.[2] They are typically made of carbon with additives to adjust the resistance, or they may be made from high-resistance wire. In electronics circuits, they are used to divide voltages or to restrict the current flow in certain components.

Another common device in electronic circuits is the capacitor. Capacitors are used to block direct currents but will pass alternating currents. In other words, a capacitor has a very high resistance to direct current but a low resistance (actually the correct term is low *impedance*) to a high-frequency alternating current. Capacitors can also be charged with electricity.

I stated earlier that lightning is capricious; somehow, with seemingly uncanny calculation it seeks out the lowest resistance path to ground and does so in microseconds, whereas when we look at the path it took after the fact, it can takes hours or certainly dozens of minutes to deduce why it flowed the way it did. Usually, our interest stems from the fact that someone was injured; scant attention is paid to the devious paths followed by lightning when no damage is done. One recent case illustrates this point, but fortunately the victim suffered a near miss and escaped unharmed.

Seven-year-old Kaylee Shriner was asleep in an upstairs bedroom when lightning struck the roof of her home in Tongannoxie, Kansas, in July 2005. The current traced a path through the attic, and then found a convenient path to ground through—of all things—the thin sheet metal angle used to trim the corner of the drywall in her bedroom. From that it jumped to her steel bed frame and ignited the mattress of her bed. Kaylee jumped up unhurt and called her father, who first tried to smother the fire and then dragged the mattress outside of the house. Kaylee, with remarkable poise for one who had had such a close call, was later interviewed by the local television station. She said that after seeing the blazing mattress, her dad said a bad word, and after that a number of bad words were said before everyone calmed down and the fire was extinguished.[3]

Less fortunate was Robert Ireland, an electrical contractor, who lived alone in a rural area north of Chattanooga, Tennessee. His house occupied high ground; in addition, he had a high antenna mast to take advantage of the many TV signals from around the area. In mid-April 1987, he came home from work and turned on his television to watch the evening news. Hearing thunder and recognizing the approach of an electrical storm, Ireland disconnected the antenna cable from his television and connected an internal ("rabbit ears") antenna so he could continue to watch the news. He left the antenna cable lying on the floor, rather than grounding it or dropping it outside the window.

As the storm intensified, Ireland decided that even watching TV was hazardous, so he reached down to unplug the television from the power outlet, not even taking time to turn it off, as the storm had suddenly become very violent. At this moment he felt a discharge of electricity pass out of his knee and as best he could tell, into the picture tube of the television set. The next thing he could recall was that he was standing dazed on the other side of the room. He speculates that lightning struck the antenna, then flashed from the cable end to his right foot, and out his left knee to the television, which was ruined. The storm died down and Ireland went to bed. He did not try to get medical help.

The next day as he resumed work on a house repair project, he began to feel more fatigued than usual. After several more days, his fatigue not only increased but his productivity declined. He would go to his truck to get some materials, then have to return to the job to try to remember what it was he went to the truck for in the first place. By the end of the week the job was nearly finished, and Ireland was so fatigued that he quit at noon and went home to bed. He is not certain of the details, but thinks that he slept for about a week. He said he felt awful—like the worst hangover he could imagine, although he does not drink alcohol.

At this point he sought help from his local general practitioner, who found no visible physical damage, and therefore treated Ireland for depression. Nothing seemed to help; Ireland was unable to work, and for a time was unable to even drive to town for groceries. Friends and neighbors helped him until, six months after he'd been hit, he sold his business and returned to his family home in Orlando, Florida. Gradually he was able to return to work over the next three to four years, but then a combination of growing disabilities— fatigue, memory loss, balance problems, insomnia, back pain —made work impossible. The Social Security Administration denied his request for disability on the basis "there was no medical evidence to support his claim." Ireland stated "...I am able to work less and less as each month and year passes by, to the point that I am becoming a pauper."[4]

Electrical Model of the Human Body
Writing in *Poor Richard's Almanac*—before conducting his own experiments on lightning—Benjamin Franklin described a lightning strike on a boy that melted the pewter buttons on his pants. In typical Franklinesque humor, Poor Richard added "Tis well nothing else thereabouts was made of pewter." [5]

Today, lightning strikes that flash over have been known to melt and fuse metal zippers.

On July 22, 1972, staff sergeant Gem L. Poe and his wife Mary Louise were at a resort property they owned near Canyon Lake, north of San Antonio, Texas. Note the month— *July*. He had cut the grass under a big oak tree on the property, had a picnic lunch, and then Poe decided to trim a few low-hanging branches from the tree. Above them, there was clear blue sky, although Poe could see lightning striking far away in the distant hills.

Poe was standing on the ground, arm upraised to cut a branch, when a bolt of lightning struck the tree, knocking him and his wife—who was standing 25 feet away—to the ground. When Poe came to his senses, he was paralyzed from the neck down. He could hear and speak, but could not move. He felt like his body was on fire and screamed to his wife to remove his boots because his legs and feet were on fire. Mrs. Poe was unhurt and was able to remove his heavy boots. His socks had holes burned through them. She tried to remove his pants, but found that the zipper was welded closed.

At this point it began to rain heavily. She tried but could not move her 6-foot tall, 215 pound husband. What to do? She wanted to go for help but did not want to abandon him in the downpour. Finally, after an hour had passed, Poe's paralysis began to fade and he was able to crawl to their truck so she could take him to the hospital. The examination and tests showed that physically he was in good condition. He had some singed hair, red streaks down the side of his body where the lightning current passed before exiting his feet, but otherwise seemed okay. He returned to work a week later with a black eye, and sore knees, ankles, and feet. Following the strike, Poe had persistent pain, primarily in his right thigh, where he says it feels as if someone is sticking a knife in the muscle, and there is a burning sensation. He is more cautious since the strike, but stated that he is not obsessed with fear of thunderstorms or lightning.[6]

The human body is composed mostly of water with a few kilograms of calcium and other chemicals mixed in. To understand the effects of electrical trauma on the human body, this knowledge of the body's composition can be used to construct a simple model that does not require medical knowledge to understand. Let us strip away all the complications of tissue, arteries, veins, and organs, and reduce this complex organism wherein resides human intelligence, passion, and the soul, to a much simpler structure: a cylindrical container of water. With this elementary model, we can begin to understand the nature of the electrical currents that flow in the body during a lightning strike, and can gain insight into the nature of injuries caused by lightning.

Resistivity in liquids is measured in ohms per cubic meter. Very pure water (distilled water) has a high resistivity: 500 billion ohms per cubic meter. It is the addition of such impurities as salt or a weak acid that makes water a good conductor of electricity. Once the impurity dissolves in water, its molecules dissociate into positive and negative ions—that is, a molecule either lacking or having extra electrons—and it is then able to conduct electricity.

Although high-purity water has a very high resistance to electric current flow, with the addition of a small amount of salt or other chemicals, in general it becomes an excellent conductor—ordinary tap water being an example. Blood is a good conductor; such other components as bone have higher resistivity and are less conductive.[7] Human skin is a dry layer of fused squamous epithelial cells approximately 100 to 500 microns thick. These cells form a relatively well-insulated (electrically) shell around the body. Skin has a higher resistance compared to internal tissue, depending on whether skin is dry (high resistance), wet or oily (less resistance), or sweaty (low resistance). The palms of the hands and soles of the feet are two to three times greater in resistance than the skin in general.

Despite the differing resistances described in the preceding paragraph, as a first approximation the resistance of the human body—say, from head or hand to foot—is relatively low, so large electrical currents can flow easily if the voltage is high enough. The model I propose to use consists of cylinders of slightly salty water (tissues and organs) contained within a somewhat flexible membrane (the skin), representing

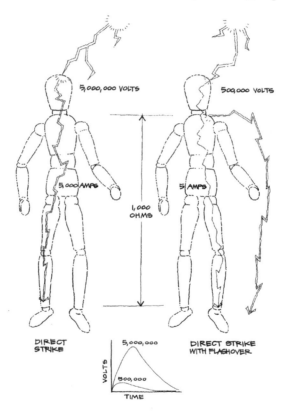

Figure 12: Simplified Electrical Model (Equivalent
Circuit) of the Human Body

the legs, arms, trunk and head, with an overall height of 6.5-foot (2-meters). We can adjust the resistivity of the saltwater in this hypothetical model to equal the internal resistance of the human body, and likewise give the outer membrane the resistance of the skin. To keep the analysis simple I will approximate the body's resistance as 1,000 ohms and neglect for the moment the higher resistance of the skin. Figure 12 is a sketch of this model, which is properly referred to as an *equivalent circuit*.

There are five different modes by which humans can be struck by lightning. A description of each, in approximate order of severity, follows.

Direct Strike
In a *direct strike*, the lightning current attaches to some point (usually the head or shoulder) at which time, a large current flows through the body. Using an equivalent circuit similar to Figure 12 and typical lightning stroke parameters such as the average current duration, current rise time, and typical lightning voltage, scientists predict that the voltage at the victim's head (in other words, at the top of the individual sketched on the left side of Figure 12) will rise to 5,000,000 volts. Within about 8 to 10 microseconds this high voltage creates a 5,000-ampere current flow through the body that lasts for a very short time and then decreases to zero around 100 microseconds later.[8]

It is rare for a victim to survive a direct strike. This becomes more obvious when you consider the fact that the heat and mechanical stresses from a lightning strike fracture concrete, shatter masonry, and split and fell large trees. Such a strike to a human would most likely be lethal. With the high voltage, high current flow of a direct strike, the heart may be stopped, a condition called asystole (cessation of heart contractions), rather than commencing ventricular fibrillation.

Direct Strike with External Flashover
The second and more likely condition is a *direct strike with a flashover*. As in the direct strike case, the lightning current

attaches to the head (head in this example; it could be an arm or shoulder, or other location) and the voltage at the head rises rapidly, but before it reaches 5,000,000 volts the high electric field created by the lightning strike causes the air to break down, creating an ionized path in the air alongside the body. This occurs when the voltage at the head has risen to around 500,000 volts. (See individual sketched on right side of Figure 12.) At this moment the current flashes over on an external path along the skin or clothing. The ionized air created by breakdown offers a path to the lightning current that has lower resistance than the internal path, so most of the current flows outside of the body, along the surface of skin or clothing. When flashover occurs, the voltage at the head drops to around 5,000 volts in less than a microsecond. Meanwhile, the internal body current, which had only risen to around 800 amperes, drops instantly to 5 amperes (5,000 volts divided by 1,000 ohms) and then drops to zero. Meanwhile, the voltage on the skin jumps to 5,000 volts and most current flows along the outside of the body.[9]

Another way of looking at flashover is to consider the electric field on the surface of the membrane (skin). At flashover it is equivalent to a field strength of 250 kilovolts per meter (500,000 volts divided by 2 meters); this is sufficient to cause the current to "flash over," or jump to the surface of the skin by breaking down resistance along a path outside of the body. When this occurs, an electric arc with a field strength of around 2.5 kilovolts/meters is established in air along the skin's surface. The ionized air has much less resistance, so the preponderance of current flow is outside of the body, and the voltage at the top of the cylinder of water instantly drops to around 5,000 volts (2.5 kilovolts/meter times 2 meters), causing the current through the body to decrease. This current flow continues for a few fractions of a second until the energy in the strike is dissipated.

The current inside the body divides in unpredictable ways—potentially flowing through the head, limbs, heart, lungs, blood vessels, nerves, or other internal organs. The current is usually high enough to cause cardiorespiratory arrest, and can damage the heart and respiratory system. This is a common occurrence, and underlies the need to provide prompt cardiopulmonary resuscitation (CPR) to lightning victims. In rendering care, there is no danger involved in touching the victim; there is no residual electricity in the body.

The equivalent circuit shown in Figure 12 can be modified so that the current flowing through the limbs or other parts of the body can be estimated. Researchers have measured the resistance of the skin of the scalp, hands and soles of feet and have found that they have a relatively high resistance—namely, 10,000 ohms.[10] The neck and arms are around 200 ohms, while the trunk and the legs are 300 ohms, respectively. Researchers also found that for the high-frequency impulse associated with lightning, the human body does not respond as a pure resistance. Instead, it behaves as if it has some low values of capacitance associated with the skin resistances. In the equivalent circuit of Figure 13, the 10,000-ohm resistor representing the head and scalp is shunted (paralleled) by a 10-microfarad capacitor. The 10,000-ohm resistors representing the hand and the feet are shunted by 0.25-microfarad capacitors. Because capacitors have low impedance at high frequency, they conduct the fast impulse of the lightning current extremely well. Thus for lightning strikes (but not for other types of electrical shocks) the capacitance provided by the skin and other organs of the body becomes important. What happens is that within microseconds the skin capacitance charges up to a high voltage until a threshold for breakdown is exceeded and the lightning current can flash over or through the skin.

In summary, the most common situation for lightning-strike victims is a high initial current flow (for a few microseconds), followed by external flashover on the skin's surface. A variation of this is an internal flashover during which the lightning current traverses the body for a certain distance and then flashes over to the external surface, producing considerably more trauma and potentially fatal consequences. In either of these situations there can be a broad

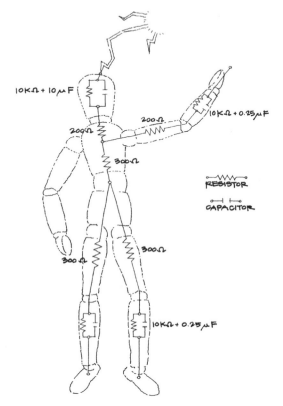

Figure 13: Detailed Equivalent Circuit of the Human Body

range of injury severity, depending on the magnitude of the lightning current, the situation (weather, altitude, et cetera), and the health and age of the victim. A surprising number of victims survive, but some do die.

The violence of a high-intensity electric arc traversing the body surface can cause burns; shred clothing; melt metal jewelry, buttons, or zippers; and in some cases blow off shoes or other articles of dress by the force of steam generated by the heat of the arc. Frequently the skin is left with fernlike burn patterns characteristic of lightning.

Finally, the reader may be wondering why anyone is killed by a direct strike, given that the mechanisms for flashover exist? All I can say is that some individuals are simply in the wrong place at the wrong time.

Side Flash

A *side flash* results when an individual stands next to a stricken object (such as a tree, metal pole, metal object inside a building, or another person) and the flash jumps to the victim. The maximum surge from a side flash to human being is estimated to be about 8,000 amperes with the most likely value being approximately 400 to 800 amperes. If this current flows internally, the effects are like a direct strike and can be very serious. If the side flash raises the body to 200,000 volts or more, breakdown will occur and the current will flow externally to the body and pose much less likelihood of serious injury.[11]

Dana Larson never considered himself a tree hugger, but became one some months after August 20, 1985. After finishing work that day at his Exxon Corporation office in downtown Houston, Dana left for his customary 6 mile jog along the edge of Memorial Golf Course, a route followed by thousands of other joggers, including the first President Bush. It was hot and humid, but otherwise, the weather was not threatening. Along the route there was a stately pine tree, known to locals as Bush's Pine, since it marked the location where the Secret Service always dropped off the President for his jogs. On the fateful day, as Dana passed Bush's Pine, it was struck by lightning and the side flash impacted Dana. He was unaware of what happened until five hours later when he "woke up" in a hospital.

I met Dana in Tennessee where we were both attending the 2006 meeting of the Lightning Strike and Electric Shock Survivors International, Inc. He was there as a survivor, while

I was there as an observer. Both of us were trying to learn more about what happened when lightning strikes a person. Somehow we got talking about exercise and I told him I was getting up early and swimming laps in the hotel pool. He said he was going jogging, and that was when he told me about what happened in 1985.

Dana: "On separate occasions, many months after I got hit, both the runner who was behind me and the runner who had been approaching me introduced or reintroduced themselves. They had seen the whole thing and gave me aid before I lost consciousness. The runner who had been behind me said that there were storm clouds about 5 miles south of us. He said a single bolt came across the clear blue sky. After I was knocked backwards to the ground, the runners took me into the nearby Memorial Park Tennis Center for assistance. Ironically, the club refused me admission because I didn't have a shirt on. The club did call an ambulance, however. One of the runners told me that I gave them my name before becoming really obnoxious.

"Somebody called my wife. After my wife and son arrived at the hospital, the doctor briefed my wife on the fact that short-term memory loss was a common aspect of lightning injuries.

"With my wife standing at bedside, the doctor asked me: 'Do you know who I am?'

"I replied, 'No dude, who are you? I'm glad to meet you.'

"The physician then said, 'I'm your doctor Mr. Larson. Now I'd like to ask you a favor. Would you please look out that window over there?'

"I turned and looked out the window.

"Then the doctor asked me to look at him: 'Now, Mr. Larson, do you know who I am?'

"I said, 'No dude, who are you?'

"I 'came to' later that evening when a friend entered the room."

Dana recovered, eventually seeing his memory improve, although remembering names was frustratingly slow. He also slowly recovered the use of his shoulder, which "froze." For several months, he had headaches that came every four hours and reminded him of the worst of any cheap booze hangover. He frequently contemplated suicide, he said, because the pain was so intense. When I met him, he was in good health and had recently retired. He considers himself extremely fortunate—he survived a potentially deadly lightning strike. Three other individuals that were hit that afternoon died.

I joked with Dana: "Better that you were hit than the President."

"I don't know," he said. "It might have changed the course of history if it had been the other way around. Anyway, it turned me into a tree hugger. For the next two years, every time I ran by that tree I stopped to give it a hug. Thanks for taking the hit for me, I told it. I would have continued, but the poor tree died. Thank god it was the tree and not me."

Capacitive Coupling by Telephone

In a sense this is a special case of a side flash. However, since a number of telephone-related injuries occur every year, it is important to understand the mechanism. If lightning strikes a telephone line at the same time an individual is using the telephone, it is possible for a voltage surge of 5,000 to 10,000 volts to occur at the handset. In this instance the earpiece may be thought of as one plate of a capacitor and the victim's head as the other plate. Above about 5,000 volts this "capacitor" breaks down and a current of up to 12 amperes will flow through the head and body. The skin however, is unlikely to reach 1,000 volts and therefore flashover along the skin and clothing is unlikely. Principal damage is to the ears and frequently to the eyes, as well as superficial damage to the face and scalp. Injuries may include hearing impairment or loss, corneal flash burns or tearing of the retina, and burns.

There is some possibility that ventricular fibrillation will occur. The injuries can be serious but such a strike is usually not fatal.[12]

Step Voltage

The fifth case is that of a *step voltage*. This situation arises when lightning strikes or enters the ground but does not directly strike the victim. Instead, the victim receives a shock from the lightning current traveling in the soil. Such a strike causes injuries to animals and to people walking or running in open areas. Using the equivalent circuit model, assuming typical soil resistance, and assuming that the victim is standing 33 feet distant from a 5,000-ampere strike—his or her legs 3 feet apart—the voltage between the feet would be 800 volts and the current flowing through the legs would be 1.05 amperes (1,050 milliamperes). The current could cause muscle spasms, knock the victim down, and might induce ventricular fibrillation or render some victims unconscious. A victim experiencing this strike will probably survive, because the current in this case generally is not lethal. If the strike is more energetic or the victim closer, a higher current might be experienced, but again, it is generally not fatal. Lightning striking an athletic field is a typical example.[13]

The BBC reported that on October 26, 1998, in Johannesburg, South Africa, in the midst of a soccer game between the Morokoa Swallows and the Jomo Cosmos, a bolt of lightning struck the ground. Fortunately, no players were hit directly, but as a result of step voltage about half of the players from each team fell to the ground and lay there twitching in agony. A referee seemed badly shaken up by the incident and ran around blowing his whistle at random. A photograph of the incident shows the injured players writhing on the ground. Several of the players were taken to local hospitals and treated for shock and irregular heartbeats. Two days later the BBC reported a second strike on a football team. Allegedly, two teams were playing in eastern Kasai Province, Democratic

Republic of the Congo. Lightning struck and killed all 11 members of the visiting team, leaving the home team uninjured. One presumes that this was a direct strike on a group of players standing close together.[14]

Why is it that some people on a playing field are struck while others are not? The voltage applied to the feet depends on the position of the victim's feet. Imagine that lightning strikes a lamp post and that the surrounding soil is flat and homogeneous. The electric field in the ground decreases with

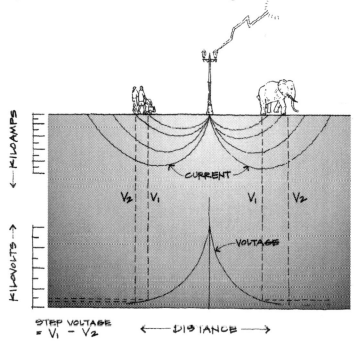

Figure 14: Soil Voltage Gradient (Step Voltage)

the radial distance away from the lamp post. (Refer to Figure 14.) Depending on the resistivity of the soil, a voltage gradient is established in the soil, the highest voltage being closest to the point of impact. An individual who stood facing the lamp post—feet together—would experience the same electric field gradient with both feet and would not experience a significant step voltage. An individual walking directly away from or toward the lamp post—feet apart—would experience a step voltage as a result of making contact with the electric field at two different points.

In the case of such livestock as cattle, the situation is much more serious, because with the greater distance between hind and forelegs—in the case of cattle perhaps 10 to 12 feet—the voltage they experience is much greater, and in addition, the path of the current from hind to forelegs or vice versa is through the thoracic region containing the heart and other critical organs. Both domestic and wild animals are victims. Remember the elephants described in Chapter 2! A small sampling of news reports in 2005 described the deaths of a herd of elk in Wyoming; half a herd of beef cattle (16 animals) on a farm in Pickens, South Carolina, and 17 dairy cattle in Vermont. Lightning killed 11,000 turkeys near Hayfield, Minnesota, and 17,000 chickens on a Swedish egg farm.[15]

Medical Effects of Lightning on Humans[16]
When the human body is exposed to electric shocks, serious injury or death can result. The effects of lightning and conventional (household or industrial) alternating current are similar, but there are important differences. Lightning exposes the body to a very high-voltage, unidirectional current for a brief instant, whereas in an alternating-current electric shock the voltage and current amplitudes are smaller but the exposure is generally longer. Also, alternating current can produce different effects in comparison to the unidirectional current of lightning. There is no "standard" injury; the effect depends on where the lightning strikes the victim, the intensity of the strike, and the path taken by the current in the victim. Electricity will seek the path of least resistance, which may be through blood vessels or organs. The effects of electricity can be classified as *stimulation* and *heating*. The discussion that follows pertains to the medical effects of lightning strikes.

A lightning strike can affect the functioning of virtually any part of the body, depending on the path and intensity of the current. In order of importance, the functions of greatest concern are:
- Cardiorespiratory (heart and lungs)
- Neurological (nervous system, including the brain)
- Connective tissue (skin, muscles, bone, and blood vessels)
- Kidneys and other internal organs
- Ears and eyes
- Psychiatric and psychological behavior

The passage of low-voltage, minute electrical currents within the human body is normal and essential to function and well-being. Nerves function by passing electrical current to the muscles. Currents are conveyed by the nervous system to muscles that are composed of many thin, elongated fibers capable of contracting. There are three types of muscle fibers. The first, and perhaps best known to each of us, are the striped (striated is the medical term) or voluntary muscles, voluntary meaning they are under our conscious control. My hands and fingers, keyboarding these words, are driven by voluntary muscles. The second type of muscle fibers are plain or unstriped, and are not under voluntary control—they react automatically to such stimuli as pressure and expansion, the bowels and bladder being examples. Finally, there is a third type, found only in the heart. Cardiac muscle fibers are transversely striated, smaller than other muscle fibers, and are very compact and overlaid tightly to make up this critical organ.

The heart is an incredible organ. It begins pumping at an early point in the life of the fetus and continues nonstop until death. Control of the normal heart's pumping action is accomplished by minute electrical signals generated in a region of the heart referred to as the sinoatrial node. The sinoatrial node is called our heart's pacemaker. If this pacemaker fails, we need a battery-operated one to start each heart beat. Impulses from the sinoatrial node travel through a relay station—the atrioventricular node—which coordinates the contractions of the top chambers and bottom chambers of the heart. The atrium and ventricle. To understand how the heart works, refer to Figure 15, which is a sketch of the human heart. The heart comprises two upper chambers and two lower chambers, the upper chambers being the right and left atria

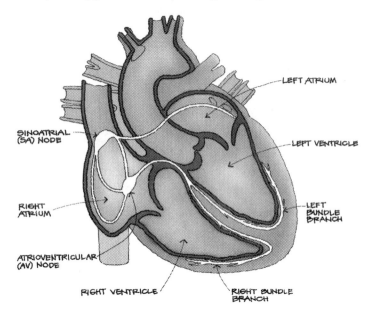

Figure 15: Sketch of the Human Heart

and the lower chambers being the right and left ventricles. Circulation commences when blood is pumped by the right ventricle through the pulmonary artery into the lungs, where the blood is freshly oxygenated and gives up carbon dioxide. From the lungs the blood is returned to the left atrium, into the left ventricle, and then is pumped under higher pressure into the aorta and its various branches to deliver fresh oxygenated blood throughout the body. The veins collect blood from various regions of the body and return it to the right atrium through the superior and inferior vena cava. The right atrium transfers blood to the right ventricle, whereupon the cycle is repeated.

Figure 16 shows one cycle of the electrocardiogram (ECG) of a healthy heart (mine). The vertical axis of the chart is the signal strength in millivolts and the horizontal axis is

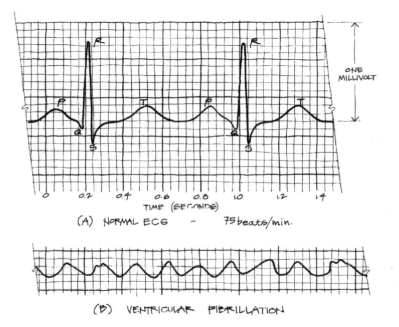

Figure 16: Normal Electrocardiogram and ECG Showing Ventricular Fibrillation.

time in milliseconds, the time for one complete cycle being about 1.25 seconds (corresponding to a heart rate of 75 beats per minute). The point labeled P corresponds to the atrium contracting; the impulse QRS corresponds to the contraction of the ventricle, while at T the ventricle is repolarizing, getting ready for the next contraction.

If these electrical signals are disrupted or stopped, various types of irregular heartbeats, or arrhythmia, can occur. Ventricular fibrillation and asystole are the deadly ones that can occur after lightening strikes. Fibrillation is a condition whereby the ventricle muscles twitch or contract spasmodically (fibrillate), causing a greatly reduced pumping action. The rate of beating is about 360 beats per minute, which is too rapid to provide an effective contraction force or to move the blood effectively. The resultant reduction in flow of oxygenated blood to the brain can lead to serious damage within minutes. It is for this reason that cardiopulmonary resuscitation (CPR) needs to be initiated immediately. Often, lightning victims who appear dead can be resuscitated if the CPR is administered quickly enough.

Cardiorespiratory System
The greatest danger to the human heart during a lightning strike is that it stops beating; the second danger is ventricular fibrillation. From the preceding description of how the heart functions, you can understand why timing is important. If the electric shock lasts for just a few microseconds and is not overpowering, the heart can recover and continue beating, whereas two seconds—two heartbeats—creates a more difficult recovery situation. Also, if the lightning strike occurs during the T phase it is more likely to cause ventricular fibrillation.[17]

Following a lightning strike the victim is typically unconscious, the result of stimulation (or perhaps we should say overstimulation!) of the central nervous system. In severe cases cardiorespiratory arrest occurs—the victim is not breathing, has dilated pupils, and has no pulse. In some cases, such as Gretchen Ehrlich (see the Preface), the heart restarts spontaneously, perhaps as a result of a fall. In any case, immediate action to resuscitate the victim should be taken; there is no danger in touching the victim.

In summary, the response of the cardiorespiratory system could follow several different paths:

- Strike→ heart stops beating (asystole)→ heart restarts, but beats at an abnormally slow pace (sinus brady-cardia)→ heart is overcome by oxygen deficiency (secondary hypoxic arrest) due to cardiopulmonary or circulatory blood not pumping.

- Strike→ heart stops beating (asystole)→ small period of bradycardia→ abnormally rapid heart action (ventricular fibrillation)→ then oxygen deficiency (leading to hypoxic arrest, or heart stoppage due to lack of oxygen).

When an unconscious lightning strike victim is examined in a hospital, ventricular fibrillation or other arrhythmias are visible in an electrocardiogram (ECG). Often, ECG readings return to normal after a period of months or a year.[18] The literature contains descriptions of various clinical observations and the changes in electrocardiogram patterns that can occur following a lightning strike.[19]

The human brain requires a continuous flow of oxygen. In the absence of other conditions, when blood flow to the brain ceases, the victim loses consciousness within 8 to 12 seconds, possibly followed by convulsions (20 seconds), cessation of breathing (30 to 45 seconds), and dilation of pupils (45 to 60 seconds). If the victim is deprived of oxygen for a period of from 4 to 6 minutes, brain injury or death will most likely result. For this reason immediate cardio pulmonary resuscitation (CPR) is imperative, followed by professional medical treatment at the earliest possible moment. CPR should be continued until the arrival of paramedics or other medical practitioners, even if the victim shows no sign of responding. Remember the ABCs of CPR:

- Airway—Clear airway by tilting the victim's head back and removing any obstructions in mouth or throat (this alone may restart spontaneous breathing).

- **B**reathing—Check to see if victim is breathing. Some authorities say that mouth-to-mouth resuscitation is no longer recommended unless the victim's medical history is known, due to hepatitis and HIV risks; others state that there is no known instance of hepatitis and HIV infection via CPR.
- Circulation—Check for heartbeat. If heart has stopped, administer chest compressions in accordance with the latest guidelines of the American Heart Association until circulation resumes.

If you live or work in a lightning risk area you should take a CPR course through your local hospital, Red Cross chapter, or the American Heart Association. Hands-on training in the presence of an instructor is the best approach, but the American Heart Association offers self-learning modules.[20] If available, a defibrillator can be used to stop fibrillation.

The dual nature of electricity is interesting. As noted in the preceding paragraphs, low voltages are part of the normal functioning of the body. If the current is too high, the victim may develop ventricular fibrillation or a fatal arrhythmia. Yet there is an intermediate high current that is a lifesaver. Defibrillators apply a current of 20 to 30 amperes for 20 to 30 microseconds to a victim's heart. The shock is produced by charging a capacitor and delivering 200 to 400 watt-seconds of energy. Electrodes are placed on the chest of the victim and the shock is delivered automatically. The effect of this shock is to cause a violent contraction that stops fibrillation and gets the heart going again.[21] Home defibrillators feature a built-in microcomputer that detects fibrillation and then administers the shock automatically; a recording gives instructions so an untrained person can operate the machine.

The Neurological (Brain and Nervous) System
Lightning can affect the brain and nervous system by causing changes in the electrical state of brain cells (cerebral depolarization).[22] The prevalent symptom is that the victim is

rendered unconscious for a few minutes, hours, or even days. The electrical disturbances of the brain may be the cause of the cardiorespiratory arrest. Interestingly, many victims who suffer cardiorespiratory arrest for a number of minutes experience full neurological recovery and suffer no loss of memory or reasoning ability. This suggests that depolarization may decrease cerebral metabolic activity and permit unusually long survival of neurons despite the shortage of oxygen. The condition is similar to cold water drowning or near drowning during which vital nerve tissues survive. In other cases, victims experience amnesia and have no recollection of the lightning strike. Some victims have continuing memory problems. Frequent headaches may occur. Other consequences of a lightning strike include temporary abnormalities of the eye, especially dilated or nonreacting pupils.

After regaining consciousness, the victim may experience partial paralysis of limbs. Temporary paralysis of the legs is common, usually accompanied by a diminished arterial pulse in the legs. However, after a few hours, when the arterial pulse returns, the lower limbs also regain their power. While full neurological recovery often occurs, in some cases neurological problems develop a year or more after an apparent recovery. Problems such as epileptic seizures, partial paralysis, palsy, or symptoms resembling Parkinson's disease have been reported.

Connective Tissues: Skin, Muscles, Bone, and Blood Vessels

As mentioned previously, muscle and nerve cells use minute electrical voltages for control signals. Thus, when lightning interferes with the cell-generated voltages, muscles and nerves may not function normally. Depending on the magnitude of the interfering electric current, the damage may be reversible and recovery may occur within a few hours or a few days. In the case of a more serious situation, permanent damage may result.[23]

Lightning has diverse effects on muscles and bones, ranging from fractures, lacerations, and contusions—directly or indirectly the result of stimulation—to external and internal burns that result from heating. The calves and forearms are the muscle groups most often affected by lightning strikes. In addition to direct damage caused by lightning there can be indirect damage to the musculoskeletal system. The sudden flow of a high current through muscle tissue can cause an intense contraction. There are cases in which an individual is "thrown" across a room in reaction to being struck. This can rupture skeletal muscle and break bones.[24] Current flow can damage tendons and muscles (usually legs and forearms) by heating; this happens more often in electrical shock cases because of the longer duration of the exposure. Internal muscular damage can be identified by blood and urine tests. Fractures also result when the victim loses consciousness and falls. Skin often exhibits puncture wounds at points of current entry and exit. Contusions (internal bruising) of the heart, lung, and other organs can occur.

High electric fields in tissue damage cells either through heating them to temperatures higher than the normal physiological body temperature or by breakdown of cell membranes through a process called *electroporation*.[25] Cell damage depends on the duration of the exposure above 109° Fahrenheit (43° Celsius). Electroporation is the rupture of cell membranes. It is similar to dielectric breakdown in other materials, and is found to occur at millivolt levels within susceptible cells. It occurs when electric forces drive water molecules into the cell membrane, causing it to expand and rupture. You can visualize this as being similar to rupturing a soap bubble by pricking it with a pin.[26]

Burns are a significant consequence of lightning. During a flashover, the skin surface can reach 1,000° Celsius and vaporize almost instantly. This explains how burns from lightning can arise. Burns can be classified in six categories.[27]

- Flash burns
- Feathering or arborescent burns
- Erythema and blistering—flowerlike burns
- Linear streaking
- Punctuate full thickness skin loss
- Contact burns from metal or other materials

Flash burns, erythema (similar to sunburn), and blistering are common. Flash burns occur when the victim is close to a lightning flashover arc, either on his or her body or on a nearby object. The most unusual burns are those that leave a characteristic fernlike pattern on the skin, sometimes called Lichtenberg figures, feathering, or aborescent burns. Linear burns occur on the skin along the path followed by the lightning current. Contact burns result when hand-held tools, such metal fasteners as belt buckles or zippers, or such jewelry as bracelets, ear rings, or necklaces arc heated to a high temperature by the discharge and burn the underlying skin. Unusual effects sometimes result from contact burns resulting from traces of jewelry burnt onto the skin.

Clothing can literally be blasted from the body by steam formed by a surface discharge on wet or perspiring skin. If clothing is ignited by the flash, serious burns and even death can result. Perhaps most serious are punctuate burns—deep wounds produced by lightning entering and exiting the body. At these locations the current is concentrated, the wound is deep, and the full thickness of the skin is involved in significant tissue destruction. Entry points can be at the head or arms, while exit points are typically at the leg or foot, for cloud to ground strikes. The reverse would be true for ground to cloud flashes. In the case of severe burns, they often resemble icebergs in the sense that most damage may be concealed within the body.

One of the more unusual examples is the experience of Matt Thomsen, of Bailey, Colorado, who was 17 when he was struck on August 24, 2003. He was in the Colorado mountains on Webster Pass—elevation 12,800 feet—when he was struck.

Lightning struck him on the chest, burned a hole in his shirt, ripped his pant leg, and then made a hole through one shoe. Fortunately, two friends were nearby and witnessed the strike. They reacted quickly and saved his life by promptly giving him CPR, although neither had any formal training and had never done it before. "We saw it on television," they said. But the metal tongue ring that Thomsen had been wearing was missing. Apparently the lightning blast blew it from his mouth, leaving a black spot on his tongue marking the spot.[28]

Several of the references I consulted showed actual pictures of various types of lightning burns; I will spare the reader graphic details. However those that are unique to lightning are of interest for that reason. Most interesting are aborescent or fernlike burns mentioned previously. It seems that skin damage traces the spidery network of electricity as it flashes across the skin.[29]

Kidney, Stomach, Intestines, and Hormone Systems
Lightning can affect these internal systems—known in medical terminology as the renal, gastrointestinal, and endocrine systems—in a multitude of different ways. There is no set pattern. Effects, if they occur at all, vary widely with the individual and with the path followed by the lightning current. Abdominal injuries including gangrene of the bowel have occurred but are rare. Kidney problems may be an indirect result of toxins released by other injuries. It is possible that lightning has triggered leukemia or autoimmune disorders on rare occasions. Blood changes, usually clearing in a few days, have been noted.[30]

Ears and Eyes
Ears and eyes are susceptible to lightning injury, particularly when the head is struck.[31] Ear damage, including rupture of the eardrum (tympanic membrane) can result if the victim is struck while holding a telephone to the ear. Tinnitus, a continual ringing or buzzing sound in the ear is another

consequence of lightning damage. There can be delayed facial nerve palsy.

Eye damage can include corneal flash burns, punctures, or tearing of the retina. Tissues in the eyes are good conductors of electricity and may serve as an entry point to the cervical cord or pharynx. More than one-half of all lightning strike victims sustain eye injuries.[32]

Psychiatric and Psychological Impacts

There are definite psychiatric and psychological effects on lightning strike victims. It seems that the psychiatric and psychological responses of lightning strike survivors are poorly understood but are now seen to be extremely important to long-term recovery and functioning. On the basis of my discussions with a handful of lightning-strike survivors, it appears that the importance of these effects is frequently not appreciated by the victim's physicians.

Immediately following the incident, most victims are unconscious for a short period of time and then may be delirious, disoriented, or suffer from amnesia for a few days. They typically do not recall what happened, or may only remember hearing a loud noise. Following the initial recovery they may experience anxiety and restlessness—combined with an inability to sleep for a week or more. Following an event, children may be fearful of storms, or even of sleep or noise. In some persons anxiety is so great as to preclude them from venturing outdoors. Flashbacks reliving the event are common. The strike is typically so violent, so random, and comes without warning, so that the victim might wonder, "Why me?" In some cases temporary blindness, slurred speech, tinnitus, deafness, or paralysis reappear after the incident. In one-third to one-half of the cases headaches and partial paralysis occur. Anxiety, fatigue, and deafness may occur in 10 to 30 percent of the cases. In the longer term, depression, anxiety, and post-traumatic stress disorder are frequently observed.[33]

In a somewhat unusual case, John Corson, a resident of Madison, Maine, who was 56 at the time, was struck by lightning in August 2004 and thrown to the ground. When he regained consciousness, he said that he felt a new surge of energy, that he felt younger and lighter. He went on to say that "It's the best I've probably felt, as far as energy, in 10 years."[34]

Individual case histories or interviews with lightning strike survivors usually reveal changes in psychiatric functioning. There is no single pattern. Some patients described feeling curiously energized; others were lethargic and depressed. Some individuals stated that they became more aggressive, irritable, or unpleasant to be around, and lost friends as a result. Others seem to withdraw within themselves. A number reported being divorced by the spouse who could not cope with their changed personality. Several of these remarried, commenting "I married a wonderful person who aided in my recovery." A few contemplated suicide. Having difficulty in performing the job they held before the strike is reported by many victims. "I can't remember dates and meetings; I just don't seem to do as well with arithmetic; I can't concentrate; I'm easily tired and distracted; I forget the names of people I know"—all are typical of the complaints of lightning-strike victims.

In the extreme situation over the longer term, some individuals experienced other psychoses, such as an acute manic episode, paranoia, pathological hypochondria (hypochondriasis), fear of open spaces (agoraphobia), and long-term depression.[35]

There seems to be no uniform medical opinion on whether the cause of mental problems following a lightning strike is organic or psychological. Electroencephalograms (EEGs) taken after the incident sometimes show abnormal response and sometimes do not. From a practical perspective, it is unimportant whether the cause of psychiatric change is physical damage or psychological change. What is important is to realize that psychiatric problems frequently follow lightning strikes. They are not imaginary and require thoughtful, supportive, professional care.

While some people struck by lightning recover without any psychiatric complications, my discussions with survivors indicate that most suffer from multiple problems that originate one or more years after apparent recovery from the incident. Many experience problems that are severe enough to prevent them from resuming their former careers. Memory loss, inability to concentrate, and anxiety were cited as typical concerns. Individuals told me that they were not the same person after the lightning strike. Many complained that their concerns were ignored or dismissed by medical practitioners who told them in so many words, "You are healthy—I've run all the tests and there is nothing wrong with you."

Christine Fram was struck by lightning in 1997 while at work in a tire and auto shop in Vancouver, Canada. Even though she was inside a building, lightning reached her by traveling through the external power lines and eventually flashing from a metal work bench to her. She did not pass out, but experienced pain and numbness. She was taken to a hospital, treated, and then released. As lightning strike victims go, in a certain sense she was fortunate in that her physical injures were not as serious as they might have been. Yet, the after-effects she experienced were similar to those of hundreds of other lightning strike survivors. Months later, she had this to say about her condition: "Sometimes, I know I seem dense," she says. "I see an apple in the store, and I can't think of what it's called. And sometimes when somebody says something to me, it takes me longer to figure out what was said. I have trouble with hearing and seeing too, not with the senses themselves but with the brain's interpretation. I can't distinguish conversation from background noise or judge distances so well. I follow a checklist when I get up and get dressed in the morning. I lost my ability to multitask. Things are very much one at a time now. It is a life-changing experience. You have to start all over again"[36]

The lack of detailed psychiatric and psychological follow-up studies of lightning strike victims appears to be an area in which considerably more research is needed. Existing studies have been limited to small groups of individuals— often those involved in a single lightning strike that produced multiple injuries. Very few studies have extended over a term of years with follow-up, and almost none have included a control group.

General Medical Treatment Sequence and Priorities
Treatment of lightning-strike victims can be broken down into four phases. The initial phase involves restoring cardio-pulmonary function and providing medical support for vital organ systems, assessing other injuries, and correcting fluid pH and electrolyte imbalances. The next early phase involves treatment of cardiac muscle damage and removal of dead tissue or foreign matter from wounds (debridement), if necessary, followed by dressing and wound closure. The intermediate step is to begin necessary surgical reconstruction, provide nutritional support, muscular skeletal splinting, and physiological studies as required. The late phase would involve rehabilitation of the individual, psychological testing, and the management of neurological after-effects ("sequelae"). If the symptoms suggested brain injury, positron emission tomography (PET) scans of the brain would be indicated.[37]

When lightning kills, relatives and families must bear the burden of a loved one suddenly and inexplicably taken from them. In the case of children, the burden of grief, no doubt is magnified by a sense of guilt, second guessing the event: "I should not have let him go outside and play today;" "I should not have camped where we did," and so on. Parents will wonder if they could have prevented the death, perhaps wonder if it might be divine retribution for some earlier transgression. I've seen no reports on treatment and support for bereaved parents whose children were victims of lightning strikes.

For survivors, being struck by lightning is a life-altering experience. For many, the memories will fade with time, health recovers, and adjustments will compensate for physical disabilities. For others, the fears remain, and sometimes emerge years after the event.

5

Reasons for Keraunophobia

B y its very nature, a lightning strike is one of the most traumatic assaults a person can experience. It is all-powerful, deadly—rendering victims insensible, unconscious if not dead, temporarily paralyzed, perhaps blind or deaf. Such strikes occur randomly and almost always unexpectedly. The victims must ask themselves, Why me?

The odds are greater that a lightning strike will claim a victim outdoors, but being indoors is no guarantee of safety. Likewise, there is more danger of being struck in a rural area

Figure 17: Various Lightning Strike Positions

than an urban area. This creates a real conflict in obtaining care, because a rural hospital typically lacks the specialized equipment and experienced personnel essential to adequately treat lightning injuries and trauma, and prompt treatment is often critical. Gretel Ehrlich's story (see the Preface), told so movingly and articulately, brings home this sobering reality. As medical practitioners gain more experience with treating lightning-strike victims, more attention is being paid to the psychological care of these victims. All lightning-strike victims should be considered candidates for post-traumatic stress disorder and should be followed in case they develop delayed symptoms.

Figure 17 illustrates various ways in which people are killed or seriously injured by lightning. Hopefully, these examples will serve as reminders of what not to do and places to avoid the next time you hear thunder. Their purpose is to instill a healthy sense of keraunophobia within every person who reads this book.

Keraunophobia (fear of lightning) or *brontophobia* (fear of thunder) are but two of the symptoms that victims might exhibit.[1] A greater sense of vulnerability is another likely consequence, combined with flashbacks of the event or disturbing dreams.[2] Children as well as adults may be adversely affected.

Outdoors
The island of Huahine, Tahiti—sometimes called the Garden of Eden Island—seemed the perfect spot for Jeff Stevens and his friend Jeff Harrison for idyllic surfing.[3] That day in mid-February 1985 started out as a perfect one for surfing—sparkling water, soft breeze of the trade winds, clear skies. The two friends were staying in the town of Fare and watched the waves breaking beyond the reef on the north side of the channel through the reef. Jeff left his camera, towel and sandals on the beach before they made the 15 minute paddle out to the waves. The reef channel was marked by a large

metal marker pole. They were joined by two local surfers, a Tahitian youth named Lemaire Smith and a French inhabitant, Jean-Pierre (not his real name) who had been living on the island for a year and a half. What happened next is best told in Jeff's own words: "As the morning progressed, I saw clouds building over the mountain at the center of the island. In a short time, they turned into a black, threatening mass and I knew we were in for a bunch of rain. At that point I remembered my camera sitting on the beach, and decided I better go in and get it. Plus, we had already experienced some pretty violent rain and thunderstorms and I did not want to be out there in it.

"About the time I made it back to my hotel room, it was really raining hard. There was thunder that shook the building and I could see lightning flashes all around. I began to worry about Jeff, hoping he'd make it back soon but it had cleared and he was nowhere in sight. Then I saw a wooden launch coming back in to the beach with several people in it, and someone was on his knees giving CPR to someone else lying in the bottom of the boat. That really scared me.

"Right after that scare Jeff returned and told me what had happened. When the storm struck suddenly, he tried to paddle in against the wind, but found it was hard going back through the pass and shallows. He was tempted to grab on to the channel marker pole and wait out the storm, but then decided with the lightning hitting it probably wasn't a good idea, and he let the wind carry him back out to sea. When the storm passed he paddled back in. Meanwhile, Smith and Jean-Pierre, who were surfing the point break on the other side of the channel, waited out the storm.

"When the sky cleared, Smith saw Jean-Pierre's surfboard sticking up vertically in the water. Smith paddled over to see what the problem was and found the Frenchman underwater and hanging from the end of the board. Smith got the victim up on his board, and shortly thereafter a boat came out looking for the missing surfers. Unfortunately, it was too late—efforts to resuscitate Jean-Pierre were unsuccessful. From the nature of his injuries—a circular burn mark on his back and burns on his extremities, it was obvious that he'd been hit by lightning while laying or seated on his surfboard.

"We were all saddened by this tragic death. Jean-Pierre was apparently well-liked in the village and two days of mourning ensued. Everything closed down—shops and restaurants. We had to scrounge for food, since nothing was open. But we were thankful that we were still alive."

A lot of people are killed by lightning strikes around water, in part because water provides an excellent path to ground for lightning current, and in part because the victim falls into the water while unconscious and drowns.

A South African policeman was fishing at the shore of a lake with his father on Saturday, July 12, 2003. When it began to rain they retreated under a shelter. However, at this moment the father hooked a fish. The son offered to hold an umbrella while his father landed the fish. Lightning struck the umbrella. The son fell into the lake, and his father was knocked down and suffered serious burns on his shoulders, back, and hands. He was transported to the local hospital, placed in intensive care, and was expected to recover. His son did not survive. The news report made no mention of the fate of the fish.[4]

In Southeast Asia, local fishermen fish from platforms called *kelong* that are set up in shallow waters. During the first two weeks of April 2006, three fishermen died from lightning strikes on these platforms. In the first instance, there were two coworkers who had gone fishing together every couple of weeks for almost a year. One man, T. Y. Chan, told his wife that this would be his last fishing trip. He could not have imagined that his statement would come true in such a horrible manner. Chan and his friend's burnt bodies were found by other fishermen on the *kelong* where they fished about 40 miles east of Singapore. A day later, lightning claimed another fisherman. This time two friends were fishing near the village of Kukup, west of Singapore, when lightning hit them. One man was seriously injured but survived; the other was killed.[5]

A nine-year-old girl was struck by lightning as she sat on a metal slide in a playground.[6] Observers stated that she "lit up" at the moment of the strike. She immediately went into convulsions and lost consciousness. Forty-five minutes elapsed before she was admitted to a hospital. She was hysterical, semiconscious, and her pulse was twice the normal rate. She had suffered second-degree burns on her abdomen and thighs, and her feet were cold, mottled, and blue, lacked sensation, and there was no detectable pulse below the femoral artery. After about eight hours, normal circulation returned and after four days her laboratory and clinical results were normal. It would be interesting to know if there was any psychological follow-up with this young patient. What were her feelings, six months later, as she approached that same metal slide? Would she ever use that slide again?

A more remarkable case is that of a 10-year-old boy struck in July 1959 while cycling home from school in Baltimore County.[7] He was found slumped over where his bicycle had come to rest against a tree. With no apparent pulse, he was given artificial respiration and then transported by ambulance to a hospital. In the emergency room he was to all appearances dead. His chest was opened and his heart massaged. It was now approximately 20 to 30 minutes poststrike when heart contractions resumed. He was packed in ice and administered other emergency measures, including being placed on a respirator. He remained comatose for three days, but by the fourth day he managed to breathe on his own. After 16 days he was able to sit up and eat. He was discharged after 29 days, with a moderate tremor of his hands, and a peculiar nasal quality to his voice. He showed no evidence of emotional or personality changes, and was able to perform at his previous level in school.

Bob Ruffolo was deer hunting with his son in Pennsylvania in October 1994. He was positioned in a tree stand about 15 feet above the ground, armed with a hunting bow and arrows. Late in the afternoon it began to drizzle and he thought about climbing down, but at that moment he saw a doe approach and decided to wait a few moments longer to see if a buck followed. The next thing he knew as he regained consciousness was that he was on the ground, he was paralyzed from the waist down, and his vision was blurred. Lightning had hit the tree and unfortunately he had forgotten to wear his safety belt. It is possible that the impact of hitting the ground restarted his heart.

His 15-year old son Bobby was nearby and witnessed the entire incident. He managed to get his father into their car and to a hospital, where Ruffolo recovered after several days in intensive care.[8]

Earlier I mentioned the dangers of hiking in the wilderness during thunderstorms. Horseback riding is just as dangerous, as the examples I cited previously indicate. There was one group of 18 people, however, that miraculously escaped serious injury in 1911. On July 21—(there it is, July again!)—the party left the floor of Yosemite Valley on horseback, accompanied by several pack mules. They wound their way along scenic trails past Illilouette Falls, heading toward Vernal Falls, the Merced River, and the high country beyond. They were near Glacier Point when they were caught in a sudden thunderstorm. Lightning struck a tree by the side of the trail and then passed to the mounted caravan. Seven horses and two mules were killed instantly, the force of the lightning current literally blowing the metal shoes off of their hooves and cracking their jaws. They fell with their legs and hooves pointing to the middle of a half circle. Although badly frightened, none of the riders were injured. There was one ranger in Yosemite at that time. He came up and stayed with the party for several days. It took 20 gallons of kerosene and a number of large logs to cremate the dead animals on the spot.[9]

Lightning has been known to blow off shoes and other articles of clothing, or to burn clothing or leave it in shreds.

But what if you were not wearing clothes? In 2003, two nudists discovered that removing jewelry, metal items, and even all their clothes did not make them impervious to lightning. They were sunbathing near a Moscow river in July—of course, when else? A sudden thunderstorm caused them to scurry under a nearby tree to seek shelter from the rain. Lightning struck the tree, injuring both but not killing them. One can imagine that there were many bystanders of both sexes willing to come to their aid.[10]

A Bad Year for the Boy Scouts

The year 2005 was a bad one for the Boy Scouts. On July 25, four scout leaders were electrocuted in Virginia while attending the National Boy Scout Jamboree. They were attempting to erect a large tent when a metal support pole slipped and hit a power line. Three days later lightning struck a group of seven scouts and five adults as they huddled beneath tents to wait out a storm in Sequoia National Park, California. I described this incident in Chapter 2. Just five days later, on August 2, another scout was killed and three others injured while they slept in a log shelter during a thunderstorm. The incident occurred at Camp Steiner, located in the Uinta Mountains of Utah, at an elevation of 10,400 feet. The four victims were in one corner of the cabin. Lightning reportedly struck a nearby tree and then flashed to the log structure. Two other scouts and a scout leader in the same structure escaped injury.[11]

Persons outdoors during a thunderstorm should immediately seek shelter in a car or building. Taking shelter under a tree is not a good idea, especially if the tree is isolated—or worse yet, on top of a hill and higher than the surrounding countryside. There is a natural tendency to try to "get out of the rain" during a thunderstorm—under a tree, in a shelter, or by use of an umbrella. Under a tree, the danger is that in the event of a lightning strike, the current will flash from the tree to the victim. At this juncture, the path of the current is unpredictable. If the victim is wet or perspiring, the current may flow outside the body to ground; otherwise it could flow internally. An umbrella with a metal handle provides a dangerous path for lightning directly into a person. Individuals should disperse and not bunch together. (A pessimist might observe dispersion is necessary so that some individuals will remain alive to administer CPR to those who are stricken.)

Finding a safe shelter on a high mountain top or in the middle of a lake or harbor in a sudden storm is not an easy proposition when lightning strikes. (See Plate 9.) About the only safe alternative is to monitor the weather carefully, don't plan trips when thunderstorms are likely, and if the weather starts to change, get off the mountain or off the water immediately. Cultivate an active keraunophobia!

Indoors
The experts say, "Get indoors when thunder roars." Usually this works, but not always. Even indoors, a strong sense of keraunophobia is healthy.

Betty Smith was employed by a drug store in Kent, Ohio. On June 6, 1986, the weather was hot and muggy and the sky became very dark. Moments later she heard thunder in the distance and then looked out her office window as rain and hail fell in the parking lot next to the building. The noise of the rain on the roof was so loud that it frightened her, and she decided to move into an interior office. As she did so, she heard a crack and a sizzling noise. In her own words: "I stepped forward and in a split second saw a ball of fire. I felt an excruciating pain as the lightning bolt entered my body. I felt as if I was being burned alive, that my head and heart had exploded. Every muscle in my body seized up and I heard my teeth shatter. A loud popping noise came from my chest and I knew for certain that I was dead. The bolt thrust me backwards as if I were being shot from a cannon. I flew against the wall with such a driving force that the shock of the impact started my heart again but I was sure my neck and back were broken."

I have chosen to recite Smith's story in some detail because she eloquently describes what a lightning strike is like. Almost any victim will cite some or all of the same feelings and experiences that she mentions, but her memory is clearer than that of many victims, some of whom were rendered unconscious.

Smith also has memories of the ambulance ride, the hospital treatment, and the agonizing pain. Perhaps worst of all was the smell of "seared steak cooking" that she could not escape for days afterwards. She survived and began a lengthy process of recovery from her multiple serious injuries. She has suffered occasional seizures, lightning-induced brain damage, and periodic blindness in one eye, but she is now able to walk with the assistance of a cane. She hides when a storm is near.[12]

Mary Frederick was working in a penitentiary in Atlanta. She had been a career employee of the prison system for 10 years and loved her job. In June 1994, while sitting at her desk inside the prison, the building was struck by lightning. The strike set off the fire alarm and somehow made it through the building electrical system to strike her where she sat at her desk. She had symptoms similar to those described by Betty Smith but not as severe. She walked to the safety office to make a report, then called her husband, got the name of a doctor, and drove to his office. He gave her a cursory examination, said she was fine, and sent her home. Over the next several months her condition deteriorated. She experienced dizziness, hair loss, blackouts, and disorientation. Several doctors dismissed her concerns as "emotional, due to menopause."

Frederick's most frightening experience occurred three years after she had been struck. She was away from home to visit her son on his birthday when she became completely disoriented while running a quick errand. By the time she realized something was wrong, she was 50 miles away and completely lost. She called her husband's office but he wasn't in. She explained her dilemma to another friend, who in an effort to help her, arranged for an ambulance to come pick her up. She was taken to a hospital, where she descended into a comalike state for 19 hours. When she came out of it she found herself in a psych ward at another hospital, and was told her family had committed her! (Not true.) In desperation she tried to climb out a window. Finally her husband located her and she found a psychiatrist who recognized the symptoms of lightning strike victims and was able to secure her release. Today she carries a medical card explaining the symptoms and treatment. She also hides during storms.[13]

Usually, but not always, as the preceding examples demonstrate, you are safe inside a building, because metal pipes, electrical conduits, or steel reinforcing rods or beams will provide a low resistance path to ground for the lightning current. However, there are hundreds of cases in which people inside buildings have been injured because lightning jumped from a window frame, pipe, or other metal object and hit them. People talking on the telephone have been killed or injured when lightning hit the telephone lines and jumped from the receiver (ear piece) to the head of the victim. The ear provides a convenient entry into the body, so the current flows internally instead of flashing over.

Telephones are only one example; a similar scenario can be envisioned for a person typing on a computer keyboard, or turning on the water faucet, or taking a shower. People have been struck while fiddling with televisions or radios. Thus, to ensure safety avoid close proximity to or contact with any metallic objects in the building. When thunderstorms appear, go indoors, but find a safe location indoors. Even inside a building, let keraunophobia be your guide!

Motor Vehicles
Conventional wisdom has it that you are safe in motor vehicles. Generally this is the case. Even though there is some

risk, it is far better to be in a car or truck (with a metal roof and body) than it is to be in the open or under a tree. In June 2005, a woman was driving on Highway 22 near Cochrane, Alberta, Canada, when her car was struck by lightning. The driver saw the flash and heard a loud bang as lightning struck the vehicle. The car lost power and smoke started pouring from the dashboard. The driver was able to pull over to the side of the road and call for assistance. The fire department extinguished the blaze and the occupants of the car were uninjured.[14] Two vehicles traveling in Florida in September 2005 were hit by lightning but the occupants escaped injury. Driving on the Florida Turnpike, a mother and her baby daughter escaped injury when lightning struck the vehicle, blowing a hole through the rear window near where the child sat in her car seat. Fortunately, neither was hurt.[15] Another Florida driver was hit on "Alligator Alley" while driving a pickup truck near Davie, Florida. Lightning struck the truck and completely fried the electrical system. The cab filled with smoke but the startled driver was able to pull over and get out of the vehicle without injury.[16]

Finally for close calls, nothing beats this story. Firemen were fighting a blaze in April 2006 in a suburb north of Memphis, Tennessee. Fire fighters were in several locations around the burning building trying to extinguish the blaze when a tornado warning siren sounded. Several firemen immediately climbed down from the fire truck's extended ladder from which they were hosing water onto the fire. Seconds after the last fireman was off the ladder, there was a loud boom and a bright flash as lightning struck the ladder and damaged it so badly that it was inoperable. The building burned down.[17]

In summary, as the previous examples show, being in a vehicle during a lightning strike is probably a pretty good bet. It might be scary, but you have a good chance of walking away uninjured. Just be sure it isn't a convertible.

Divine Intervention

Thunder and lightning have symbolized the power and wrath of the gods since ancient times. The Bible contains dozens of references, such as *Psalm* 18:14, "The Lord...sent out his arrows and scattered them; and he shot out lightnings, and discomfited them." Or, in *Revelation* 4:5, John describes his vision of a throne in heaven: "And out of the throne proceeded lightnings, and thunderings and voices..."[18]

The image of an angry god, hurling thunderbolts at mortal men, is an ancient one dating at least to the Greeks and Zeus. The idea of a lightning strike as a natural disaster, classified as "an act of God" is more than a legalistic definition; it is also a way of rationalizing the capricious nature of lightning, its seemingly heartless lack of concern in choice of victims. Historically, lightning has shown a callous disregard for even the most solemn occasions.

In 2005, a man attended a funeral near the town of Ljubljana, in Slovenia. He was struck while holding aloft a metal cross. He died a few hours later in the hospital. In another tragic incident the same year, an elderly man visiting his son's grave at a cemetery in Tucson, Arizona, was struck and killed by lightning. Maintenance workers discovered his body lying near his son's grave on a Sunday morning. In July 2003, a guest evangelist was preaching at a First Baptist Church in Forest, Ohio. The preacher's message concerned penance, and to emphasize his point he raised his arms in prayer and called to the heavens for a sign. At this moment lightning struck the church steeple and flashed through the electrical system, including the microphone he was using. He was startled but not injured. He was illuminated by the resulting flash and the noise of the strike rang through the church. Worshippers were awestruck by the timing. The service continued for another 20 minutes before the congregation finally realized that the building was on fire. Another tragic event took place on Sunday morning in April 2006, in the town of Santa Maria Dell Rio in central Mexico.

A group of young people gathered around a metal cross to pray and clean and decorate the cross for an upcoming Catholic celebration. Lightning struck; five were killed and nine others were injured.[19]

In December 2003, lightning struck the Zionist Church at Mankayane, Swaziland, during church services. Fifteen people were stricken; of these, 9 were killed, including the priest, five children, and three other adults, while six other victims were taken to a local hospital. Sadly, three of the nine fatalities—a mother and her two children—were from the same family.[20]

However, when actor James Caviezel, who played Jesus in Mel Gibson's film *The Passion of the Christ* was hit by lightning during filming in Italy, he was not injured. Lightning hit an umbrella being held above him by another man. Both escaped injury.[21] I leave the interpretation of these events to the spiritual inclinations of my readers and others who are wiser than I.

In summary, individuals can become lightning casualties outdoors or indoors—more fatalities, as opposed to injuries, occurring outdoors than indoors. As the examples in this chapter indicate, that is not necessarily a good thing; many of the injuries are debilitating and can result in pain and disabilities lasting a lifetime. There is little else that can be said for individuals who might be struck outdoors on golf courses, under trees, in the mountains, or on beaches or lakes, other than watch the weather and cancel dangerous activities when thunderstorms are likely. For individuals in buildings or otherwise associated with human-made infrastructure such as roads, bridges, or transportation systems, understanding how lightning interacts with buildings and infrastructure may save your life. That is the subject of the next chapter.

6

The Lights Flickered and Then Went Out

The lights flickered and then went out. It was 5:16 P.M. on November 9, 1965, and the worst blackout in the history of the United States had just begun. A backup relay near Niagara Falls tripped, causing a circuit breaker to disconnect a transmission line, which caused other transmission lines to be overloaded and shut down as power flowed to them, resulting in generators shutting down because there was no place for the power to flow, and within minutes power was lost in Ontario, New York, most of New England (except Maine), and portions of New Jersey and Pennsylvania. More than 30 million people were without power—many for as long as 12 to 13 hours. No one knew for certain what had happened, but it was obvious that it had been a costly failure—the economic impact later was estimated at $1 billion.

National concern was so great that President Lyndon Johnson directed the Federal Power Commission to conduct an immediate and detailed investigation, involving the FBI if necessary. Was it sabotage, lightning, or equipment failure? The Federal Power Commission and the northeast and Canadian utilities conducted exhaustive studies and simulation. Two years after the event, the Federal Power Commission published a review of the incident and had this to say about the backup relay that started the entire debacle:

> "The precise cause of the backup relay energization is not known. A momentary and relatively small change in voltage might have been responsible as the pickup setting is inversely proportional to the square of the voltage."[1]

A momentary change in voltage could well have stemmed from a lightning strike somewhere on the system, or it could have resulted from some other cause. We'll never know. Nonetheless, the great Northeast Blackout had significant ramifications. Congress held hearings and debated the wisdom of creating an electric utility research organization to improve utility reliability. In response, the nation's electric utilities organized the Electric Power Research Institute (EPRI), a nonprofit organization funded by utilities. Thus it could be said that a lightning strike may have triggered the greatest impetus to advance electricity research and development in decades.

Despite numerous improvements, lightning struck New York again on a hot summer night—July 13, 1977. With lights out and no air-conditioning, resentment built until this blackout unleashed a firestorm of riots and looting in the poor sections of New York City. Nine million people were without electricity for more than 24 hours. Rioters and vandals started more than 1,000 fires; 2,000 stores were broken into and pillaged; 3,700 people were arrested. Losses were in the millions of dollars.[2]

Table 4: Economic Losses Due to Lightning

	$ millions/year
• Electric utilities	1,000
• Annual insurance claims (homes, farms, equipment)	1,000
• Forest fires	1,000
• Personal computers	100
• Other	1,900
TOTAL	**$5 billion**

These two examples point out the costly impact that lightning strikes can have on infrastructure. When the effects on infrastructure, buildings, and sensitive electronics equipment are combined, the total is staggering—estimated to be $5 billion per year in the U.S. alone.[3] Major areas of loss are tabulated in Table 4.

Lightning flashes can inflict damage on infrastructure, people, or livestock, by one of three means: by a direct strike, by indirect strike (flashover), or by indirect effects resulting from the intense and rapidly changing electromagnetic field that is produced by the flash.

Direct strikes are mitigated by lightning-protection systems that are designed to intercept the lightning strike and channel the current to ground, where it can be safely neutralized, protecting the structure or equipment that falls under the shielded zone created by the lightning arresting system. The problem of indirect effects is more complex and today has become more important due to the widespread use of solid-state electronic devices for businesses, factory automation, home entertainment, and communication. As microelectronic components have become smaller and smaller, the amount of electrical power that it takes to damage them has correspondingly decreased. Very small surface-mounted semiconductor components used in microcomputers and related devices can be destroyed by the minute energy created by a static electric discharge.

If an electrical conductor such as a wire or coil is moved rapidly in a magnetic field, a voltage is induced in the wire. This is a basic principle by which electric generators work. Conversely, if a magnetic field expands or collapses near a stationary conductor, a voltage is likewise induced in the conductor. If the field is strong and the change very rapid, momentary high voltages can be produced.

A secondary indirect effect is what is known as *capacitive coupling*. Remember that a capacitor consists of two parallel metal plates separated by a dielectric. So if a rapidly changing electric field is impressed on a conductor or metal surface, other nearby conductors separated by a dielectric will have an induced voltage, just as occurs in a capacitor.

A tertiary indirect coupling effect occurs at high frequency, wherein a burst of high-frequency energy radiated by the flash is absorbed by nearby conductors acting as antennas.

Direct and indirect effects are of concern in a number of situations, these being the ones of greatest interest:

- Buildings
- Commercial/industrial facilities
- Personal computers, fax machines, and other sensitive electronic devices
- Public assembly, athletic, and recreational facilities
- Agriculture and forest lands
- Bridges, highways, railroads
- Aircraft and boats
- Electric transmission and distribution lines, substations, and related equipment
- Telephone and cable television systems
- Antennas
- Pipelines, oil, and hazardous material storage facilities
- Mines and underground structures

I believe that the reader will find it interesting to see how lightning impacts each of these areas.[4]

Buildings
The vulnerability of buildings and structures to lightning strikes would have been foreseen in ancient times by observing lightning setting trees ablaze. Leonardo DaVinci's notebooks, written in the 15th century, describe a lightning hit on the Torre della Credenza in Milan. The bolt tore away a section of a brick wall about 6 feet wide and 6 feet long and 4 feet deep.[5] Three centuries later, Benjamin Franklin writing in

1752, described lightning strikes on two houses in Philadelphia, as the lightning:

"...seem'd to go considerably out of a direct course, for sake of passing thro' metal; such as hinges, sash weights, iron rods, the pendulum of a clock, etc., and that where it had sufficient metal to conduct it nothing was damag'd; but where it passed thro' plaistering or wood work, it rent and split them surprizingly."[6]

Residential buildings, being the most numerous and often unprotected, are damaged more often than other types of buildings that are hit by lightning. Sometimes lightning-strike effects border on the bizarre.

A pre-Christmas hit on a home in New Orleans ravaged the structure. The strike originated in Christmas lights decorating a large oak tree in front of the house. From the lights, the current passed into the house. On the way, a side flash blew a decorative reindeer located in the front yard into the air, breaking it into several pieces and scorching the grass. The timer controlling the lights blew off the wall and flew into a neighbor's yard. The Christmas wreath was thrown from the front door and the blast tore the door from its hinges. The current also jumped to a metal bolt in the front porch concrete slab, shattering the surrounding concrete and blasting pieces of broken concrete into the ceiling. Within the house, windows exploded, nails were pulled from the walls, shelves and pictures were knocked down, and curtain rod brackets flew off the walls. The owner of the house was watching television with his two children when the bolt struck. He recalled that "suddenly there was a bright flash and then darkness." The family was spared injury by blinds that deflected the window debris.[7]

Fires in buildings may be the direct result of lightning, as when flammable materials are ignited by an arc, or an indirect result, as when the lightning damages electrical or fuel systems to the point that they ignite a fire. Spalling, meltdown, and fractures are due to heating caused by the flow of electricity through a conducting material. This is called resistance heating and is the same process used in an electric toaster or skillet. Intense heat causes rapid expansion of materials or generates steam if moisture is present. The effect shatters concrete, ejects bricks from walls or fascia, or splits boards or trees. Pressure built up in structures or chimneys can blow them apart violently. High currents that jump to wiring, plumbing, or other metal objects can melt them. Indoors, one is in greatest danger near windows or doors, on the telephone, or in contact with plumbing or electrical equipment. If struck indoors, you are more likely to be hurt than killed; injuries outrank deaths by a ratio of 20 to 1 indoors.

Lisa Cunningham—a teenager at the time—was at home in West Virginia with her younger brother when a thunderstorm began abruptly in 1977. Some of the windows were open, but they waited for a break in the lightning before closing them. As she stood in the living room with a bowl of salad and a fork in one hand (they had been eating lunch at the time), there was a bright flash, a loud bang, and she flew through the air about 12 feet into the next room. For an hour or so her entire body felt numb, but by the time her parents returned she appeared to have recovered. She had no external signs of injury. She subsequently completed high school and college, got married, had a career. All was well for 18 years, until she was hospitalized with ulcerative colitis. As part of the therapy, she was given a steroid. Upon release from the hospital, she felt worse rather than better. Her condition gradually deteriorated until she terminated her job. By then she needed a wheel chair and suffered from memory lapses and other problems. A three-year series of visits to neurologists and other specialists ensued as she and her husband tried to identify her medical problems. Finally she determined that as a result of the 1977 lightning strike she had suffered damage to the limbic and temporal lobes of her brain.

The effects lay dormant until triggered by her 1995 illness. Today, although she has seen steady improvement in her condition over the last several years, she feels as though she is functioning at 50 percent of her normal capacity.[8]

Commercial and Industrial Facilities
The electric fields due to nearby lightning strikes induce electric currents that can burn out electronic control systems or instrumentation and can be very disruptive to manufacturing plants. Hollow or flat conductors can be crushed as a result of heating and magnetic effects. Fires that result from the lightning strike are even more serious problems.

In April 2005, 19 people in northern Spain were injured—four seriously—when lightning struck a grain silo that was part of a flour factory. The lightning strike caused an explosion and fire, and the force of the blast also broke windows and damaged nearby cars.[9]

A lightning strike near Louisville, Kentucky on August 4, 2003 resulted in *truly* disastrous effects! The bolt hit a storage facility operated by the Jim Beam distillery, causing a fire. The flames were fed by more than one million gallons of fine Kentucky bourbon. The total loss was in the millions of dollars.[10]

Personal Computers, Fax Machines, and Other Sensitive Electronic Devices
Damaging effects of lightning on electrical and electronic systems are the result of voltage surges, or induced currents. Voltage surges can travel long distances over electrical distribution systems. The resulting high voltage will damage computers, radios, televisions, and other electronic equipment.

Bailey Greene-Kouri lived in Atlanta, Georgia, and worked in a steel and glass high-rise building for an insurance company. Her desk in an office on the top floor was located near a window. At noon one day as she typed at her keyboard, a summer thunderstorm approached. She was concentrating on her work and did not pay much attention to the approaching storm until suddenly she sensed a hot white light and knew something was very much the matter. She managed to pull her hands away from the keyboard (coworkers said that they saw a bright white light that went from the keyboard to the tips of her fingers). She felt as if she was a piece of charcoal pulled glowing from a fire. The lightning current exited through her left foot resting on the base of her roller chair, leaving a smoking hole in her shoe. Her left side was numb, she could not see out of one eye, and she was in intense pain. An ambulance was called and she was taken to the hospital. Following her release from the hospital a neurologist found that her left arm had sustained severe nerve damage and she had suffered injury to her brain. She has some ongoing vision problems, headaches, insomnia, intense mood swings, and memory impairment. Despite all of this, however, she reports a happy marriage, has a new job, and feels that she continues to make progress in recovering from her injuries.[11]

Public Assembly, Athletic and Recreational Facilities
Some years ago, I joined a Masters swimming program. The team works out early in the morning in the outdoor swimming pool of the local high school in Newport Beach, California. One morning as I drove to swimming practice it started to rain, and before long I could hear the first peals of thunder. As I parked the car, I saw several flashes of lightning in the distance. Entering the area, I saw that two swimmers were already in the pool, and a number of others were standing by on the concrete deck trying to make up their minds. As I timed the interval between the lightning flashes and subsequent thunder, it was apparent that the lightning strikes were a few miles north of the pool—too close for comfort in my opinion. We suggested to the swimmers that they vacate the pool, but they declined to do so. Along with a number of the other swimmers, I waited inside the locker room for the storm to pass. The storm was unusual because thunderstorms are

infrequent in Southern California. Fortunately, no one was hurt in this incident.

The danger of swimming during a thunderstorm was dramatically brought home to a group of people—one of them a pregnant woman—swimming at the beach near Clearwater, Florida. The month? As you might guess, the incident took place in July 2005. Lightning struck the water, injuring all five swimmers. Fortunately, they were able to get out of the water and no one drowned. They were all taken to a local hospital and were expected to recover from their injuries. News reports did not state the distance between the swimmers and the point of impact of the lightning flash.[12] When lightning strikes water, it establishes an electric field gradient similar to that created in a ground strike. (See Figure 14 in Chapter 4.) The shock hazard is therefore analogous to the "step voltage" discussed later in this chapter. At some distance, depending on the intensity of the strike and the resistivity of the water, the electric current in the water is dissipated by the water's resistance (the lightning energy is converted to heat in the water). It is impossible to stipulate a "safe distance" because no one can predict where lightning might strike. Certainly, if lightning hit a swimming pool—even an Olympic-size pool—everyone in the pool would sustain injuries, and the victims closest to the point of impact would likely become fatalities.

Indoor pools should not be considered safer than outdoor pools. There are many different pathways whereby lightning energy can be conducted into the pool building through buried metal water pipes and telephone or cable television lines, wet ground, or metal parking lot lamp poles, to cite a few examples. Consequently, if lightning strikes a building or strikes the ground next to the building, damage to equipment or personal injury can occur.

Athletic facilities can be hazardous during thunder-storms. The hazard is all the greater because large numbers of people may be attending events. In September 2004, about a year before the swimming pool incident described above, lightning struck a football playing field at the Grapeland High School in east Texas. Practice was nearly over, it had started to rain, and the players were preparing to head for the locker room when lightning struck. The bolt struck in the middle of a massed group of players, knocking many of them to the ground. Newspaper reports indicated that 40 people were injured—both players and coaches, several seriously. One of the players subsequently died from his injuries.[13]

This was an incident during which thunderstorms were nearby but had not yet reached the town of Grapeland. "There was no warning," the coaches said.

Agriculture and Forest Lands
Lightning claims many victims among agricultural workers and livestock. Farm workers are further at risk because they are often in an area where medical assistance may be at some distance and furthermore may not have the sophisticated diagnostic tools necessary to evaluate the victim's condition. Livestock are frequently killed by step voltages (See Chapter 4) or by proximity to metal fences or rails that are struck.

A teenager by the name of Barry W. Smith was riding a horse during a Montana cattle roundup on the family ranch when it began to thunder. The riders were told to dismount and seek shelter in a low wash or other unexposed spot, but before doing so Barry took a direct hit on his head. The rider with him heard a loud noise and saw a brilliant flash as Barry and the horse went down. The current burnt Barry's hat, singed his face, burned and matted his hair, and then flashed down his back, shredding his pants and shirt and burning him in numerous locations. It appeared that the flash had also jumped to the "D" ring of his saddle and killed his horse. His partner rode back to the ranch for help and by the time Barry's mother arrived in a pickup truck to help him he was conscious but did not know what had happened. She took him to the nearest hospital, 31 miles away at Lewiston, Montana. After spending nearly a week in the hospital recovering from his burns and other injuries, Barry was finally able to go home. He eventually recovered from most of his injuries and was able to return to rodeoing and other sports. However, he had sustained severe damage to one ear and had to undergo surgery (tympoplasty) to repair his ear.[14]

Lightning is a major cause of fires and is typically responsible for 10 to 20 percent of all wildland fires (80 to 90 percent are of human origin), but lightning typically results in one-half to two-thirds of the total burnt acreage. In the five-year period from 2001 to 2005 there were 58,000 wildland fires started by lightning in the United States. The southern and eastern United States only accounted for 8 percent of these, while Alaska, the western states, and the Great basin area had 92 percent of the lightning-induced forest fires. At first this seems surprising, but the majority of wildlands are in Alaska and the West. During this same five-year period lightning-caused fires burned more than 22 million acres of wildlands. The cost to the United States federal government for fighting wildfires (of all sources) ranged from $0.9 billion to $1.7 billion.[15] More than 7 million acres were burned as a result of lightning strikes in 2004 and in 2005—two of the worst years since comprehensive records have been compiled. The largest reported fire occurred in Alaska in 2004. It was called the Taylor Complex fire and burned more than 1.3 million acres. In June 2004, Alaska was particularly hard-hit: 15 forest fires burned 80,000 acres of spruce and tundra during a period of unusually hot and dry weather.[16] There were also major fires in British Columbia, Canada, that month.

The summer of 2005 exemplifies a bad year for lightning-induced wildland fires. Fires occurred near Durango, Colorado, early in June. By mid-July they were ravaging Arizona (60 fires at one point), Utah, Texas—even Indiana. August 9 saw hundreds of fires raging in Ontario, Canada. On August 18, there were 11 fires in Yosemite National Park; August 23, 7 new fires in eastern Oregon; August 24, 20 fires near Elko Nevada; August 25, a group of fires in the vicinity of Cook County, Wyoming; September 5, 2005, 11 fires near Billings, Montana, with 300 to 400 lightning strikes reported on one afternoon alone; September 10, fires near Great Falls, Montana. Then, on the other side of the world on November 23, Sydney, Australia, was bombarded with 750 lightning strikes in a matter of several hours. There was no significant damage, but on November 28 and for the next month, Victoria and New South Wales suffered a series of fires—sometimes as many as 25 to 33 per day burning at locations near Warrnambool, Melbourne, and other parts of eastern Victoria. In January and February 2006, Victoria and New South Wales were again stricken with a series of devastating wildlands fires.

We know from backpacking and camping experiences that it is difficult to start a campfire with green wood. How is it then that lightning starts so many forest fires, since living trees are the ones most often struck? Many trees that are hit by lightning are damaged but still survive. In May 2005, I took a hike on a trail named "The Shadow of the Giants," which passes along Nelder Creek and through the Nelder Grove of Giant Sequoias, located just south of Yosemite Valley, California. There you can see trees that have been felled by a lightning strike and others that have survived. (See Plate 10.)

About one-half of the mass of living trees is water, either absorbed into the porous cellulose cells that form the structure of wood, or chemically part of cellulose molecules, or free flowing in pores and fibers. When a tree is harvested to produce lumber—or firewood for that matter—it is first seasoned—either by kiln drying or sun drying—to reduce its water content. Dry wood has good insulating properties; however, green or wet wood is more susceptible to damage.

The amount of moisture in the wood has an important bearing on its response to high voltage. Consider first a green tree: the resistance to ground is on the order of 1,000 ohms due to water content. An electric field in the range of 150 to 250 kilovolts per meter will cause breakdown to occur. In this case the path of the electric arc will be internal—deep in the trunk—or near the surface, depending on how the moisture is distributed.[17] Internally the intense heat of the arc turns moisture to steam and the resulting pressure often shatters the trunk. If the arc is near the surface, bark and outer fibers will be blown from the tree, leaving a characteristic furrow that traces the path of the lightning current as it flows to ground. The tremendous heat of the arc (temperature in excess of 2,000 degrees Celsius) can ignite fragments of the tree and start a forest fire, or the bolt can side flash to another tree or bush, starting a fire, especially if there is dry brush or dead branches nearby. For the tree to burn, conditions must be such that the strike duration is sufficiently long to raise the temperature of the wood to its flash point.

There is considerable test data concerning the effects of high voltage electric currents on wood, since wooden poles are used in the electric utility industry for distribution and transmission line supports. Wooden poles have been extensively tested in the laboratory using high voltage arcs. In seasoned wood that is wet, if the field strength reaches 200 to 300 kilovolts per meter, there will be a breakdown over the wet surface (similar to flashover on a human). In dry seasoned wood, flashover requires 500 kilovolts per meter. In the case of seasoned power or telephone poles, the current path depends on several variables. If it is raining and the wood surface is wet but the pole is well-seasoned with low moisture content, the electric arc will travel on the surface of the wood and there will be little resulting damage. If, on the other hand, the pole moisture content is appreciable, the lightning current can flow internally, shattering or splitting the wood. The likelihood of this effect is increased if lightning enters the pole through metal bolts or lag screws that penetrate to the moist core wood.

This topic interested me so I decided to take some measurements of my own. I bought an eight-foot-long Douglas Fir 2"x 4" from my local home-builders store, knowing that the wood you buy today is typically "green" (not well-seasoned). I weighed this board and found that it weighed 12.63 pounds and with a volume of 0.281 cubic feet had a specific weight of 44.93 pounds per cubic foot.[18] I applied either direct current (14 volts) or alternating current (120 volts) through brass screws embedded in either end of the board, measured the current flow, and calculated the resistance. The resistance was 313,000 ohms (average of alternating and direct current measurements). I set this piece of lumber aside in my study and let it dry out over the winter. Three months later in the spring I repeated the measurements and found that it now weighed only 9.32 pounds, having lost 26 percent of its initial weight. The new resistance was over 10,000,000 ohms—more than 30 times greater. If the water content was converted to saturated steam, it would occupy a volume more than 300 times as great as the size of the original board. Given that fact, it is easy to see how a lightning strike can split and shatter large trees!

Lightning in Soil and Rock
When lightning hits the ground, soil breaks down (due to groundwater content) at a field strength of 50 kilovolts per meter. Powerful current flows through the soil can heat it to temperatures as high as 10,000 degrees Celsius. (The temperature in a lightning bolt is estimated to be 30,000 degrees Celsius, five times hotter than the glowing surface of the sun (but not as hot as the coronas that flash out from the sun). If the lightning current passes through sandy soil, it can melt the sand and fuse it into a tubelike glassy or vitreous material called *fulgurite*. Fulgurites as long as 3 meters have been found. (See Plate 2.)

The high magnetic field created by a lightning strike can induce magnetism in rock. This effect is noticeable in certain rock formations, especially basalt. Archaeologists investigating ancient petroglyphs in California and Oregon have made a fascinating connection with lightning strikes.

Rock carvings at Petroglyph Lake in southeastern Oregon, Boles Creek Canyon in Northern California, and other locations in California appear to be associated with magnetic anomalies in the basalt. Archaeologists and anthropologists studying the rock art observed that a compass brought near the carvings will swing wildly. In some instances, researchers are able to trace the path of the lightning strike over the face of a canyon wall. The glyphs contain both abstract and realistic motifs, the abstract ones resembling various geometric figures, the realistic ones portraying humans, various quadrupeds, and snake lizards and horned lizards.

As I noted in Chapter 1, early humans attributed magical power to lightning. On the West Coast of the United States early humans are believed to have been the Hokan peoples, followed by the Penutians and then the Paiutes, the Hokan prior to 1000 A.D. and the Penutians and Paiutes following 1000 A.D. From legends and verbal histories of descendants of these early humans (Paiutes are still found in California), we know that shamans and others sought power by visiting trees struck by lightning or looking for fulgurites when lightning struck the ground. It could be that by placing rock art over lightning strikes, the artist believed that his carvings were imbued with a special power. It is interesting that many of the panels feature a snake lizard, a common reptile found even today in the petroglyph area. Many of the lizard figures are drawn head-down, and are thought to symbolize lightning. Measurements showed that a number of the petroglyphs were associated with magnetic anomalies in the underlying rock.[19]

Bridges, Highways, Railroads
Lightning strikes are responsible for damage to every type of infrastructure, not just the electric grid. Transportation systems, even though they are generally constructed with lightning-protection measures, are not invulnerable. Bridges and highways have been struck by lightning, as have cars,

motorcycles, and bicycles—both stationary and in motion on highways. Plate 11 shows a lightning strike on the Queensboro Bridge in New York City. When bridges are struck by lightening there is usually little damage as they are constructed of steel and are grounded. When highways are struck, large chunks of concrete can be dislodged when the lightning current produces high-pressure steam from moisture that has seeped in through cracks in the concrete.

An exception is the Rion-Antirion Bridge, a new cable-stayed bridge that crosses the Gulf of Corinth near Patras, Greece. The 1.4-mile-long bridge, which opened in 2004, was hit by lightning on January 27, 2005, resulting in a fire in one of the suspension cables. This is an unusual occurrence and suggests that the bridge's lightning-protection system was inadequate. The bridge was closed for five days for inspection and repairs.[20]

Vehicles traveling on highways during thunderstorms have also been struck, although occupants within a metal vehicle are generally safe. It is a different story for cyclists or motorcycle riders. For example, on August 12, 2003, a man riding a motorcycle near Sozopolis, Greece, was struck by lightning and killed. Robert Davidson endured a similar experience, but miraculously survived. It was June 1980, and he and his wife were riding a Honda 500 motorcycle down I-74 near Indianapolis, Indiana when it started to rain. He pulled over and stopped so they could put on rain gear. As he started to step off the bike, he was struck on the left shoulder. The bolt blew holes in his right leg (still across the motorcycle seat at the time) and then down his left leg to the wet pavement. His shoes were blown off and he was catapulted about 20 feet from the motorcycle, coming to rest on the highway in full cardiac arrest and paralyzed. Fire department paramedics were summoned but initially were unable to get a pulse. A mysterious woman dressed in black materialized from the onlookers and placed a bible on his chest. She said a few words and then the paramedics were finally able to get a pulse.

Moments later the woman had disappeared. The freeway was closed and Davidson was flown by helicopter to an Indianapolis hospital. A doctor performed an emergency tracheotomy during the flight so that Davidson could breathe. Davidson—in a coma—remained in the Indianapolis hospital for five weeks, and was then transferred to a hospital closer to home, where he remained in a coma for two more weeks. Once released from the hospital he was unable to function well, struggling with continuous headaches. His wife divorced him and he contemplated suicide. Three years after the incident he remarried, and credits his new wife with turning his life around. He returned to work six years after the lightning strike. He still tires easily, suffers from memory lapses, but as he says, "I am coping, knowing I do have a purpose in life."[21]

Automobiles and buses provide a good measure of protection to occupants because of their metal shell. In fact, if unable to get into a protected building at the onset of a thunderstorm, taking shelter in a vehicle is the next best alternative. Just be careful not to touch any of the metal components of the vehicle.

Heavy-rail locomotives and cars are generally not prone to damage because they are grounded by the track work and usually do not present a high profile. However, signals and communication systems are vulnerable. On June 6, 1950, lightning struck a railroad signal tower in Alexandria, Virginia. As a result, two trains crashed, injuring hundreds of passengers.[22] Light-rail systems in use for public transportation in many cities use an overhead line to supply traction power. This line and the substations that feed it are protected in much the same manner as utility distribution lines.

More recently—in November 2005—during an early morning thunderstorm over Melbourne, Australia, a lightning strike disabled a portion of the CONNEX train-control system. (CONNEX is an international company that operates transportation systems in 25 countries.) As a result, full service on the extensive Melbourne commuter rail system was delayed and not resumed until three hours later. More than 150 trains—and an estimated 20,000 riders—were affected by the delays.[23]

Boats and Aircraft

I was in *Sitting Tall*, a 46-foot Bertram sport fishing boat about 60 miles west of the Southern California coast, and not far from the island of San Clemente. It was early in the afternoon of Monday, September 19, 2005, and we were trolling for marlin when we saw the first lightning strikes over the mainland. We were aboard my friend Andy Youngquist's boat, and he had recently installed a new radar system. The radar provided a good indication of the distance and direction being taken by the thunderstorm. Throughout the day we kept an eye on the storm, as we made our way back to Avalon Harbor on Catalina Island. Monday night, secure at our mooring in Avalon Harbor, we watched spectacular fireworks as the lightning illuminated the mainland 30 miles east of us. It was a truly impressive storm as captured in Dev Gregory's photographs. (See Plates 2 and 9.) By coincidence, my wife Nancy was aboard a Jet Blue flight scheduled to land at Long Beach airport at 7:00 P.M. Monday evening. More on that later.

Sometime during the late evening of Monday night, the Coast Guard received a distress call stating that a sailing vessel had been hit by lightning and a four-person crew was abandoning ship about 15 miles west of Dana Point. Throughout the next day we monitored the VHF radio listening for further reports about the crew of the sailboat. The Coast Guard and other vessels conducted a search over a broad area, and we also maintained a watch, although we were some distance from the location where the boat reportedly sank. No sign of the boat or the crew was found, and the Coast

Guard subsequently determined that the report had been a hoax.

Thunderstorms are relatively infrequent in Southern California, but this storm arose when a cold upper-level, low-pressure area interacted with tropical moisture from Hurricane Max, coming up from the south. As far as I know, no boats were hit during this particular storm, although many sailors took precautions or avoided the area.

Lightning strikes less frequently over the ocean than over the continents, but boats at sea are not immune. The crew of one long-distance cruiser had an unforgettable Christmas Eve in 2002, while sailing just south of the Bay of Bengal. The sea was flat and there was very little wind, but in the distance lightning could be seen for miles and miles along the horizon. Thunder kept cracking and a blue-white light illuminated the boat. As the captain later described events, when it seemed the lightning strikes couldn't get any closer, they did. The concussion rattled the boat, and even the water around the boat. In the distance an occasional bolt came down and hit the water. The air surrounding the boat was heavy with the pungent smell of electricity—ozone. Unable to stand this nerve-racking demonstration of nature's power any longer, the crew went below and tried to sleep. A few hours later, when they awoke, the storm had passed by them and was moving away. They were lucky; the boat was never struck.[24]

Nonetheless, boats are frequently hit—particularly those in inland waters and marinas in areas prone to thunderstorms. A major marine insurance firm cites these statistics for the period 2000-2005: the odds of your boat being struck by lightning in any year are about 1.2 in 1,000. Insurance claims for lightning strikes on boats come from all over the United States, but 33 percent of all lightning claims come from Florida, where the incident rate is 3.3 boats per 1,000. The second most frequently struck area in the United States is the Chesapeake Bay region, which accounts for 29 percent of the claims recorded. The majority of strikes are on sailboats, with an incident rate of about 4 per 1,000. Powerboats are also struck, of course, but at a lower rate of about 5 per 10,000. One interesting statistic is that multihull sailboats are struck more than twice as often as monohulls, possibly because their wider beam lessens the shielding effect afforded them by adjacent boats (when docked).[25]

A remarkable survival story is that of Ron Griggs. One Saturday in August, Ron and his wife and daughter were netting bait in the Indian River in Florida. Ron is an experienced boat captain and on this day the sky was clear and no thunder could be heard. Out of the blue a lightning strike hit the boat, momentarily deafening Ron's wife, Char. After a moment Char recovered her senses and saw that Ron had been thrown in the water by the force of the blast and was drifting away from the boat. Their nine-year-old daughter, Linsey, was uninjured. After instructing Linsey to dial 911 on a cell phone Char dove into the water, reached her husband, rolled him over on his back, and swam with him back to the boat while trying desperately to administer mouth-to-mouth resuscitation to him. Some nearby boaters came to her aid and helped lift Ron into the boat, where they gave him CPR until a sheriff's boat arrived and took him to waiting paramedics. Ron survived, thanks to Char's quick action that was based on a course in CPR she had taken *25 years ago!*[26]

Although mast-mounted equipment is most likely to be destroyed, almost any electronic device or metallic item in a boat can be damaged or destroyed. Examples include (in addition to the obvious ones of radios connected to external antennas) battery chargers, auto pilots, radar, switch panels and circuit breakers, as well as navigation instruments. If the boat is struck but no damage is observed, it is still a good idea to haul out the boat and make certain that there is no underwater damage where the lightning exited the vessel.

In some instances lightning can start a fire. The worst case of course is when fuel vapors are ignited by a side flash. A 25-foot fishing boat was struck at a dock in 2004. A small

Plate 1 Lightning Strikes Near Dana Point, California During a Winter Storm

Plate 2 Fulgurite

Plate 3 Lightning Strike on Empire State Building, New York

Plate 4 Rocket Launch Tower

Plate 5 Lightning Strike in Desert Near Lake Havasu,
California

THE EIFFEL TOWER AS A COLOSSAL LIGHTNING CONDUCTOR.
Photograph taken June 3, 1902, at 9.20 p.m., by M. G. Loppé. Published in the *Bulletin de la Société Astronomique de France* (May, 1905). [*Page* 82.

Plate 6 Lightning Strike on the Eiffel Tower, Paris, 1902

Plate 7 Spider Lightning Over Norman, Oklahoma

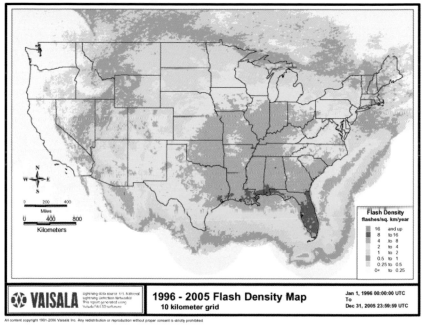

Plate 8 Lightning Flash Density Chart for the United States

Plate 9 Lightning Flashes Over Dana Point Harbor, California

Plate 10 Lightning Damaged Tree, Lewis Creek Trail,
California

Plate 11 Lightning Strike on the Queensboro Bridge, New York City

Plate 12 Oil Storage Tank Damaged by Lightning Strike

Plate 13 Cloud-to-Ground Lightning, Oro Valley, Arizona

Plate 14 Test House Lightning Protection System

amount of fuel in the bilge exploded, blasting pieces of the boat nearly 100 feet away.[27]

A notable incident of this type occurred on September 1, 1979, at the Deer Park Shell Oil terminal on the south side of the Houston ship channel. The weather was warm and windy with heavy downpours and lightning. A tanker, the *Chevron Hawaii*, was discharging crude oil and catalytic cracker feedstock at the terminal, when it was struck by lightning. Apparently vapors that had accumulated on the cargo deck ignited, causing a tremendous explosion. The vessel burned and sank. The explosion was so powerful that a large segment of the vessel hull flew 600 feet and penetrated the roof of a petroleum product storage tank on shore. This tank, containing 26,000 barrels of ethyl alcohol, also ignited and burned. Meanwhile at the dock, the fire spread into a nearby barge slip and four more barges discharging cargo caught fire. Three of these exploded and sank. On the *Chevron Hawaii*, 3 persons were killed and 13 injured.[28]

The morning following the September thunderstorm I'd experienced on the boat at Catalina Island, I called home to let my wife, Nancy, know that: 1. unfortunately we hadn't caught a tournament-winning marlin; and 2. we were fine following all of the lightning. She'd been on the East Coast with some friends, and I'd forgotten exactly what time she was scheduled to return. When I called, she said something about "...a plane being hit by lightning." (The telephone connection from the boat wasn't the best.) I was in the midst of writing this book and said "Oh! Wow! Be sure to save the article for me!"

"No," she said. <u>My</u> plane was struck by lightning."

"No big deal," I said, knowing that she was obviously okay. "It happens all the time. Planes are designed to withstand lightning."

As one might imagine, that was the wrong thing to say. Then she told me the entire story.

"September 19, 2005, just before sundown—I was on a Jet Blue Airlines flight back from New York to Long Beach. It had been a smooth, uneventful flight up to the point when the pilot announced that in a few minutes we would begin our descent into Long Beach Airport. He told us he didn't expect any turbulence, but some scattered showers had been forecast for the foothills and coastal area. I looked out the window and the sky was clear. I estimate that we had just passed over Palm Desert, when suddenly: FLASH! BANG! then a sucking sound as all of the passengers collectively inhaled. Immediately all of the little seatback television screens went blank and the passengers began speaking softly to each other. What was that? We flew in silence for a few minutes and then a woman across the aisle jumped up, ran to the flight attendant in the rear of the plane and began demanding that we be given some information. After a few more minutes a flight attendant got on the intercom and said the flight crew was checking things out. She told us not to worry, the plane was flying normally and the televisions were turned off just as a precaution. She escorted the woman back to her seat and told her to stay there. But the woman would not be quiet. Finally Karen, my seatmate, shouted to her, 'Shut up! You are frightening me and the rest of the passengers.' Perhaps five more minutes went by and then the pilot made an announcement. He said that in all his years of flying, his plane had never been struck by lightning, 'But this was about as close as it gets.' He went on to explain that aircraft are designed to withstand a lightning storm and that he and the crew had checked out all systems and reassured us that everything was normal. That was as close as he came to telling us that we had been hit by lightning.

"The weather still appeared clear out the window of the aircraft—no evidence of a thunderstorm could be seen. A few minutes later we were on the ground after a smooth landing. As we touched down, the passengers applauded loudly. There were a few clouds in the sky by the time we landed, but no rain.

"We collected our baggage and were about halfway home when the fireworks began, and we were treated to a most spectacular show of lightning. However, the rain didn't begin to fall until we reached our destination in Newport Beach about an hour later. All night long and well into the next morning there was loud thunder, lightning and rain."

Airplanes are not immune to lightning strikes; in fact it is estimated that on average there is one airplane hit per year for every commercial airliner flying. Scanning the headlines, you can see that there are newspaper reports of planes being hit by lightning on average about once per month. Checking the Internet for the period from April 2005, to April 2006, I found 15 incidents reported, four in Japan, one each in Iceland, Nigeria, Australia and the United Kingdom; and in the United States, incidents occurred in Alaska, Tennessee, Illinois, Ohio, Massachusetts, and Hawaii (two). The United Kingdom incident on April 27, 2005, involved Prime Minister Tony Blair's aircraft.

In addition to Nancy's experience on September 19, 2005, three other recent examples come to mind: in February 2004, a Hawaiian Airlines Boeing 767, en route from Portland, Oregon, with 270 passengers on board, made an emergency landing at Kona, Hawaii. Lightning struck its nose, causing instruments to malfunction. Two months later a Boeing 757 carrying Mexican President Vicente Fox and other officials and journalists was hit on the wing. Passengers heard a loud bang and saw the flash, but the plane landed safely about 15 minutes later. Then, on August 2, 2005, an Air France Airbus A340 (flight 358) carrying 309 passengers and crew skidded off the runway while landing in a thunderstorm at the Toronto Airport and burned. Miraculously, all of the passengers and crew survived with no major injuries. The initial reports indicated that lightning may have struck the aircraft, disabling some of its electrical systems. Earlier the airport had issued a warning concerning lightning. There was also speculation that a powerful downdraft or wind shear generated by the storm may have caused the crash or contributed to it. The real cause may never be known.[29]

From 1959 until 2005, a search of various databases reveals a total of 13 airline crashes attributed to lightning, an average of one every 3 to 4 years. (See Table 5.) A milestone crash was the December 8, 1963, crash of the Pan Am Boeing 707 that went down near Elkton, Maryland, resulting in 81 fatalities. Lightning struck a fuel tank and caused a fire. As a result of this incident, fuel systems were redesigned with lightning-protection measures. Fuel systems still remain areas of potential danger despite the attention focused on them. The 1976 crash of an Iran Air Force Boeing 747 near Madrid was attributed to a lightning flashover that ignited fuel vapors in the number 1 fuel tank. This modified the shape of the wing, causing it to vibrate strongly and eventually fail.

Aircraft flying through thunderstorms or charged clouds can be hit by lightning or can themselves trigger lightning. (See Plate 3.) In general such strikes are intracloud strikes, meaning the strike passes from one part of a cloud to another part rather than to the ground. Military aircraft have been deliberately flown into thousands of thunderstorms (without crashing) to gather data concerning the effects of lightning on aircraft *avionics* (aircraft electronic systems). Typically, the lightning will hit near the front of the aircraft, flow over the surface, and exit near the tail. Modern planes have a distinct advantage in that improvements in onboard radar systems, better weather forecasting, and the ability to fly higher and faster enables them to avoid most thunderstorms.

In general, an airplane's aluminum skin forms a protective shield for the contents of the plane. Special protection is required for such nonmetallic areas as the radome on the nose of the aircraft as well as for the fuel system. Aircraft systems undergo extensive testing and checks to ensure that

Table 5: Aircraft Crashes Attributed to Lightning Strikes

Date	Airline/ Location	Aircraft Type/ Registration	Fatalities vs. No. Passengers
06.26.1959	TransWorld Airlines Milan, Italy	Lockheed L-1549A N7313C	68:68
07.19.1961	Aerolineas Argentinas Azul, Brazil	Douglas DC-6 LV-ADW	67:67
12.19.1962	LOT Polish Airlines Warsaw, Poland	Vickers Viscount 804 SP-LVB	33:33
08.12.1963	Air Inter Lyon, France	Vickers Viscount 708 F-BGNV	20:20
12.08.1963	Pan American Elkton, Maryland, USA	Boeing 707-121 N709PA	81:81
12.24.1971	Lineas Aereas Nacionales Puerto Inca, Peru	Lockheed L-188A OB-R-941	91:92
05.09.1976	Iranian Air Force Madrid, Spain	Boeing 747-131F 5-8104	17:17
02.08.1988	NFD Mulheim, Germany	Swearingen 226 D-CABB	21:21
05.05.1998	Peruvian Air Force Andoas, Peru	Boeing 737-282 FAP-351	74:87
06.22.2000	Wuhan Airlines Wuhan, China	Xian Yunshuji Y7-100 B-3479	44:44+7
10.25.2000	Russian Defense Ministry Batumi, Republic of Georgia	Ilyushin IL-18 ---	82:82
12.04.2003	Kato Airline Bodoe, Norway	Dornier DO-228-202 LN-HTA	0:4
08.02.2005	Air France Toronto, Canada	Airbus A340-313X F-GLZQ	0:309

Source: http://www.airdisaster.com (Airdisaster.com is dedicated to aircraft safety)

lightning cannot affect sensitive electronic devices used for navigation and control.

Jim Whitehead, a former Navy flight engineer and commercial airline captain, is familiar with lightning strikes on aircraft. His closest call occurred in the late 1970s, when he was flying in a P3B Orion (a Navy search aircraft used to detect and locate submarines). The plane, with a crew of 10, took off from Moffett Field Naval Air Station in Northern California. The weather forecast indicated storm conditions and the aircraft soon encountered turbulence along the Pacific Coast near Half Moon Bay.

Whitehead recalled seeing a few flashes of lightning in the distance. As the flight engineer, he was seated behind and between the two pilots. Suddenly a bolt of lightning struck the belly of the plane, in the area beneath the cockpit.

"It was as if someone hit the underside of the plane with a hammer—a big hammer," Jim said. "I felt the impact with my feet, saw a flash. At the same time the instrument warning lights all lit up because of the induced voltage from the lightning flash. These were false readings, and the instrument lights faded back to normal in a few seconds. We made checks and there seemed to be no damage to the plane's controls or instruments. Still, we didn't want to take a chance on losing the plane over the ocean, so we returned to Moffett Field. After we landed, I checked the belly of the plane and saw where the lightning strike had hit on the nose gear door. There was a multicolored ring about four inches in diameter. Aircraft maintenance personnel later found burnt areas on the 'spinners' located at the center of the propellers and burnt spots and pitting around various antennas on the aircraft.

"Another time, we left at night on a tactical flight out of the Philippines and were at low altitude when I saw a spectacular display of Saint Elmo's fire. Most Saint Elmo's fire that I've seen streaks across the windshield like lightning, but this was different. It was in the form of small, brightly illuminated 'raindrops' that hit the windshield of the aircraft and exploded in a shower of sparks with no apparent damage to the plane.

"Commercial airliners have static discharge whisks at various locations for dissipating static electricity. After a lightning strike, these are frequently burned off and have to be replaced."

In his years as a commercial pilot, Jim had other experiences with lightning, but none that were as "close-up and personal" as these. He told me that captains are obligated to report every strike and its effects on the aircraft to the U.S. Federal Aviation Administration. The information is compiled and used to design further improvements in aircraft systems.

Electrical Transmission and Distribution Systems
Since 1861, when the intercontinental telegraph line was completed, it has been known that lightning could strike and damage overhead electrical systems. One of the men in charge of constructing the western half of the transcontinental telegraph line, James Gamble, described what happened when a thunderstorm occurred during construction. The storm was some distance away, but still induced a voltage on the telegraph wires the men were stringing from pole to pole, causing them to get shocks unless they wore heavy gloves and boots.[30] Fifty years later—in 1915 AT&T completed the first transcontinental telephone line. At the same time, electrical transmission lines were spreading across the United States. As use of electrical power and telephone communications continued to grow, methods of protecting overhead lines became important.

Lightning strikes generate voltages in excess of 1,000,000 volts and can damage insulators. Wires and related hardware can melt, burn, or become pitted, weakening them so they are susceptible to later failure during wind or ice storms. Flashovers onto phase conductors can create a high-voltage wave that is capable of traveling long distances and damaging substation equipment. Even if the lightning flash does not hit the line directly, a nearby ground stroke can induce high voltage on the line by electromagnetic coupling. In the regions of the world where there is a high incidence of lightning, it is one of the main causes of electrical system outages.

If the voltage is high enough, flashover (jumping from the ground wire to the tower or to a phase conductor, et cetera) can occur; however, this is usually less of a problem for high-voltage transmission lines since the insulators are designed for high-voltage. The likelihood of this happening is influenced by a number of factors, including how clean the insulators are and the altitude where the line is located.

In the case of distribution lines that operate at lower voltage, this is not the case and flashover can be a more serious problem since insulators are designed for lower voltage. In the case of indirect strikes, if the lightning flash strikes in the vicinity of the distribution line, a high voltage (easily as much as 50,000 volts) can be induced in the line (even though it is not directly hit). This over-voltage or surge will travel down the line and can damage the line, insulators, and associated equipment.

Modern utility systems employ a variety of sensors on distribution lines to measure the load, detect faults, and for control purposes. But this type of equipment is vulnerable to damage from the lightning-induced over-voltages or transients; sometimes the failure of secondary equipment can render a line inoperable, as in the old adage, "For want of a nail, the shoe was lost..."

Telephone and Cable Television Systems
Telecommunication networks are also vulnerable, but the probability of damage is less because many are underground or in the case of overhead systems are not as high as electrical distribution lines. Still, direct strikes can occur, but induced voltages are more common. High voltages can be induced in cable television or telephone systems. It is this over-voltage surge that travels down the line, enters the building, and leads

to injuries to any unfortunate individual who happens to be near the television or telephone. This is the reason why telephones should not be used during thunderstorms except in emergencies.

My good friend and neighbor Howard Wells recounted that his mother, Gladys, was struck by lightning when she was six years old, in 1916. She was sitting under a wall-mounted telephone in the kitchen of their home in Kemp, Oklahoma. The telephone lines ran through a nearby tree. A lightning flash hit the tree, causing a high voltage on the telephone line. Inside the house, there was a bright light as the lightning flashed from the telephone to Gladys. She was injured, unable to move because her left side was paralyzed. The family moved into the storm cellar, carrying Gladys, who began to recover after a couple of hours although she noticed that her teeth seemed loose. She mentioned this to her uncle, who happened to be with them at the time, and he pulled out two of the teeth before her mother yelled at him to stop! Gladys recovered, kept the rest of her teeth, and lived for 88 more years.

Nothing could justify being on the telephone more than working in a hospital emergency room during a major storm. This was the situation one August 1996 night in Minnesota when physician's assistant Bonnie J. Bartos came to work. In the midst of the storm she was on the phone talking to a patient when there was loud crack and the lights went out. She felt as if both hands and the left side of her face were on fire. Lights flashed in her eyes and her head spun with vertigo. When the lights came back on Bonnie had her head down on the desk; she was groaning and holding her bleeding left ear. The melted telephone equipment she'd been using was smoldering. Following this incident, Bartos suffered from dizziness, tinnitus (buzzing in the ear), hearing loss and other medical issues including nightmares and memory loss. After surgery she found her condition somewhat improved but she still suffers from the after-effects of the lightning strike. She emphasizes, however, that she is happy to have come away from the incident alive.[31]

David Smith had a similar experience while on duty as an emergency medical dispatcher for 911 service in Martin County, Florida. In a horrendous storm during August 1992, as he was talking to a man in a burning building, lightning struck the phone line and he was tossed backward 15 to 20 feet. Following numerous visits to a dozen or more doctors, Smith was finally diagnosed with a perforated tympanic membrane, hearing loss, short-term memory loss, and central nervous system damage. After struggling to work for three more years despite his medical problems, Smith finally had to retire as 100 percent disabled. He believes that his condition has worsened with time.[32]

Antennas
There are numerous incidents of lightning striking unprotected antennas and entering buildings or boats and destroying antenna tuners, radios, televisions, or other equipment. In one case, lightning struck the antenna of radio amateur Andrew Flower of Rogers, Arkansas in 2003. As Flower described the experience, he had heard distant thunder, but was not concerned. The next thing he heard was "the loudest noise I had ever experienced." It was accompanied by a very bright light—then the room was filled with smoke and all of the lights were out. When he tallied up the damages, neither his high-frequency shortwave radio nor a VHF (2 meter) radio was functional. A power supply and other equipment had been zapped. The current entered the house, leaving burn marks on the wall, and then jumped to equipment. Fortunately no one was injured. Since then the cables have been modified and there are disconnects both inside and outside the house. When a thunderstorm threatens, all cables are disconnected.[33]

As a 10-year-old in the 1960s, Gerrie Catolane liked to watch storms. Once, as she knelt next to a metal sash window, lightning struck the TV antenna, traveled down the antenna wire that entered a nearby window, and side-flashed to her. She recalls a bang and being thrown across the room, then a pain in her chest like she'd had the wind knocked out of her. A neighbor who was a doctor came to the house, examined her and told her that she'd be just fine. Years later she started experiencing insomnia, headaches, and leg cramps. Now she realizes that she probably suffered some type of permanent neurological damage, and as a result had a learning disability. She managed to overcome the problems and went on to a career in graphic design and desktop publishing.[34]

Pipelines, Oil, and Hazardous Materials Storage Facilities
Lightning can cause explosions in facilities where volatile products are manufactured or stored. Special cases are military and commercial facilities storing munitions, explosives, or fireworks: These are at risk and require carefully designed lightning-protection systems—not only to protect their contents, but also to avoid risk of injury to the public. Fires and explosions have frequently resulted from lightning strikes on petroleum facilities.

Dr. Frank Coffman is one of my colleagues at DMJM and a talented physicist. He was formerly an assistant secretary in the United States Department of Energy, where one of his most interesting challenges was to oversee the cleanup of the Three Mile Island nuclear power plant accident. He is also the owner of Coffman Oil Company in Kentucky, a small family-owned production company.

One spring day in 2004 I visited Coffman in his office and saw him studying his blackboard, covered with a drawing of a tank surrounded by Maxwell's equations in various forms.

"Lightning hit one of my oil-storage tanks," he said, "and I'm trying to figure out what happened." (See Plate 12.)

There had been a thunderstorm a few weeks earlier in Livermore, Kentucky, a small town with a population of a few thousand persons. The installation consisted of two storage tanks, an oil-water separator, and connecting piping—all surrounded by a concrete block retention basin and grounded electrically. It was located at the end of a gravel road, about one city block from a paved highway. Between the tank farm and the highway is a mobile home occupied by a man and his wife. At the time of the incident, the man was sitting on his porch. He was barefoot.

"Suddenly there was a loud explosion—the detonation was heard all over the town and as far away as two to three miles," Coffman told me. "From his vantage point on the porch, my neighbor saw one of the tanks launch into the air and fly toward the mobile home. It crashed into an open area a few hundred feet away. The man was so startled the he leaped from his porch and ran in the opposite direction, toward the highway, somehow oblivious to the rain and the pain of the gravel road cutting his bare feet. He was fortunate in two respects: he was not struck by lightning and he happened to have a cell phone with him. Later he was able to use it to call his wife to bring him some shoes. Meanwhile the fire department, the police, and the sheriff arrived."

A lightning flash had struck the tank and somehow ignited vapors inside it. The resulting explosion separated the tank from its the bottom—which was bowed out—ripped it from all its connecting piping, and blew the tank into the air. The blast demolished a portion of the concrete-block retention basin, allowing some burning oil to spill. Fortunately the tank was nearly empty at the time so the fire was quickly extinguished and the spill contained.

At the blackboard, Coffman was speculating about the exact mechanism that triggered the explosion. At the bottom of the tank was a thin layer of salty water—thus a good conductor. Above this was a layer of crude oil, and above that petroleum vapors. The metal tank was grounded.

Coffman's suspicion was that the tank functioned much like an oil-filled capacitor, the oil serving as a dielectric. The lightning strike induced a charge; the resulting high voltage flashed over to some point within the tank, igniting the vapors. Also, for the gas mixture to detonate, air had to be present, indicating that somehow the tank had been improperly sealed.

"Fortunately no one got hurt this time," Coffman said. "Now I'm looking into other forms of lightning protection, for this and my other tanks farms." Then he chuckled. "You know, when we were kids, we used to put one of those big firecrackers—cherry bombs—in a tin can filled with water, light the fuse, and run like heck. That old can would rocket up a hundred feet in the air. Well, that tank must have done the same thing—I bet it was quite a sight—Cape Canaveral in Kentucky."

A more serious incident occurred at an ExxonMobil tank farm in Marion County, Indiana, during a thunderstorm on the evening of March 30, 2005. Lightning struck a five-million-gallon tank and ignited the crude oil within the tank. The tank was not full and was believed to contain only about 20,000 gallons of crude. Still, it was enough to create a blaze that produced a glow seen from more than 10 miles away. The next day the fire was still burning. But it had not spread and no oil was spilled.[35]

Other vulnerable components of infrastructure include pipelines, liquefied natural gas storage tanks, and refineries. Lightning has the ability to traverse pipelines, and can then jump to equipment or systems at some distance from the original point of impact.

Magazines used for the storage of explosives and munitions require lightning protection. Historically, there have been several notable disasters when magazines were detonated by a lightning strike. In 1926, a lightning strike at a Naval Ammunition Depot located at Lake Denmark, New Jersey resulted in the death of 21 people, injured 51 more, and destroyed the depot. The adjacent Picatinny Arsenal was also damaged as were nearby communities. In June 1998, lightning struck a Russian Army munitions depot in the Ural Mountains near Jekaterinburg. The depot was destroyed and 14 military personnel were killed. The fire spread to nearby forests and 1,300 villagers were evacuated.[36]

Mines and Underground Structures

Since the earth is a terminal point of lightning-grounding systems, you would think that being underground would be safe, and in most cases it is. But it is important to recognize that a direct lightning strike on the ground can create high electrical currents that travel some distance before ultimately dissipating as heat in earth and rock. If an underground cavern contains flammable liquids or gases, lightning can cause a fire or explosion if the current jumps a gap, for example, from the earth to a metal pipe. Metal pipes or vents exhausting mining vapors also could be ignited by lightning.

A lightning strike was the cause of the Sago mine disaster, in which 12 people perished. The mine, located near Tallmansville, West Virginia, had just begun operations at around 6:00 A.M. on January 2, 2006. Two crews were descending into the mine when there was a loud explosion at 6:30 that was heard and felt by persons outside the mine. The explosion trapped the first crew of 13 men deep in the mine; the second crew was not trapped and was able to escape. Rescue efforts were hampered by high levels of poisonous carbon monoxide gas in the mine, but one miner was eventually rescued and recovered following a lengthy hospital stay. The North American Lightning Detection Network recorded 100 lightning strikes in the vicinity of the mine within 40 minutes of the explosion. Three lightning strikes carrying an estimated 35,000 to 101,000 amperes hit near the mine at 6:26:36 A.M. It appears that the explosion occurred two seconds later. The electric power distribution system and telephone cables for the mine passed close to the two of the strikes. The most intense strike was 1.9 miles from the site of the explosion, which took place in an abandoned and supposedly sealed-off portion of the mine. Lightning current could have entered this area through the mine electrical systems, through steel reinforcing mats on the mine ceilings, or by some other means. As of this writing, state investigators concluded that a lightning strike had ignited methane gas underground, causing the explosion.[37]

In the air, in buildings, on the water, underground—is no place safe from the capricious, erratic, unpredictable force of lightning? Like a fast-striking snake, lightning seems to jump this way and then that to strike at long distance where least expected. Yes, protection is possible—in most cases. But first it is necessary to understand the phenomena that guide the lightning flash in the final microseconds of its journey to earth.

7

Dodging the Electric Bullet

Some cultures have held the belief that the chief or king could ensure protection against lightning. A century ago, on the upper Zambezi, certain tribes would gather in the chief's compound when dangerous storms threatened, seeking to place themselves under his protection. In medieval times oak trees were thought to be preferentially struck by lightning, and thus oak was a favored wood for winter solstice celebrations that later transformed into Christmas celebrations. In many countries, by one name or another, the Yule log formed a central part of these celebrations. In some countries it was removed from the fire only partially consumed and then set aside to be relit when lightning threatened; in others, charcoal remnants served the same purpose, the belief being they would protect the house against a lightning strike.[1]

Lightning strikes cannot be prevented, and as we have seen, lightning is capricious and can strike anywhere, even though certain areas are more prone to lightning strikes than others. The basic principles of lightning protection were discovered by Benjamin Franklin in 1750 and are still valid today. The changes that have occurred are primarily improvements in materials and equipment. Succinctly stated, protection requires: placement of lightning rods (called *air terminals* by lightning engineers) at locations where they will intercept a lightning strike, provide a means to conduct the lightning current safely to ground (down conductors), and provide a means to discharge the current into the earth through a grounding system (sometimes called *earth terminals*). These three points can be summarized as:

- Intersecting the lightning strike

- Providing an adequate, isolated, current-carrying capacity
- Connecting to a low resistance grounding system

Lightning current will follow the lowest impedance path to ground; if this is through the protection system, buildings and equipment will sustain little or no damage. It is only when a lower impedance path to ground is through a building or its contents that damage can occur.

In Franklin's time buildings and boats were the primary focus of lightning protection. In the ensuing 250 years many new technologies have been deployed that require lightning protection. Each has certain peculiarities, but the basic principle is the same. Today, in addition to buildings and water craft, we are concerned with protecting electric utilities, telephone and communication systems, computers and other electronic devices, pipelines, airplanes and airports, and structures housing petroleum products or their derivatives and other hazardous materials. In the past, lightning struck harmlessly in open fields. With increased urbanization, there are more points of vulnerability as indicated in Plate 13, which shows three simultaneous cloud-to-ground strikes over Oro Valley, Arizona.

Buildings
Consider Figure 18, which indicates five potential entry points for lightning—namely, antennas, a direct strike on the building, coupling into the building via overhead utility lines, an indirect strike on the ground or a nearby tree, or coupling into the building by underground utilities.

A typical protection system involves grounding of the antenna mast, air terminals to intercept a direct strike on the building, and surge-protection devices on each point of entry into the building, including any antenna cables, incoming power or telephone lines, and the underground utilities such as water, sewer, and gas lines. The surge-protection devices, the air terminal system, and the underground utilities are bonded together and connected to a suitably designed earth terminal or grounding system. (See Plate 14.) Assuming the structure is a typical wood frame residence and the electrical conduits and water pipes are properly grounded, the occupants are provided

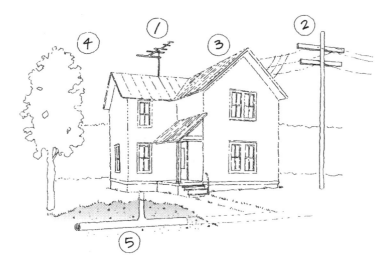

Figure 18: Lightning Entry Points in a Building

a fair degree of protection from a lightning strike as long as they maintain a distance from walls, telephones, electrical receptacles, faucets, showers, or metal casement windows—or from any location where lightning could flash over to an individual within a room.

It is important to understand that a lightning-protection system will not *prevent* a lightning strike. Its purpose is to reduce the danger to the building occupants and contents. One way of visualizing the area protected by an air terminal system is to imagine a sphere with a radius of 150 feet that is touching the earth on one side of a building and touches a roof air terminal on its other side; anything under the sphere is protected. (See Figure 19.) Likewise, for a sphere just touching the tips of two air terminals—say, above a roof—

anything under the sphere is protected. Cables connecting air terminals to the grounding system should have good connections and adequate current-carrying capacity, should keep the distance to ground as short as possible, and should avoid sharp bends. Television antennas, roof gutters, and downspouts should be connected to the system.

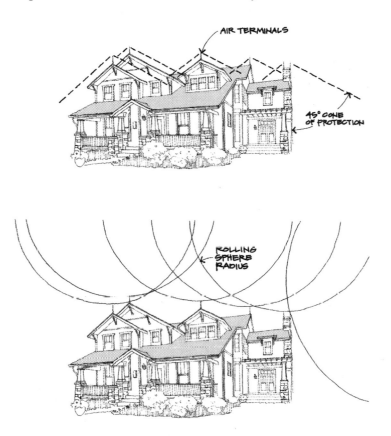

Figure 19: Areas Protected by Lightning Arrestors

Another way of visualizing the protected area is to imagine a cone with an apex at the highest air terminal. The area under the cone is protected. Experts disagree about the size of the protective cone; some say the angle with the vertical is 45 degrees, others say 60 degrees.

Guidelines for protecting buildings against lightning strikes are provided by building code authorities in most countries. Codes and standards are used by architects and engineers throughout the world to design protection systems. The International Electrotechnical Commission in Geneva publishes "Protection of Structures Against Lightning," while in the United States the basic guide is the "Standard for the Installation of Lightning Protection Systems," published by the National Fire Protection Association.[2] Lightning-protection standards also describe a risk assessment procedure that can be used to determine the relative degree of risk to a given structure. The risk is calculated on a scale of 0 to 7 or greater, 0 to 2 being low risk and over 7 being severe. The risk index is computed by taking into consideration the type of structure, type of roof and materials of construction, location, building occupants and contents, and lightning frequency of occurrence at the building location.

The degree and type of protection is determined by the three most important variables, which are: the expected frequency of lightning at the building location; the building type; and the building contents.

Consider in general terms the import of each of these variables. In areas with low kerataunic activity (infrequent thunderstorms and lightning strikes), an extensive and expensive lightning-protection system is probably not justified economically. Some of the standards provide guidelines for assessing cost-benefit ratios for various situations.

The building type has a great deal to do with the lightning hazard. Height is the first consideration; tall, multistory structures are more likely to be struck. Building materials are another important consideration; wood structures pose a greater fire hazard than reinforced-concrete or steel-frame buildings.

Finally, the building contents may or may not justify extensive protection schemes. Within a single-family residence it is likely that the cost of replacing a damaged appliance once in a great while may be far less than the cost of a lightning-protection system. In a bank computer center, extensive protection may be required not only to safeguard equipment, but to prevent interruption of operations or loss of data.

As described above, a lightning-protection system consists of air terminals, interconnecting cables, and a grounding system. In the United States, the current-carrying capacity of lightning-protection equipment is greater for larger structures. The distinction is based on height, so that for buildings not exceeding 75 feet in height, class I materials can be used. For buildings and structures exceeding 75 feet in height, including stacks and tall radio masts, class II materials are required.

Class I air terminals are either copper or aluminum rods that are tapered at one end and generally resemble a wooden pencil in shape. They are either 3/8 inches or ½ inches in diameter and are available in lengths ranging from 10 inches to 48 inches. The conductors that connect the air terminals to other metal systems on the building and to the grounding system are either copper or aluminum cables that are 3/8 to ½ inches in diameter. Associated with the air terminals and the conductors are a wide variety of specialized copper or aluminum fittings that adopt the cables to the configuration of building roof, parapets, and chimneys. These types of hardware ensure good electrical connections and avoid sharp turns or bends whereby the lightning current might jump from the conductor. There are also special air terminals and conductors available that protect trees.

The most common type of grounding devices are copper rods that are driven into the soil. These are typically ½ to 1 inch in diameter and 8 to 10 feet long. Ground rods can also be sectional—in other words, 5-foot to 10-foot sections that can be threaded together to produce greater lengths. For rocky soils or areas where driving long ground rods is not feasible, other types of grounding devices are available. One is a solid copper ground plate, which can be mounted in shallow or rocky top soil conditions. Ground plates are typically 1.5 feet square, but can be 2 feet by 2 feet or 3 feet by 3 feet in size as well. Another grounding device is fabricated of four copper sheets placed together in a cruciform shape. Each of the four "wings" of the cruciform is 3 or 4 inches wide and 18 inches long. This type of grounding device can be placed in a predrilled hole and backfilled in locations where driven ground rods are not practical.[3]

In reality, designing adequate grounds is far more complicated than just pounding a metal rod into the soil. Since it is the earth that has the ability to accept and safely dissipate the huge electrical charge transported by a lightning flash, soil electrical properties must be known. Assuming that the lightning-protection system safely conducts the lightning current to earth, it will propagate away from the point of connection of the grounding system and eventually will be neutralized by the existing charge in the ground. The effectiveness of this process is influenced by the soil resistivity measured in ohm-meters. Soil resistivity can vary widely and is an important consideration in many engineering situations. For example, in electrified rail systems, track work is *insulated* from the earth to prevent stray currents from coupling into the ground and causing electrical interference in adjoining property or buildings. Rail systems are typically specified to have resistances of 100 to 250 ohms per 1,000 feet of track or higher to ensure that unsafe stray currents are not created. The resistivity of soil, measured in ohm-meters, ranges from 30 to 30,000. Given such a wide variation, it is imperative that the appropriate value of soil resistivity be used in the design of grounding systems. This is necessary to determine how many grounding rods are needed.

In grounding systems for lightning protection, the goal is to create a low resistance path to ground, preferably 10 to 20 ohms or less. If soil resistivity is low, fewer attachment points (grounds) are required than if the resistivity is high. The resistivity of soil depends on a number of factors including its composition (rock, sand, clay, et cetera), concentration of dissolved salts, and most importantly, water content. For critical installations, soil resistivity must be measured to obtain accurate values. To be conservative, measurements would be made during the dry season, when soil moisture is at a low value.[4]

Under dry conditions (water content 5 to 10 percent), soil resistivity can be several thousand ohm-meters, while in the moist condition (water content 20 to 40 percent by weight) it drops to 200 ohm-meters or less for sandy soil and clay. Rock has high resistivity unless by chance it has minerals or ores that are good conductors. Electrical engineers think of soil as a "lossy" dielectric material, meaning that rather than being a perfect dielectric, some current will flow. Engineers might model a unit lump of soil as a capacitor connected in parallel with a resistor, the resistor representing the lossy part and the value of resistance determines the current that will flow. Normally no current flows through an ideal dielectric, but if the current density is high enough, the dielectric breaks down and the resistance drops. The point where the soil breaks down is called the critical soil ionization potential E_o.[5] A typical value for E_o might be 500 kilovolts per meter, but could be as low as 300 kilovolts per meter or as high as 1,500 kilovolts per meter. Using an appropriate value of E_o and measurements of soil resistivity, the soil resistance can be determined and this information used to establish how many grounding rods are needed to provide a low resistance path to ground.

Resistivity is measured by inserting four electrodes or probes along a line in the ground. By applying a voltage to the two outermost electrodes, a current will flow through the ground between them. The voltage difference between the two middle electrodes is measured and the resistivity is calculated by making use of the known distances between the electrodes, the current applied, and the measured voltage.

Figure 14 in Chapter 4 illustrates how the electric field changes if one were able to insert a probe in the earth at various distances from an electrode that was delivering current into the soil.[6] The figure also shows a voltage difference that exists at various points along the surface of the earth. This figure is important because it illustrates the concept of the *step voltage*. Imagine now that the electrode is actually at the impact point of a lightning flash. If an individual is walking nearby at the time of the strike, and had one foot at the point labeled V_1 and the other foot at point V_2, a potential difference would exist between the feet and a current would flow up one leg and down the other, from the high voltage to the lower voltage. For this reason the situation is referred to as a "step voltage."

As noted in Chapter 4, step voltages have been known to injure humans walking in the open when lightning flashes occur, but are more dangerous to livestock and other four-legged animals, as the current flows through the chest, heart, and vital organs.

Lightning current can penetrate soil to a depth depending on the average soil conductivity and the predominant frequency of the flash. Soil penetration is in-versely proportional to the square root of frequency and soil conductivity.[7] Some typical values of depths reached at the point where the lightning current has dropped to 37 percent of its initial value are:

100 kilohertz: depth is 150 feet, when conductivity = 0.001 Siemens per meter.
1000 kilohertz: depth is 50 feet, when conductivity = 0.01 Siemens per meter.

Today there are even more elaborate systems for protecting structures housing high-value contents. One device is the Faraday Cage, named after Michael Faraday (1791–1867), a British scientist who made many fundamental discoveries in electromagnetic induction and electrolysis. (The *farad*, a unit of capacitance, is named in honor of Faraday.) Faraday knew that charge resided on the outside of a conductor and postulated that a conducting screen or cage around a building would protect its contents from lightning strikes. This is the same principle by which the body of a metal vehicle or aluminum airplane protects the occupants. Faraday's idea was ignored for a long while, but recent research has demonstrated its practicality and improved understanding of how to design reliable systems. As a simple example, the reinforcing rods in reinforced-concrete buildings can be employed as a Faraday Cage if they are spaced correctly and if they are all bonded together electrically and connected to ground. Penetrations into the building—electrical conduits and pipes—also need to be bonded to the reinforcing rods and grounded.

Unconventional Systems
There are several commercially available unconventional lightning-protection systems. Rather than use Franklin's approach of air terminals, down conductors, and ground terminals, these systems use specialized hardware that is a variation of the conventional air terminal design. The manufacturers claim that this equipment "eliminates" lightning, discharges clouds or dissipates the ground charge, or provides a protective zone greatly in excess of conventional methods.

The proponents of lightning elimination systems (sometimes referred to as dissipation arrays or charge transfer systems) claim that their equipment eliminates lightning strikes by creating conditions in which strikes cannot occur. The equipment in essence—there are various shapes and forms—consists of a large number of sharp spikes similar to barbed wire. These spikes create myriad points of corona discharge—that allegedly discharge overhead clouds or reduce the field intensity at the protected structure so an upward connecting leader cannot occur. A variation of this concept is a field array of dozens or hundreds of small lightning rods in the ground surrounding a building that serve the same purpose.

A key element in the theory of the systems is that the spikes "leak" charge into the atmosphere, in much the same manner as do blades of grass and trees. (See Chapter 2.) While this may be true, measurements show that a palm tree can produce a greater discharge current (measured in millionths of an ampere) than the lightning-protection system.[8] We know that trees in a forest are frequently struck by lightning even though surrounded by dozens of natural dissipaters–namely, more trees—so common sense says that such a system does not have much value. There are more extensive scientific reasons why these systems do not discharge thunderclouds or limited lightning, but they are beyond the scope of this book.[9]

The Federal Aviation Administration, the National Aeronautics and Space Administration, and other researchers have tested dissipation arrays installed at airports, the Kennedy Space Center, and at a nuclear power plant. No benefit was found when compared with conventional systems.[10]

The second class of nonconventional systems is known as "early streamer emission," or ESE. The basic idea is that by initiating an upward streamer earlier, or before the electric field strength has built to the value at which a lightning strike might normally occur, the streamer event has a few additional microseconds of travel time and will rise higher before the lightning strike occurs. This supposedly creates a larger zone of protection when compared to conventional systems. Some of these systems use lightning rods tipped with radioactive materials to increase ionization at the early streamer air terminal.

A number of studies and tests show that there is no advantage to early streamer emission systems, and that in fact, they are struck as frequently as conventional systems.[11]

Commercial/Industrial Facilities

The basic principles of protection for commercial/industrial facilities are the same as those described above for residential buildings. Differences arise in the size and number of air terminals, conductors, and grounding devices, and in the need to protect sensitive equipment and machinery. With respect to plants with a large electrical demand, there may be a substation dedicated to the plant housing transformers and switchgear that require protection. Some industrial processes, such as those that involve metal or chemical production or processing, require a constant flow of electrical energy. If the electricity supply is interrupted, expensive equipment can be damaged irreparably. Such plants usually have an on-site emergency generator as a backup source of power. The emergency equipment must be isolated and protected so that it is not put out of commission by the same lightning strike that interrupts the regular power source.

Another important protection concept is guarding against electrical transients ("surges") that can damage industrial equipment. The development of semiconductors has revolutionized industrial equipment in much the same manner as it changed automobiles and consumer electronic devices. Virtually every piece of machinery in a factory has microprocessor controls, electronic sensors, and other low-voltage devices that are easily destroyed by high-voltage transients. Examples include variable-speed drive systems, programmable controllers, analog-to-digital converters, remote and wireless controllers, and countless other devices, including the ubiquitous laptop computer. Protection of equipment requires the use of surge-protection devices that ground spurious high voltages before they can cause damage.

Tall smokestacks or chimneys constitute an example of a special structure found in many industrial facilities. Since they are by design normally higher than adjacent structures, they are particular targets for lightning. They are constructed either of steel or reinforced concrete, and are protected at the top with air terminals. In the case of a steel smokestack with steel walls more than 3/16 inch thick, the only requirement is to bond the base of the tower to a good ground connection. In the case of a reinforced-concrete smokestack, it is important that the steel reinforcing be bonded together electrically—that is to say that the reinforcing must provide an uninterrupted path to ground. Air terminals placed on top of the smokestack are connected electrically to the reinforcing steel at the top and bottom of the smokestack and to the grounding system. All metal components on the smokestack—ladders, hoists, platforms, and so on—should also be connected to the grounding system.[12]

There are so many thousands of variations in types of equipment and manufacturing processes that are found in industrial and commercial facilities that it is impossible to describe how to protect every single one. A detailed discussion of the design of lightning-protection systems is beyond the scope of this book in any case, but it is important for readers to understand the importance of having such systems, and then knowing how to reach experts who can provide the details.[13]

Personal Computers, Fax Machines, and Other Sensitive Electronic Devices

Electrical utility systems—transmission and distribution lines—act as extensive lightning collection systems capable of bringing surge currents into buildings through the electric panel. Televisions, fax machines, personal computers, printers, and many other electronic products use low-voltage semiconductors, integrated circuits, or surface-mounted devices that are extremely sensitive to even moderately high voltages. (For this reason, technicians working on these devices use special grounds so that static electricity from their clothing or shoes does not burn out delicate components.) Most household devices are adequately protected when plugged into an approved surge-protection device.

Even with the building-protection system described above in place, damage could occur to such sensitive electronic devices as microcomputers as a result of induced currents or high transient voltages. Some protection against induced currents would be afforded by moving sensitive devices away from walls that might incorporate current-carrying conductors (pipes or conduits). All such devices should be connected to the power source through a surge-protection device. Separation distances to avoid shocks or induced currents depend on the intensity of the lightning strike, the effectiveness of the lightning protection system, and the resistance of the grounding system. There are computer programs that can calculate safe distances. The discussion of these is beyond the scope of this book. To provide a greater degree of protection, sensitive electronic devices can be placed in the shielded room (one enclosed by a grounded metal wire mesh or grid work) that is itself protected by surge-protection devices.

Public Assembly, Athletic, and Recreational Facilities
Such public assembly buildings as churches, theaters or sports arenas—buildings in which large numbers of people con-gregate—require adequate lightning protection, otherwise people can be injured even when indoors, as demonstrated by the examples in Chapters 5 and 6. The principles of building protection discussed earlier in this chapter apply to public assembly buildings. This has been known for centuries.

On the west coast of France there is an impressive medieval abbey known as Mont Saint-Michel. The abbey was constructed over the course of several centuries on a tidal island in Normandy. The tide change around Mont Saint-Michel is substantial, so centuries ago at high tide the abbey was isolated by the sea. Today a causeway connects the abbey to the mainland.

The abbey is in an imposing structure towering hundreds of feet above the surrounding salt marshes and visible for many miles. During a recent visit I climbed stairs worn by the feet of numerous pilgrims and visitors up to a point where I could see a panoramic view of the stormy Atlantic Ocean and the surrounding French countryside. I saw that the abbey's tall spires and steeples are protected against lightning by an extensive grounding system. Copper bars approximately 1 inch wide (25 mm) and 1/8" thick (3 mm) serve as the conductors. These are attached to the stonework by lead staples. I do not know the date when the lightning protection system was installed, but by the materials of construction it would appear that it is several hundred years old.

Outdoor recreational facilities, especially golf courses, represent a unique hazard, since typically there is "no place to hide." At a golf course in New Zealand, lightning struck a huge macrocarpa tree near the 11th fairway a few days before Christmas 2005, blowing telephone-pole-size splinters out of its massive trunk. Damage to the tree was so extensive that it is unlikely to recover. The greenkeeper and another employee were near the 12th hole when they heard a large bang and saw a bright flash. The greenkeeper stated that he felt an odd tingling sensation and saw his colleague's head light up. Elsewhere, another man was knocked to the ground, but fortunately no one sustained serious injuries. The flash was so bright that it was noticed even in the clubhouse. The club manager was quoted as saying that the club's procedures advise golfers to "gather under trees during thunderstorms." But then he added, "We'll have to think about that one again."[14]

Obviously, "gathering under trees," is ill-advised. Today, many golf courses use a system of loud warning horns to alert golfers to impending thunderstorms. When the horn sounds, golfers are to suspend play and leave the course. Such systems are not infallible, and golfers are still struck, either because the horn did not sound early enough or the golfers could not reach shelter quickly enough. Some consideration has been given to placing metal lightning shelters or bunkers at strategic locations around courses to provide golfers with safe havens. An alternative solution would be to station a couple of secondhand buses at suitable locations to provide golfers with a refuge. Positioning a bus in the middle of a golf course might not be aesthetically pleasing, but it could save lives.

Other outdoor sports involve athletic fields, swimming pools, and stadiums. These also have had lightning casualties. The National Collegiate Athletic Association takes lightning seriously. The latest version of the NCAA's *Sports Medicine Handbook* includes a guideline for lightning safety.[15] This publication reminds coaches and athletes that blue sky and the absence of rain do not indicate that lightning will not strike. Lightning can strike from distant storms 10 miles away, either as a storm approaches or from the trailing edge as the storm departs.

The NCAA guidelines provide an excellent planning basis for any type of athletic event—indoors or outdoors. As a first step, the NCAA recommends that a chain of command be established to designate who will monitor the weather and who will make a decision to cease activity during an athletic event. Weather reports should be obtained prior to the event or prior to practices in the event that the potential for adverse weather exists. The guidelines suggest monitoring thunderstorm "watches" or "warnings" issued by the National Weather Service. A "watch" indicates that conditions are favorable for severe weather to develop in an area; a "warning" indicates that severe weather has been reported in an area and proper precautions should be taken. When the safety monitor has reached a flash-to-bang count of 30 seconds (implying that lightning is striking six miles away), players and spectators should have reached a safe structure or location.

The authorities monitoring an athletic event need to know the locations of the nearest safe structures. Generally speaking a "safe" structure is any building that is suitably protected against lightning. In the event there is no safe structure that will accommodate spectators, the procedures outlined in Chapter 9 should be followed. Swimmers should exit pools. Danger areas are any contact with pool sides or bottom, metal ladders or railings, or light standards. Wet floors at pool facilities are good conductors.[16] Athletes should avoid using shower facilities as shelters and definitely should not take showers during a thunderstorm. Spectators seated in metal bleachers are at risk and should evacuate the bleachers to a safe structure or location. Shelter should not be sought in the area beneath metal bleachers. Activity should not be resumed until 30 minutes has elapsed since the last flash of lightning or sound of thunder.

Agriculture and Forestlands
Farm buildings should be protected against lightning strikes. Field work should not be undertaken when thunderstorms threaten. If caught out in the open by a sudden thunderstorm, seek the shelter of an enclosed metal vehicle. Have a means of communication, either a cell phone or two-way radio on hand.[17] Also make sure someone knows your destination and expected return time. This latter precaution saved the life of Garry Rudd.

Garry Rudd is a wildlife officer in Colorado. On July 28, 1999, he was in the process of irrigating several hundred acres of hay ground used as a wildlife habitat. Having worked outdoors all of his life, Rudd was mindful of weather conditions. The sky was clear, but there was a thunderstorm about 30 miles to east that was moving away from him and did not appear to present a risk. In addition to the actual irrigation, his work involved cleaning brush and debris from the irrigation ditches as required. In the course of this work he realized that he had left his two-way radio in the truck. He stuck a pitchfork in the ground and left his backpack and other equipment by the side of the ditch while he walked back to retrieve his radio. Upon returning, he reached out his hand to take the pitchfork. What happened at that exact moment is unknown.

What Rudd does remember is waking up, flat on his back, smelling burnt hair and feeling as if he was on fire. He crawled to the irrigation ditch and plunged into the water. Then he crawled back out and tried to figure out what happened. His first thought was that he had slipped and fallen. He noticed his right hand appeared to have sustained a compound fracture. He alternately felt like he was on fire and yet was shivering and in a tremendous amount of pain. He tried calling on his radio and while it seemed to be working he could not hear any reply. (Later he realized his hearing had been affected.) Still in great pain, he resigned himself to dying and lay there on the ground as darkness fell.

Meanwhile, Rudd's wife realized that something was amiss when she hadn't heard from him by 5:00 P.M. She tried his pager and cell phone but there was no response. Knowing where he had planned to work, she drove to that location, but in the darkness failed to see his truck. She then called his supervisor and reported him missing. He was finally located just before midnight by a search party. At the hospital, doctors determined from his various burns that a lightning strike must have entered at his hip, flashed from the chest area to the pitchfork—shattering it—and exited from his leg. The "bone" protruding from his right hand was actually a 5-inch-long splinter of the pitchfork handle that had penetrated his hand.

Since his release from the hospital Rudd has been coping with memory problems, severe headaches, a painful hip condition (he walks with a cane), hearing loss, and disorientation. He has had several seizures resulting in unconsciousness. He also suffers from dizziness and balance problems.

"I want to thank my wife," he wrote. "Without her I would have never been found alive."[18]

In another incident, Susan Woods and her family were camping by a small lake in Nova Scotia one summer. Her father was in the Navy and was stationed in a nearby town for summer training, so the family took advantage of the situation for an extended camping trip. On this particular afternoon Susan's mother had left Susan, her older sister, and her younger brother at the campsite while she ran some errands. They were playing by the lakeside when a sudden thunderstorm came up and it began to rain. They ran to the tent to seek shelter. The wind was so strong that the tent was swaying back and forth—so Susan and her sister tried to hold up the tent by steadying the center wooden pole. They could hear thunder and saw a distant flash of lightning, and a few moments later the tent was struck by lightning.

In discussing it afterwards, Susan's memory of the exact details was hazy. She recalled hearing a loud crashing noise and having a sense that the tent pole was humming or possibly vibrating. She and her sister were thrown to the ground. When they recovered they ran into a nearby farmhouse and awaited the return of their mother. Neither seemed to be seriously injured by the incident, but they recalled a tingling sensation in their arms. The tent fabric was burnt at the point where it was supported by the tent pole.

Today the advent of lightweight down sleeping bags and lightweight tents that roll up into very compact shapes have made backpacking and overnight stays in the wilderness a popular sport. Such equipment provides warmth and comfort under extreme weather conditions including snow and rain but provides no protection against lightning. It is doubtful that the typical backpacker would be willing to carry the added weight required for an effective lightning protection system. However, hikers expecting to camp at high elevations above the tree line during summer months when thunderstorms are possible should give serious consideration to bringing lightning protection equipment. A better alternative would be to avoid high-altitude open areas when thunderstorms are possible. Thunderstorms are an almost daily occurrence in many mountainous areas during the summer months, so the probability of encountering one is significant.

When camping in areas accessible by automobiles, lightning protection is easily arranged. A heavy wire, supported by poles, should be placed above the ridge line of the tent. This should be grounded by wires connecting to metal stakes driven into the earth at the four corners of the tent. The tent should be circled with the bare wire buried a few inches in the earth and wrapped around or otherwise connected to each of the ground rods. If the camp site is rocky so that driving metal stakes is impossible, a long wire, say 50 feet long, can be substituted for a ground rod if it is buried in the topsoil. Similar arrangements could be used to protect cabins in the mountains or other wilderness shelters.[19]

For the backpacker unable or unwilling to carry the added weight of a lightning protection system, the best recourse would be to make camp in a grove of trees (not under a tall solitary tree), maintaining a safe distance to avoid a side flash from any tall trees that might be struck. Some back-packing tents are designed to be supported by a metal arch which is assembled using short sections of aluminum rod. With the addition of ground rods and the ring wire described above, such a tent would provide a degree of protection.

One or more of the measures described above might have saved the lives of the Boy Scouts described in Chapters 2 and 5.

There is no practical means of protection against wildland fires caused by lightning, because wilderness areas are typically too vast and usually remote. Damage can be minimized by good wildlands management practices, including firebreaks and reducing deadwood and brush fuel inventory. Forest management techniques of preventing wildfires have recently come under question over concern that they have allowed fuel buildup that makes fires all the more devastating. This has led to experiments using controlled burns to reduce the fuel inventory, but some of the "controlled burns" have gotten out of control and the practice is still controversial.

The advances in lightning detection have helped protect wilderness areas in one way, however. By pinpointing where lightning strikes are occurring, forestry departments can anticipate where fires could arise and can pre-position firefighting teams and aircraft for an early response, hopefully stopping the fire before it becomes unmanageable.

Bridges and Highways
Bridges are fitted with lightning-protection systems consisting of air terminals and grounding systems similar to those used to protect buildings. An important detail is to ensure that all the metallic components are bonded together. This is particularly important in reinforced-concrete bridges; all of the reinforcing steel should be connected to provide a continuous path to ground. If there is a discontinuity, the lightning current could follow an alternate path through the concrete—such as a crack filled with moisture—and the resulting pressure of steam formation could blast pieces of concrete from the structure.

Aircraft and Boats
Aircraft are occasionally struck by lightning in midair—in most cases with no serious consequences. Typically, there is one such occurrence every month somewhere in the world. A Japanese engineer with a video camera actually caught the image of lightning striking an aircraft as it departed from an airport.[20]

Commercial aircraft employ radar and weather routing to avoid thunderstorms as the first protection measure. If unavoidably caught in a thunderstorm, the aluminum body of an aircraft acts as a Faraday Cage to shield the crew and passengers from the lightning current. The lightning strike typically occurs near the nose of the plane, flows over the outer skin of the aircraft and into the atmosphere. The inherent danger is that a lightning-induced spark could ignite the fuel, as has happened in a few cases, resulting in the loss of the aircraft, passengers, and crew. For this reason designers have paid careful attention to designing lightning-proof fuel tanks and fuel vents. The internal electronics are protected by design measures that include transient voltage surge protectors and shielding.

Aircraft lightning-protection systems are tested to verify that they comply with government and industry standards. Testing typically consists of two components. The first component simulates the effects of direct strikes on the aircraft by means of high-voltage impulse generators that produce voltages in excess of 1 million volts and simulate the high-voltage effects of lightning striking the aircraft, while high-current generators capable of producing 200-kiloamps or more simulate current effects.[21] These tests verify that metallic and nonmetallic structures as well as fuel systems and engines, are protected. The second testing component verifies the lightning protection of the aircraft electronics (called *avionics* by aircraft manufacturers). Electronic systems are divided into those that are critical to flight operations and those that are essential; a higher degree of protection must be demonstrated for critical systems. Tests are performed to verify that these systems function properly when exposed to induced currents and high-voltage transients typical of a lightning strike on the aircraft. These tests—often referred to as *electromagnetic compatibility* (EMC) tests—involve flight control systems, radar, communications, guidance, and instruments. Tests are performed on individual instruments and power supplies as well as on the miles of cables and wiring that go into a commercial aircraft.

The standards and test procedures are revised periodically to incorporate new findings from the aircraft lightning-strike reporting system described in Chapter 6. One new finding is that as electronic systems become more complex, the flight critical and flight essential functions are sometimes integrated into one system. Lightning validation and test procedures need to be updated to account for such changes.[22]

As noted in Chapter 3, the deadliest days for lightning strikes on humans are Sunday, Saturday, and Wednesday, in that order. An engineering friend and fellow sailor named Ted von Rosenvinge has a 36 foot Beneteau sloop named *Freedom*. On Wednesday the 11th of August 2004, Ted along with a 17 year old junior sailing instructor and six teenagers were preparing to sail *Freedom* in the annual Beach Point Regatta, a Long Island Sound event in the waters off of New York and Connecticut. Since it was an overnight race and would conclude before the weekend, Ted originally had reason to believe that the lightning odds were in his favor. He and his crew attended the race committee briefing prior to the start of the race. Thunderstorms were reported to be occurring in New Jersey and were projected to arrive in the local area around race start time. Safety was emphasized during the briefing.

On *Freedom* the crew was somewhat delayed in making final preparations and was still on a mooring at the American Yacht Club (Rye, New York) as start time approached. Many of the other boats were already at the starting line when the race area was blanketed by heavy rains at around three o'clock. Ted had the crew put on foul weather gear, personal flotation devices, and safety harnesses in preparation for leaving the mooring. Meanwhile, they waited for the rains to subside and visibility to improve. There was another boat nearby also waiting. While waiting, the diesel engine was idling and some interior lights and all instruments were turned on and operating. Although the crew was anxious to get out and join the rest of the boats at the starting line, Ted as captain made the decision that they would wait until the weather and conditions improved, regardless of the race start. Ted took advantage of the delay to visit the head.

At this time, approximately 3:30 P.M., a violent thunderstorm entered the harbor and multiple lightning strikes were observed. One strike hit the top of *Freedom's* mast. On hearing the noise, Ted raced up from the head to the cockpit and turned off the engine and all the battery switches. Fortunately no one appeared to be injured. Ted's initial assessment was that the boat appeared to be in a stable condition although smoke was issuing from the starboard aft cockpit locker where the autopilot and other wiring was located and from the aft cabin on the starboard side where the battery charger and other electrical connections were located. These were quickly inspected and Ted could see melted wiring but nothing on fire. As a further precaution, a fire extinguisher was emptied into a small port to blanket the engine and battery compartment.

Ted used a handheld VHF radio to calmly inform the race committee that *Freedom* was withdrawing from the race and also to summon the yacht club launch to remove the teenagers. Meanwhile they were instructed to stay in the cabin away from safety lines and any metal connections. Once the teenagers had been taken ashore, Ted and the junior instructor made a detailed inspection of the boat. Ted observed that the VHF antenna on top of the mast had disappeared and burnt and melted remnants of it were scattered on the deck and in some cases burned into the fiberglass deck.

Freedom was towed the next day to a nearby boatyard for a haul out and complete inspection. It was determined that the hull was undamaged, suggesting that the lightning discharge had exited the boat through the keel. Virtually all of the electronics instruments—autopilot, radios, wind instruments, battery charger, and so on, were damaged. A lot of wiring was damaged. The boat had to be cleaned where there was smoke and fire extinguisher residue. Among the stranger effects of the lightning strike, the running light covers popped off. Total repair costs came to approximately $20,000, and that does not include Ted's time and a lot of volunteer labor. Two other sailboats that were in the race were hit, as was one of the radio antennas at the launch dock.

Ted was philosophical about the damage. "We were pretty lucky," he said. "About 45 minutes after the lightning hit us, when the kids were ashore, things had calmed down and I knew we weren't on fire and we weren't going to sink, I looked down and saw that my fly was unzipped. Thinking back about being in the head when we got hit, it could have been worse, if you know what I mean."

Sailboats are generally struck on the mast and particularly on the VHF antenna on top of the mast; powerboats are struck on antennas, metallic towers, or cabin tops. There is no certainty as to where lightning will strike. Biminis and rigging have also been hit. In the typical case, lightning strikes the mast or the VHF antenna on top of the mast, travels down the mast, and eventually find its way to the water. It is important to provide a safe low-resistance path from the mast to the water so the lightning current can be dissipated with the least damage to the boat. Even with good grounding, there is likely to be peripheral damage resulting from side flashes or electromagnetic pulse (EMP) effects on sensitive electronics. It is common to discover that radios have been disabled, instrumentation destroyed, or fuses blown. Even hand-held radios or other instruments that are not connected to the electrical system may be damaged. Surge-protection devices should be installed to protect electronic equipment.

If the boat does not provide a low-resistance path to water, lightning will create its own path. The worst situation is for the lightning current to travel down the mast (an aluminum mast is a very good conductor) and then flash to the sailor at the tiller or exit the boat through the fiberglass hull. If the exit point lies beneath the waterline, the boat is in real danger of sinking. Moreover, if the lightning strike damages the radio and possibly puts an engine out of commission, it may be difficult to seek or summon aid at a time when the boat may be sinking. Given forewarning of a thunderstorm, some boat owners will disconnect the VHF radio and other antenna cables in order to protect sensitive electronics. One precaution: If this is done, make sure that the cable connector is not lying against the hull of the boat or in an area where it could come in contact with a person, because the lightning could flash through the hull at that point, or could injure a crew member.

In the United States, methods for protecting boats are prescribed by the American Boat and Yacht Council standard.[23] Basically this standard describes how the various components of a boat should be bonded together, both to prevent galvanic action and corrosion and to provide a low resistance path for lightning current to exit the boat via the boat's keel or an installed grounding plate. The principles are somewhat similar to building protection in that an air terminal on top of the mast or at the highest point of a power boat is required, as well as down conductors with sufficient current-carrying capacity. It is in grounding that boats differ from buildings. In saltwater, the resistivity of the water is low enough that the boat can be grounded by bronze or stainless steel grounding plates on the hull or even by a metal keel (if bonded to the mast). In freshwater, the resistivity is higher and a larger grounding plate area is required to prevent voltage flashover from rails or rigging into the water.

In a realistic sense, however, every boat operator should be aware of the fact that even the best lightning-dissipation system will not eliminate the possibility of some damage occurring. Lightning strikes can best be described as fickle; no scientist can absolutely predict where lightning will strike in a crowded marina or at sea. There are products on the market that claim to dissipate lightning or prevent it from striking the mast. As noted earlier in this chapter, there is no solid scientific data to indicate that these devices—commonly known as "fuzzy dissipaters"—have any benefit. In at least one case, the fuzzy dissipater did not prevent a mast from being struck—twice. In the first case, the mast was struck; and the following year, on the same boat lightning ignored the taller VHF antenna and struck the fuzzy dissipater itself.[24]

"One of the Most Frightening Experiences of My Life"

My friend Todd Kolber is a professional lifeguard and schoolteacher. He keeps in shape by swimming regularly in a master's swimming program at Newport Harbor High School. One day in the locker room at the pool I heard him mention the word lightning. Todd told me it was one of the most terrifying things he had ever experienced, sitting in a boat, knowing there was nowhere to go, helpless in the presence of the overpowering energy of the approaching storm.

"It was August 2003, after a long flight," he said, "I'd flown from Los Angeles to Narita, Singapore, Jakarta, and then Padang, finally arriving at the harbor, where the boat awaited. Maybe it was just being tired after the long trip, or maybe it was reality, but the 60-foot trawler *Santa Lucia* was not exactly the boat I had envisioned when embarking on this surfing odyssey. We were five guys from Southern California, planning to spend 12 days on the boat and surfing various isolated reef breaks on small islands in the Mentawai Island chain along the West Coast of Sumatra.

"The boat had a crew of 8 to take care of a total of 11 surfers, including those of us from California. After we surfed each morning, the crew would move the boat to a new location, anchoring in the lee of an island, where we would spend the night. It seemed that every night there was rain for an hour or so, usually with some lightning in the distance. On the seventh night it was different.

"That evening, the sky was illuminated for an hour by continuous lightning flashes high in the atmosphere. The sky had the appearance of a flashing strobe light. It was more than

15 miles away, because we could hear no thunder. Then the first sounds of thunder became apparent, and we could see lightning flashes reaching down into the ocean in the distance. The captain gathered us together and told us that his radar showed the storm coming in our direction, and told us what precautions to take. He said, 'Get on shoes, get under cover, stay clear of the rails and any metal objects on the boat.' When asked if the boat might be struck by lightning, the skipper replied that there was a good possibility, and mentioned that the boat had been hit once before. I think it had a lightning arrestor, but don't know the details. Another 15 to 20 minutes passed, and as we huddled back under an overhang in the central part of the boat we could see the lightning strikes hitting the water in the distance. Water would launch up into the air like a geyser when the bolt hit the sea. At that point the air was charged with electricity; we could feel our hair standing on end.

"Suddenly a flash hit the boat. There was a loud, almost deafening noise, accompanied by a sharp vibration and the entire boat lit up. Seconds later, we could see debris— pieces of the boat—landing in the water 30 or 40 yards away. Afterward, we learned that it was parts of some of the antennas and the superstructure (tower) of the boat. Made of wood and metal, this structure was mangled, twisted, melted; pieces of it were blown away, all from the force of the strike. After this initial hit, since the storm was traveling at a good speed, we next saw the strikes occurring on the opposite side of the boat in the water and then slowly disappearing in the distance.

"At first the captain thought that he would have to summon assistance to repair the damage to the vessel. But the engines still worked, and he had enough navigation equipment to continue the journey without interruption, although a good part of the boat electronics—radar, VHF radios, and other equipment—had been knocked out by the lightning strike. The crew was able to make emergency repairs and get some of equipment operating again."

"Oh," I said, "and how was the surfing?"

Todd laughed. "The surfing was great. We caught some really fine waves. So, all in all, it was a good trip. But I never want to experience another storm like that—one of the most frightening experiences of my entire life."

Todd was fortunate—the boat was large enough, the captain experienced enough to take precautions, and the boat was equipped with some form of lightning-protection system. What do you do at sea or in an anchorage when the threat of a thunderstorm suddenly looms and your boat is unprotected? First, the crew should recognize that the mast provides a cone of protection approximately equal to the height of the mast. Beneath this protected area, crew members are relatively safe as long as they stay away from standing rigging, rails, or other metal objects, whether on deck or below in the cabin. Before the storm arrives, an effort should be made to ground the mast in an expedient manner—that is, if it is not already grounded. This can be done in a number of ways, depending on the materials available. The best way would be to attach a heavy copper cable electrically to the mast at an elevated point and place the end of the cable directly into the water. Alternatively, the anchor chain can be connected to the standing rigging or mast and the anchor dangled in the water. An aluminum oar can be connected to the backstay and allowed to hang in the water. Propane systems should be secured at the tanks and spare fuel containers holding fuel for outboard motors should be moved to a location where there is no likelihood they could be ignited by a side flash from a metal object. In a well-maintained vessel, fuel vapors or fuel spills in the bilge would not be present. But if there was any likelihood of either occurring, the bilge should be vented or cleaned to avoid ignition by a side flash.[25]

Electric Transmission and Distribution Lines, Substations, and Related Equipment

Lightning ground strikes represent a major problem for utilities. In the United States, it is estimated that as much as 60 percent of all outages can be attributed to lightning, with an annual cost to the industry exceeding $1 billion per year.[26]

Lightning can affect electrical systems in three ways, either by a direct strike, flashover, or electromagnetic coupling.

Transmission line engineers adopted Franklin's principles to the protection of overhead lines by stringing an additional cable above the conductors (known as *phase conductors*) carrying electric power to shield them against direct lightning strikes. This top conductor is analogous to the air terminal on a building. The top conductor and the transmission line towers are connected together and grounded. The overhead shield line was a simple and inexpensive solution to the challenge of protecting wires against direct strikes, but it did not solve all of the problems. Experience showed that it is possible for lightning to enter the transmission and distribution system by induction (creation of a nearby magnetic field) if not by a direct strike. Lightning transients in the electrical grid can wreak havoc on such substation equipment as switchgear and transformers, causing the system to shut down. In the early 1900s, electrical engineers developed the first lightning surge arrestors, improved insulator design, and initiated research and measurements to better characterize the lightning threat.

As an undergraduate electrical engineer at Stanford University, I knew about the Ryan High Voltage Laboratory, a high-ceiling, corrugated metal building. Professor Harris J. Ryan had come to Stanford from Cornell in 1905 to pursue research in high voltage transmission of electric power. The laboratory named for him was financed by donations from several large corporations, including the Pacific Gas and Electric Company, the California-Oregon Power Company, and General Electric. At the opening of the laboratory in 1926, 300 guests watched a demonstration of artificial lightning—a 2.1 million volt flashover through 20 feet of air between two electrodes. The laboratory worked on the development of transmission tower insulators used to support high voltage power lines, and later was instrumental in solving problems related to transmitting large amounts of power from Hoover Dam to Los Angeles.

Before improved lightning-protection systems could be designed, more had to be learned about electrical properties of lightning itself. From this research, engineers were able characterize a "typical" lightning flash for design purposes. Knowledge of the magnitude of the lightning current and voltage enables them to size the overhead ground wires and the conductors that carry the intercepted current to ground. Research also provided insight into how best to insulate the phase conductors from metal transmission towers or wooden distribution system poles.

Lightning at Leadville

High-voltage transmission lines are suspended from transmission towers by strings of bell-shaped porcelain insulators. These insulator strings have to be long enough so that the high voltage on the lines does not cause an arc to jump to the tower structure (cross arms or legs). In the early days of transmission line design, the conventional approach was to make the insulator strings proportionately longer as the voltage increased.

When the first lines to operate at 500 kilovolts were being planned, several issues arose. At this higher voltage, was making the insulator strings longer in direct proportion to the voltage, the correct approach? Some lines were intended to cross mountain ranges at high elevations, where air pressure and air density were less, reducing the resistance to electric flashover. Also, lightning strikes were more frequent at high elevations. What did this imply for transmission line design?

And finally, just adding more insulators, with the attendant increase in tower dimensions, was costly; what was the most economical solution?

In 1965, the General Electric Company initiated a research program to try to answer these questions. First General Electric built a portable high-voltage pulse generator capable of producing a 3,000,000-volt surge of electricity. The unit was unique in that it could be transported on a large tractor-trailer rig to field locations.

Working in conjunction with Arizona Public Service and Public Service Company of Colorado, General Electric planned a series of tests that took place near Leadville, Colorado, at an elevation of 12,000 feet. The project engineer for the work was Richard Thompson, one of my Stanford electrical engineering classmates.

I asked Thompson about the tests and what had been learned.

"At the outset, we weren't certain that you could even build a 500-kilovolt line that would operate at a 12,000-foot elevation, where insulation strengths are reduced," he said. "There were multiple effects to consider. Besides the higher voltage, we had to design to handle switching transients high-voltage traveling waves that propagated on the line during normal operations—and of course, lightning. I spent a summer up there in Leadville, living in a motel and commuting back and forth to Schenectady a couple of weekends per month to let my new bride know that I hadn't electrocuted myself and was still alive.

"The tests were pretty exciting. Our utility partners built a section of transmission line that was heavily instru-mented. We connected the impulse generator and pulled a switch. The "bang" when the pulse generator went off was extremely impressive. We did a series of tests simulating all kinds of conditions—even sprayed water on the insulators to see what happened when they were wet. Summer storms were frequent, and when they were particularly violent we shut down the tests, but we did get a number of measurements from actual lightning strikes.

"The test program proved that extra high-voltage transmission lines could be built and operated at high altitudes, but it also showed that insulator strings had to be longer than we first thought. The relationship between the number of insulators and flashover voltage turned out to be nonlinear. We found that the tower, insulator, and conductor system had to be designed to withstand lightning-caused voltage surges on the order of 1 million volts. The test program provided invaluable design data—we could now predict how the critical flashover voltage changed with barometric pressure, temperature, and humidity. This was important because these factors have a disproportionate effect on the economics of transmission lines built at high elevations. The critical flashover voltage is a probabilistic value, not a constant. Another important result of the research was to develop statistical models that evaluated the probability of flashover occurring for a range of weather conditions, making the design of transmission lines much more reliable."[27]

Leadville was but the first step in a distinguished career in the energy field for Thompson. He eventually became president of the Caterpillar Diesel Engine Division.

Making certain that transmission and distribution lines had the right insulation properties was an important part of the problem but not the entire solution. A lightning strike could send high voltage surges down the line, even if it did not hit the line directly. As electrical systems expanded and the number of users increased exponentially, the systems became more complicated. Transformers, capacitors, switch gear, generators, control systems of various types, and other kinds of equipment were connected to the lines. These components were vulnerable to high-voltage surges caused by lightning. A disruption of the system in which current suddenly flows to ground is called a fault—for example, as when lightning causes a flashover to ground (by current jumping from a phase conductor to a metal tower). If the system instrumentation detects a fault, it opens a switch to disconnect the line in order to protect the line and any equipment connected to it. After a short time, the instrumentation automatically recloses the switch to restore service, on the assumption that the fault has cleared. If the fault persists (as in the case when an ice storm has broken the line and it is in contact with the ground) the switch opens again and stays open, leading to a condition known as an *outage*.

To prevent faults and outages from occurring, lightning arrestors are deployed at critical locations. The earliest lightning surge arrestor was similar to a spark plug. It consisted of a "tee"-shaped electrical connection. Normal current flow was along the top of the tee. The bottom of the tee led to ground. The vertical element of the tee consisted of two parts separated by an air gap, much like a spark plug. The normal voltage (say 230 kilovolts at a frequency of 60 hertz) was not sufficient to jump the air gap, but if lightning struck the system, the high voltage impressed by the lightning strike ionized and jumped the air gap and took a low resistance path directly to ground rather than damaging equipment. A problem with this type of arrestor is that the 60 hertz line voltage continues to flow down the low resistance ionized path created by the lightning until a circuit breaker on the line is opened and then closed. From the 1950s to the 1970s, surge arrestors were fabricated by using silicon carbide to provide the strength and electrical characteristics needed to withstand the lightning flash. These incorporated a means of quenching the ionization after the lightning strike is dissipated, returning the line to normal operation. An improvement over this design is a metal oxide *varistor*. Varistor is an acronym for a solid-state material that has a variable resistance. At the transmission line nominal voltage—say, 230 kilovolts—the resistance is very high and it does not conduct. But at the lightning surge voltage, the varistor switches into a conducting mode, allowing the lightning current to discharge harmlessly to the ground. As the high voltage dissipates, the varistor returns to nonconduction as soon as the line voltage returns to normal.[28]

Today, much more is known about lightning—the duration of a lightning pulse, its maximum current and voltage, and frequency of occurrence in a given area. Still, lightning is a statistical phenomenon and absolute predictions are impossible. A transmission line can be designed to withstand a certain number of strikes of a given intensity over its 50-year lifetime, but there is no assurance it will not be hit by a larger strike or by fewer or more strikes than predicted in the design process.

The Electric Power Research Institute
Utility engineers have worked hard to improve the ability of transmission and distribution systems to withstand lightning strikes. There is a strong incentive to do so; in addition to the cost of repairing outages, there is the cost of lost revenues. As noted in the Preface, it was an extraordinary outage, disrupting electric power for many hours to millions of customers that gave impetus to the formation of the Electric Power Research Institute (EPRI). The EPRI is a nonprofit research organization funded originally by American utilities, but today draws support from many international organizations as well.

Dr. Chauncey Starr, the founding president of EPRI was previously the Dean of Engineering at UCLA and in that capacity, my former boss. Since EPRI came into being as a result of the great Northeast blackout of 1965, I thought it would be of interest to hear Starr's thoughts on the subject of lightning. I was particularly interested in his views on what progress has been made in the 40 years since the blackout, and what challenges remain. Starr was the chairman emeritus of EPRI and at age 94, was still coming to his office on a daily basis when I spoke to him about his visionary work in the energy field.[29]

Chauncey Starr: "In the early 1970s, utilities were under pressure from Congress. Senators Magnuson and

Hollings were preparing legislation to set up a federal agency to do research and development for the utility industry, stimulated in part by a desire to avoid a repeat of the costly 1965 disaster. Under this impetus, the electric utility industry created EPRI and provided assurances it would be adequately funded and dedicated to problem solving. The board of directors invited me to be the Institute's first president. I accepted on the condition that I have absolute freedom in setting the Institute's research priorities for the first five years."

With his first priority that of reducing the vulnerability of the electric transmission and distribution network to failures of any type, Starr moved aggressively to recruit the best minds in the industry and to sponsor groundbreaking research and development programs in collaboration with manufacturers, universities, research organizations, and government agencies. Within a few years, Starr built an organization that had 700 employees and an annual budget of nearly $500 million.

Chauncey Starr: "We've done a lot of work to improve reliability against lightning strikes. Equipment has been improved, better computer models were developed for designing transmission and distribution lines, and we have better means to protect substations and related equipment.

"In spite of this, lightning still represents a major interruption in the electricity distribution system. Not just direct hits, but even nearby strikes that start tree fires that knock lines out of service.

"The real problem in the national electrical grid is not local short-term outages—rather it is larger area disruptions where outages of a day or more occur. These may lead to societal costs—lost revenues, repairs, business down times— of as much as $100 million. Since they occur infrequently, our system does not have an effective means to annualize costs. If it did, I'm sure the results would indicate that we should spend more on lightning research."

I asked Starr if he foresaw future technological advances that might reduce lightning vulnerability.

Chauncey Starr: "Undergrounding would help. By placing more of the electrical grid underground, we could reduce its vulnerability to all manner of natural disasters, wind and ice storm failures, as well as lightning. This is already happening in many locations for aesthetic reasons. I don't think anyone has made a systematic study of the trade-offs involved—the costs of tunneling or direct burial versus right-of-way costs, public concerns regarding aesthetics and visual effects, as well as savings on both capital and repair and maintenance costs.

"A more futuristic thought is that we need to learn how to safely discharge lightning energy in major storms. Today we have a much better idea of the electrification processes that take place in thunderstorms, even though there are still a lot of gaps in our knowledge. Hopefully, we can make continued progress in this field and learn if it might be possible to direct lightning strikes to safe paths in those parts of the world most prone to damaging lightning strikes. Frankly, I don't know if we've given our scientists sufficient incentives to pursue this line of research. This might be an area where the national academies or some other group should establish a prestigious prize to be awarded to the person who makes a significant advance in lightning mitigation."

I worked with EPRI on several projects in the energy field between 1970 and 2000, and indirectly heard about the Institute's research in the areas of electric power transmission and distribution. The person responsible for guiding much of this research was Ralph Bernstein, the program manager for severe storm, disaster recovery, and lightning effects. I met with Bernstein and asked him for his thoughts about lightning and electric power.

Ralph Bernstein: "EPRI took a broad-brush approach to addressing the lightning problem, recognizing that any actions taken would be futile until the threat was better understood. EPRI funded the establishment of a National Lightning Detection Network (predecessor to the North American Lightning Detection Network), first by supporting research at the State University of New York at Albany. As newer and better monitoring equipment was developed, a measurement system in the Northeast United States was combined with two other regional networks to provide a national system. This network has been expanded with additional sensors and now covers both the United States and Canada. [Refer to Chapter 8 for a description of the North American Lightning Detection Network.]

"The lightning detection network represented a major advance in the ability to protect electrical systems and other sensitive facilities from lightning strikes, and now has the ability to closely pinpoint lightning strikes. By tracking storm movements and comparing them with historical lightning strike records, utility maintenance planners have a better idea of where to position repair crews and equipment for fast response in case an outage occurs. By knowing where lightning strikes occur most frequently, transmission and distribution lines in those areas can be provided with a higher degree of lightning protection than lines in areas where the risk is low. Such utilities as Consolidated Edison of New York estimate that they have reduced operating costs by hundreds of thousands of dollars per year by using the North American Lightning Detection Network. For all utilities combined, the benefit runs into millions of dollars in savings per year.[30]

"EPRI also saw the need for more full-scale testing of transmission and distribution systems, since laboratory tests cannot replicate the effects of lightning. For that reason, EPRI was instrumental in funding triggered lightning research, first at Cape Kennedy, and then at the International Center for Lightning Research and Testing, located at Camp Blanding, Florida. [Refer to Chapter 1 for a description of Camp Blanding.] EPRI and several of its member utilities established the research facilities at Camp Blanding, including full-scale sections of two configurations of distribution lines, each 0.5 miles long. These lines were hit multiple times by triggered lightning in order to measure how the lightning current propagated, to get actual values of voltage and current, and to evaluate the performance of lightning arrestors.

"The facility was originally operated for one year by a private firm under contract to EPRI, but later we decided that a better arrangement was to turn it over to the University of Florida to operate. This work has yielded a great deal of valuable information about lightning effects. EPRI publishes a transmission line design guide that is widely used by the industry. This design guide includes lightning protection information based on research performed at Camp Blanding. Also, EPRI played a key role in the development of the fast zinc oxide lightning arrestor and developed several computer programs for use by utilities. One, called *Fault Analysis and Lightning Location System*, uses data from the North American Lightning Detection Network and utility recorded data to identify transmission and distribution lines that should be upgraded due to poor utility performance. Another is the *Lightning Protection Design Workstation*, a computer design system that allows utility engineers to determine the optimum line spacing, arrestor selection, grounding, and other parameters for a given lightning environment.

"Still," Bernstein concluded, "I think that lightning continues to be a major threat to electric utilities. No one tallies all of the costs, but if you considered the cost of repairs, lost revenues, customer expenses, and other hidden costs, I'm certain that the cost to the United States economy is a billion dollars per year."

Today, ongoing research with triggered lightning at Camp Blanding is occurring under the direction of Professor Martin Uman and his colleagues in Florida and at other locations internationally. When I asked Uman if he thought that all of the problems had been solved, he told me that there were still uncertainties; utility engineers still do not have a complete grasp of the physics of the lightning/distribution line interaction, and more needs to be done to understand arrestor performance.

So, on the basis of the opinions of several well-respected researchers, I conclude that despite all of the work done within the past 40 years, there is still a very real prospect that lightning will cause a major blackout at some future date.

Telephone and Cable Television Systems
These systems should be protected with surge-protection devices. Most importantly, they should not be used during thunderstorms or when thunderstorms threaten. A safe distance (6 feet as a minimum) should be maintained between any individuals and telephones, computers, televisions, or other electronic devices for at least 30 minutes after the last thunder has been heard.

Antennas
Today most residential AM and FM radios have built-in internal antennas that do not require lightning protection. External antennas—particularly those used by radio amateurs—require lightning protection. At a minimum, the antenna mast should be grounded with a suitably sized down-conductor and a ground system employing driven ground rods or other acceptable means for achieving a low-resistance path to ground. Coaxial antenna feed cables should have lightning arrestors installed. These are commercially available. Some amateur radio stations make use of antenna feed cables that are not coaxial. They are either two-wire open line or 300-ohm ribbon-type cable. Spark-gap lightning arrestors can be made for these using ⅛-inch-thick by ½-inch-wide copper sheet. The arrestors are conducted to each side of the two-wire line and to a ground.[31] In addition, radio receivers, amplifiers, trans-mitters, and antenna tuners should all be bonded together and grounded with large capacity copper conductors. When possible in advance of a storm, disconnect equipment from

power sources and disconnect antenna leads. Do not leave them lying in exposed areas where they could flash to individuals or to equipment; better yet, connect them directly to the grounding system as an added safety measure.

"Ham" (FCC-licensed radio amateurs) operators perform an invaluable service globally by providing emergency communications services in times of natural disasters. To obtain a ham license, individuals are required to know basic electrical and electronic theory. Therefore it is to be expected that they should provide a high degree of reliability and lightning protection in their stations so as to be able to operate when other communication systems have been damaged or destroyed.

Commercial broadcasting stations (television and radio stations) constitute an interesting special case. For maximum coverage, transmitters and antennas are located on mountaintops where possible. This makes them good lightning targets. Protection is compounded by the fact that such locations usually involve rocky soil with high resistivity. Protection involves the same general principles described at the beginning of this chapter, in connection with buildings—that is, air terminals, down conductors, and ground terminals.[32]

The air terminal should extend above the highest object on the tower—for example, above an aircraft warning light. All metal objects on the tower should be bonded together. The base of the tower should be grounded. A desirable goal would be ground resistance of 10 ohms, although this would be difficult to achieve with ground rods driven in rocky soil. Another approach would be to place a "cage" of reinforcing steel around the tower foundation, and extend out from it radial ground conductors buried near the surface of the soil, to achieve as low a resistance as possible.

Usually towers are strengthened by guy wires terminated in concrete foundations. The guy wires have insulators to isolate them electrically from the tower. The insulator should be paralleled by lightning arrestor so lightning current can bypass the insulators. At the ground, the guy wires are connected to the same grounding system as the tower. Cages fabricated from metal rods can be placed around the guy wire foundations as well. A cage of metal bars with the appropriate spacing acts as if it were fabricated of sheets of metal.[33]

Antenna feeds (cables connecting transmitters or receivers to antennas) also require protection. This is usually a spark gap or other type of surge protection device inserted in the connecting cable. The signal strength is such that it is unable to jump the gap. But in the case of an overvoltage impressed by lightning, the high-voltage flashes across the gap to ground. An alternate technique in the event of an approaching storm is to disconnect sensitive equipment from antenna feeds, either by electrical disconnects or manual means.

Pipelines, Oil, and Hazardous Material Storage Facilities
How does one protect against the situation described in Chapter 6 involving a petroleum storage tank that was hit by lightning and exploded? First, by ensuring that all tanks, piping, and related equipment are bonded together—especially any clean-out openings or inspection ports that might have gaskets. Secondly, by installing an overhead ground wire system to intercept a lightning flash and convey it to ground.

Ammunition dumps and other facilities where explosives or munitions are stored require protection systems to prevent fires and explosions. There are various guidelines for the protection of structures housing explosives. In the United States, these have been published by the National Fire Protection Association [Standard NFPA-780 (2000)], the National Space and Aeronautics Administration, and the United States Air Force. These standards recommend that an overhead mast or overhead wire system be used for lightning protection. The use of an overhead system with the down conductors removed from close proximity to the structure reduces the likelihood of a sideflash that could ignite the contents.[34]

Underground Structures and Mines

Storage facilities for such hazardous materials as explosives may be located underground. They can be made relatively safe from lightning strikes by constructing an underground air terminal system or Faraday cage that will intercept the current from a lightning strike on the ground and safely dissipate it, preventing it from reaching the structure. (Refer to the example given in the Preface.)

Underground mines present a special type of hazard because of the potential presence of combustible or explosive materials. As noted in Figure 14, a high electric field is created in the soil adjacent to and extending some distance from the location where lightning strikes the ground. Depending on the resistivity of the soil, the electric field gradient and hence the current may dissipate quickly in a short distance, or can extend some distance below the surface. In moist sandy soil with low resistivity, the voltage decreases rapidly in the top layers of the soil—say, from 15 to 30 feet. In rocky soil or material with high resistivity, significant voltages can be produced thousands of feet below the surface of the soil.

When lightning strikes the surface near a mine, dangerous currents can enter the mine directly by propagation through the soil or indirectly by means of electrical power lines, water pipes, or telephone connections to the mine, as in the case of the Sago mine described in Chapter 6. An example of a direct connection would be a current passing through the soil to a rail system in the mine tunnels. Danger arises when high-voltages are present in the mine and flashover occurs between metallic objects or equipment within the mine. In this case, such combustible materials as coal dust, or such gases as methane, can explode or cause fires.

Blasting in a mine is usually performed by using electric detonators. These devices subject a small electric heating element to a brief high current, causing it to detonate a blasting cap, which in turn causes the explosive to detonate. Miners have to exert special precautions to avoid premature detonation of explosives. For this reason, operation of radios is prohibited lest stray high frequencies inadvertently ignite the detonators. Likewise, stray currents from lightning can prematurely set off the blast, causing serious injuries and fatalities. Historically, there have been a number of mine disasters attributed to lightning; the Sago mine disaster described in Chapter 6 is but the latest.[35]

Mine safety depends first of all, on preventing the accumulation of combustible or explosive materials. Generally, this requires dust control and providing adequate ventilation; both measures are important aspects of mine safety in any event, because an explosion could be ignited by an electrical spark from machinery or by the impact of metallic tools on rock. Next in importance to controlling the inventory of explosive materials in the mine is to provide adequate grounding and lightning arresters (surge-protection devices) on all electric utilities coming into the mine. Ventilation pipes extending from underground chambers to above the surface should be made of nonconducting materials. The subject is too complex to address in detail in this book, but the final point is that even underground, you are not necessarily safe from lightning.[36]

8

Predicting the Unpredictable

Several years ago, while attending a meeting at the Electric Power Research Institute (EPRI), in Palo Alto, California, I noticed a large electronic map display on a wall. Every now and then a flash of light occurred on the screen. Curious about this, I asked one of the EPRI staff what it meant. He explained that it was a link to the North American Lightning Detection Network—a system used by the EPRI's member utilities to prepare for outages on the nation's electrical grid caused by lightning.

Early detection and prediction of lightning strikes has many obvious benefits. Such information enables airports to advise pilots about potentially hazardous weather, electric utilities to position repair crews in service territories where outages may occur, and operators to advise visitors and others at recreational and public facilities to seek shelter.

Some Legal Considerations
Before reviewing detection and warning instruments, I want to explore some of the legal ramifications of issuing warnings versus not issuing warnings. Under the law, a lightning strike is generally treated as "an act of God," something beyond the control of humankind. In other words, if an accident is caused by a purely natural force that could not have been foreseen or prevented by any amount of human care, it is an act of God. By installing a lightning detection and warning system a public agency might be concerned about incurring liability— the thinking being that the installation of such a system suggests that a lightning strike could have been foreseen or prevented by human care. Suppose that despite the installation of the detection and warning system, someone is killed or injured? To what extent is a public agency or

corporation obligated to warn the public or employees of natural hazards? These legal considerations can be extended to the question of providing lightning protection systems for public buildings.

Here is one example of how the courts have ruled.

It started out as a clear June day in 2001, and the manager of Smiley's Golf Complex, in Lenexa, Kansas, opened the course as usual in the morning. However, shortly after 1 P.M. he observed dark clouds and heard a weather alert on television. In keeping with the golf course's stated policy, he sounded a horn that alerted golfers to vacate the course. The course remained closed until approximately 4 P.M., when the weather cleared and the sun returned.[1]

It was around this time that two young men—Patrick Sall and Christopher Gannon—decided to go golfing. Gannon checked the weather channel on television and saw that the storm appeared to be leaving the area. After the two played one hole a light rain began to fall but they continued on to the second green. As they prepared to putt on the second green, Gannon observed a lightning bolt in the distance. It seemed far away, but nonetheless they decided to quit after the second hole.

Meanwhile, the golf course manager walked outside, noticed a lightning strike, and blew the club's warning horn in two five-second bursts.

Sall and Gannon heard the horn from their position on the second green, and a few moments later observed a second lightning strike. At this point, Sall completed play and the two started to walk back toward the clubhouse. As they were walking, Gannon saw a big flash of light followed by a loud boom. He blacked out and fell unconscious to the ground. When he came to, he found his friend unconscious and was unable to rouse him. He then went immediately to the clubhouse for emergency assistance, and a 911 call was placed. In the meantime, other golfers began giving Patrick CPR. Shortly thereafter, emergency personnel arrived and Sall was transported to the hospital. He survived, but was severely injured and required ongoing care.

Sall's parents sued the golf course, claiming it was negligent by failing to properly monitor the weather, failing to sound a timely warning, and failing to utilize lightning detection equipment. In response, the golf course filed a motion for summary judgment, claiming that it had breached no duty to Sall. In addition, the golf course advised the court that it had issued a timely warning for golfers to stop play. The trial court ruled that due to the capricious nature of lightning, businesses do not have a duty to protect or warn patrons. The Salls appealed the court's decision.

The appeals court upheld the decision of the trial court. The court was persuaded by the fact that the two young men had observed two lightning strikes and heard the horn, but still continued to play. In addition, the court noted that there is no industrywide standard for golf courses that mandates the use of lightning detection equipment. The court found that lightning detection monitors are not a guarantee for golfing safety. Even without a lightning detection system, this golf course had had a system and process in place for more than 10 years for warning golfers—namely, a system of monitoring the weather via television and the Internet and sounding a warning horn when dangerous weather approached.

The courts have heard a number of cases involving lightning deaths or injuries on golf courses, and in the sample I examined, no golf course was found liable if it implemented one or more of the following safety measures: posted warnings; declared no responsibility for injuries and stated clearly that players use the course at their own risk; provided an evacuation plan; monitored the weather; sounded an alarm if bad weather approached, or employed a lightning detection system.[2] The courts seem to indicate that if a course applies one or more of these measures, it has a duty to consistently and properly apply it/them. However, lots of cases get settled so they do not go to court and set precedent.

So, what is the answer? Install a lightning detection and warning system or not? My personal opinion—based on this limited sampling of cases from various jurisdictions in the United States that may or may not be representative of the laws in any one specific locality—is that a lightning warning and detection system would demonstrate a good-faith effort by a golf course or athletic facility to protect its patrons. But it must be accompanied by warnings that such systems are not infallible and that individuals are responsible for their own welfare, and the system must be maintained and operable at all times or the operator could be vulnerable to a claim of negligence. (Don't take my word for it, however; I am not an attorney and I am not engaged in rendering legal advice, nor should my opinion be considered a substitute for professional legal services.)[3]

Readers should be cautioned that none of these warning and detection systems are foolproof. The equipment can malfunction, operating staff may fail to turn the system on, or a random bolt of lightning may simply escape detection. Or, as in the case of Michael Utley (See Chapter 9), the warning might come too late to be of any value.

This is but one example; on balance, it would appear that the overall risk of litigation for public agencies and private companies is reduced when they take positive actions to mitigate the lightning hazard by some combination of education, warning signs and notices, and lightning warning and detection systems. These measures should be applied in relationship to the extent of the risk; workers within a factory or office building located in a low lightning risk area (infrequent keraunic activity) are obviously at far less risk than golfers in Florida. Warnings and education programs should note that there is yet no infallible system for predicting or warning of a lightning strike, and persons should seek protected areas when thunderstorms are forecast or threaten, even if the warning system does not activate.

How Detection Systems Work

Despite the claims of some manufacturers, there is no lightning detection and warning system available that will *predict* a lightning strike. No scientific means of predicting exactly when and where lightning will strike has yet been discovered. The available technology (with varying degrees of sensitivity and accuracy) detects the presence of thunderstorm activity, as evidenced by a distant cloud-to-cloud or cloud-to-ground lightning flash, changes in the earth's electric field that sometimes serve as a precursor to lightning strikes, or a combination of both. Refinements use radio direction finding or magnetic field direction finding and time-of-arrival techniques to locate distant strikes. Still, no method will provide a 100 percent guarantee that lightning will or will not strike. At best, the technology available today enables one to anticipate where lightning might strike within the next 30 minutes or so, but provides no guarantee that a strike will actually occur and no guarantee that it won't strike within the next 30 seconds and in a completely different locality. Such is the random, capricious, and unpredictable nature of lightning.

Lightning detection and warning systems sense either the radio frequency signals, changes in electric or magnetic fields, or optical signals (light pulses) emitted by a flash. The radio waves emitted by lightning do not occur at discrete frequencies, but rather cover a broad range of frequencies from 10 kilohertz to 120 megahertz. As noted in Chapter 2, radio waves propagate differently depending on the frequency. Many inexpensive detectors are sensitive to signals in the range of 100 to 500 kilohertz. This is the frequency band below the low end of the standard AM radio frequency band. If you tune your AM radio to its lowest frequency setting during a thunderstorm, you're likely to hear the crackling static sound caused by lightning. Inexpensive personal or pocket-sized lightning detectors operate on this principle, using the signal strength to estimate the distance to the lightning strike.

Several limitations are immediately apparent. A large, distant strike can produce the same signal amplitude as a smaller nearby strike. Also, the detector cannot differentiate between a cloud-to-cloud flash and a cloud-to-ground flash—the latter being less frequent but far more dangerous.

Other units use signals in the VHF range (50 to 120 megahertz. At these frequencies the range for signal detection is 25 to 50 miles and is limited to line of sight. In other words, the detector must "see" the lightning flash. Intervening mountains or other obstructions can block the signal, and at longer ranges the curvature of the earth blocks the signal.

Another problem is that these low-cost detectors are susceptible to many different types of interference. Arc welding, gasoline motor ignition systems, some computers or electronic systems, or even static electricity from clothing on low-humidity days can cause spurious readings.

The more sophisticated (and expensive) detection and warning systems use a combination of optical and radio-frequency signals or two radio frequency signals to isolate cloud-to-ground flashes and improve the accuracy of the detection system. They also may include microprocessors with algorithms that improve signal detection accuracy. To obtain a more accurate indication of a nearby hazard, the more complex instruments include a sensor to measure the electric field strength. As noted in Chapter 1, at the International Center for Lightning Research and Testing, when the electric field strength increases from a clear weather value of around 300 volts per meter to 5,000 to 10,000 volts per meter, it is a danger signal for lightning. However, even under these conditions, and with thunderclouds overhead, a rocket fired into the cloud will not always trigger a lightning strike.

Types of Lightning Detection and Warning Systems
In 1992, Richard Kithil formed the National Lightning Safety Institute. The Institute grew out of Kithil's conviction that there was a need for better and more reliable information

concerning lightning safety and design of protections systems. With the background of a lifetime interest in amateur radio and antenna theory, Kithil began assembling information about lightning. He brought objectivity to this work as he was not tied to any particular equipment supplier. Today he is widely recognized for his expertise and has served as a consultant to the National Aeronautics and Space Administration, the Department of Defense, international mining consortiums, and numerous private corporations in the United States and overseas.

I spoke with him to ask about his estimate of the economic costs of lightning and about the accuracy of lightning detections systems. He pointed out that with the proliferation of low voltage electronic devices (computers, modems, faxes, communications systems, printers, digital controllers of all types, and so on, the economic cost of lightning strikes is soaring. Users have been slow to install adequate surge protection devices to protect sensitive electronic equipment.

Most of the low-cost lightning monitoring and detection systems, in his opinion, have limited value and accuracy. As he put it: "Hearing thunder is far more accurate and useful at close range. Your ear can detect thunder at a range of 6 to 8 miles. The inexpensive instruments approximate the range by the signal amplitude, but can confuse a large distant strike with a nearby weak strike."

There are many different types of lightning detection and warning systems that are commercially available. These range from small personal warning devices that cost less than $100 to fixed location networks costing thousands of dollars. In addition, there are subscription services that will provide warnings or alerts for a specified area. The following paragraphs provide a brief description of some typical instruments and detection systems.

Personal Lightning Detectors

Personal lightning detectors range in price from $70 to $400.[4] These units claim detection ranges of from 40 to 75 miles. Typically, light emitting diodes (LEDs) display the range to the detected lightning strike. An audible alarm will sound with each lightning strike. The more expensive units will indicate the speed of a storm approach. One device—StrikeAlert—is the size of a cell phone or pager, costs $70 to $80, claims to be able to detect strikes as far away as 40 miles, and can advise if the storm is coming closer. The SkyScan lightning detector also detects radio frequency signals from lightning and claims a range of 40 miles. The cost is approximately $180. The ThunderBolt Pro unit samples primarily below 10 kilohertz and uses magnetic field detection. A detection range of up to 75 miles is claimed. The cost is approximately $430. Hand-held lightning detectors can be purchased over the Internet and are available from stores that sell outdoor recreation or boating equipment or those that specialize in weather monitoring instruments.[5]

Portable Area Detection and Warning Systems
Utility work crews, television news vans, highway repair crews, and forestry personnel are often required to perform their duties in inclement weather. Several portable instruments have been developed to enable crews in the field to monitor thunderstorm activity and stop work when dangerous con-ditions arise.

One example is a portable instrument called the SkyScan EWS-Pro early warning lightning detector. This is a portable, briefcase-sized instrument powered by a rechargeable 12-volt battery. The detection range is stated to be 40 miles and the manufacturer claims to have software that differentiates cloud strikes from cloud-to-ground strikes. The unit includes a loud warning horn and flashing lights. The cost is $800.

The fixed-mobile lightning alert system (FMLA-1000) unit is designed for use on utility vehicles and live television vans to provide early warning of approaching thunderstorms. It uses warning lights and a klaxon horn as alarms. Its stated range is 25 miles and the price is $250 to $350, depending on the model.

Another mobile unit is the model 350 lightning detector sold specifically for mining and blasting operations. This suitcase-sized unit has an external telescoping antenna and a warning strobe light and siren. It has a rechargeable battery and the cost is $2,100. Information on these types of instruments can be found on the Internet.[6]

Area Detection and Warning Systems

As noted in Chapter 1, changes in electric field near the earth's surface often (but not always) are a precursor to lightning activity. Some detection and warning systems operate on the principle of monitoring the electric field strength and providing a warning when changes occur and an alert when dangerous conditions exist. Systems of this type have been deployed at golf courses, municipal parks, airports, universities, and even ski resorts.

One commercially available system is ThorGuard, which uses a rooftop or elevated electric field strength sensor to monitor an area approximately five miles in diameter. When a change in the electric field strength is detected above a threshold value, the instrument indicates that a lightning hazard exists. When dangerous conditions exist, the unit activates amber strobe warning lights and sounds a warning using loud klaxon horns. When the threat of lightning strikes has passed, the system sounds three short blasts to signal an all clear.[7]

Many parks, golf courses, and athletic fields have installed lightning warning systems that alert visitors to impending lightning strikes. Examples include Texas Christian University, in Fort Worth, Texas, which installed detectors at a soccer field, coliseum, student center, recreation center, and several other locations. Another example is the City of Miami, Ohio, which installed warning systems in several parks.

Other Lightning Warning and Detection Systems

The Boltek LD-250 is a lightning detector system operating in the broadcast band that is designed to interface with a laptop or desktop personal computer. The system uses radio direction finding and ranging to detect a lightning strike and display the location on a map installed in the computer. The unit has selectable ranges of 100, 200, and 300 miles. The software enables a real-time display of lightning strikes on the computer and also sounds an alarm. The cost is $800. A home or business detection system called Boltek's StormTracker costs $500 and detects radio signals produced by lightning up to 300 miles away. The system connects to a personal computer and can generate maps that show where the storm is located and in what direction it is heading. The system will also activate an alarm.[8]

Such other detection systems as the Rabun model 300 or 1000 are designed to detect nearby lightning strikes and automatically disconnect, isolate, or shunt to ground such sensitive electrical or electronics equipment as computers or communications gear. These systems will also switch equipment from power lines to a separate backup battery supply in order to maintain continuity of operation. The unit has a battery backup and a "self-protect" feature that automatically disconnects the unit from the ac power lines when operating in the "protect" mode. The unit automatically restores all connections when the danger has passed. Its cost is approximately $3,000.[9]

Given the variability of lightning flashes, detection systems with a single sensor are likely to be subject to both detection failures and false alarms. Before investing in a detection and warning system, talk to other owners nearby who have the same equipment and find out how the equipment has worked for them. Ask the manufacturer for data that compares the performance of their equipment with the North American Lightning Detection Network.

The North American Lightning Detection Network

In 1975, Dr. Martin Uman and Dr. Phillip Krider co-founded a company known as Lightning Location and Protection, Inc. The company developed commercial versions of lightning direction finding equipment that subsequently formed the basis of three lightning detection networks in the United States. One, set up by the United States Bureau of Land Management, was used in 11 western states and Alaska to aid in predicting the likely locations of forest fires. Researchers at the United States National Severe Storm Laboratory established a second network covering Oklahoma and some midwestern states, while another group at the State University of New York, Albany, established an East Coast network. In the 1980s, with support from the EPRI, improved equipment was developed and deployed and the three networks were combined into a single national network operated by a new entity called Global Atmospherics, Inc., that employed both direction finding and time-of-arrival technologies for more precise pinpointing of lightning strikes. In the early 2000s Global Atmospherics, Inc., was acquired by the Finnish company Vaisala, which currently operates the North American Lightning Detection Network.

I contacted Ron Holle, a meteorologist for the North American Lightning Detection Network, and made arrangements to visit Vaisala's Tucson operations. It is here that information from the network of more than 180 North American detectors is received and analyzed. Lightning sensors distributed throughout the United States and Canada detect the electromagnetic signals created when lightning strikes the earth's surface. A sensor transmits data including the intensity, time, and other pertinent information through an uplink to an orbiting satellite. The satellite in turn relays the information to Tucson, where the control center computers calculate the location, time, polarity, and amplitude of the stroke. This information is then available in less than one minute nationwide to such subscribers as the National Weather Service and the Electric Power Research Institute. Data can be animated to display trends and indicate the potential direction in which a storm will move. Today flash detection efficiency is around 90 percent and locations can be determined to within around 1,500 feet.

In the control room, Holle showed me how the system works. A large screen flickered with spots of light as lightning flashes were detected while we watched—most were in Florida on this particular day. By tracking the direction as storms move, the center's data can be used to issue warnings to wildlands agencies, utilities, athletic events, or companies with facilities potentially at risk. Warnings permit airports, NASA space flight operations, or hazardous material handling facilities to suspend operations when dangerous conditions approach. The center's archives now contain a vast amount of historical data, so it is possible to select a given area and determine what the historic average number of lightning strikes has been. (The system is currently recording in excess of 20 million cloud-to-ground strikes annually.) To view an example of the NLDN display for the United States, go to www.lightningstorm.com and follow the links to "lightning explorer free map."

By using data gathered by the North American Lightning Detection Network, utilities alone calculate that they annually save millions of dollars in maintenance and repair costs and have been able to selectively upgrade those transmission and distribution lines with greater lightning exposure to improve system reliability while avoiding unnecessary capital costs. In addition to the United States and Canada, 40 countries have installed similar systems.[10]

Other techniques can be used to determine if weather conditions (temperature, water vapor content, et cetera) will facilitate lightning strikes. If the necessary conditions are met, forecasters can predict that lightning strikes will occur in a general area, but cannot pinpoint specific locations. A company by the name of Weatherdata, Inc., recently patented a lightning prediction methodology based on weather data. The method analyzes radar data to locate areas where cloud tops extend to a height where the temperature has decreased to a predetermined level. This information is combined with radar reflectivity data (indicative of cloud density) to forecast areas with significant lightning potential. Storms that meet the screening criteria can be tracked and future locations anticipated 10 to 30 minutes into the future, providing a degree of advance warning.

Subscription Weather Services
There are also subscription services that will monitor the weather at a given site and provide notification of impending thunderstorm activity. Extreme weather data and forecasts are available on the Internet in the United States, Europe, and many regions and countries.[11] These national and international weather services also provide storm warnings for specific areas.

There are a number of commercial services that provide weather data and alerts. WeatherData Inc. provides weather risk-management data to clients on a subscription basis. The service is called *Storm Intelligence*™ and provides site-specific warnings for tornadoes, hurricanes, flash floods, high winds, and other extreme conditions to private clients and government agencies.[12] Intelecast.com is another Internet-based weather service and can be accessed at no cost. It features maps showing current thunderstorm risk areas—called thundercasts—and also areas where lightning is currently striking or has recently struck. These maps provide a general indication, but are not detailed.[13]

Accuweather.com offers a service that enables subscribers to obtain real-time weather data and forecasts at the regional or municipal level. The data include radar maps of storm conditions, storm movement directions, forecasts, regional lightning strikes, and one hour lightning forecasts. Basic weather data cost from $7-$42 per month depending on the services requested; specialized lightning strike information and forecasts cost an additional $17-$200 per month depending on the level of service desired. The service includes an interactive map of street-level lightning strikes from the last two hours, e-mail or telephone alerts will be sent automatically to users providing estimated arrival and departure times when lightning is forecast to occur in the subscriber's area.[14]

Vaisala, the firm that operates the North American Detection Network, also provides a lightning notification service, but only to organizations with 50 or more users per account. Notification services are available online, in lightning tracking software, and in local-area lightning information systems. Notification options include short- and long-format e-mail messages. Messages are sent to a computer, pager, or cell phone. Three notification levels offer expanding areas of coverage: 8-mile radius (overhead), 15-mile radius (near), and 30-mile radius (distant).[15]

Advanced Detection Systems
The National Aeronautics and Space Administration (NASA) has a lightning research program that includes developing instrumentation for lightning detection and measurements by planes and satellites.[16] In 1995, NASA orbited an optical sensor (called the optical transient detector) capable of detecting cloud-to-cloud, intracloud, and cloud-to-ground lightning strikes from space. The satellite circled the earth once every 100 minutes and the sensor scanned an area 800 miles by 800 miles as it traveled above the earth. The resulting data have been compared with the land-based system, indicating that about 25 percent of all strikes go to ground. The data confirm that most global lightning occurs in the Intertropical Convergence Zone over the continents, more

lightning strikes occurring over land than over oceans. The system ceased transmitting data in March 2000.[17] A second lightning detection system was launched in November 1997, as part of the Tropical Rainfall Measuring Mission (TRMM). The satellite has a circular orbit over the earth at a relatively low altitude of 217 miles. While the primary objective of the TRMM satellite is to measure rainfall and gather global weather data, the instrumentation package also included a lightning imaging sensor. This sensor has a higher detection efficiency and better resolution than the optical transient detector and can scan a given point on earth for up to 80 seconds, detecting 90 percent of all lightning strikes. The instrument detects a lightning flash, estimates the location, and calculates the radiant energy.[18]

NASA recently announced the use of a new lightning index that combines measurement of water vapor in storm clouds and weather data from a global positioning system. Forecasting lightning strikes at Kennedy Space Center is extremely important to avoid damage to equipment or injury to personnel. (Figure 20 shows a lightning strike near a launch pad.) Accurate forecasts can easily save $1 million simply by avoiding a 24-hour launch delay or the expense of transporting the space shuttle back to Kennedy Space Center following a West Coast landing.[19]

These are but a few examples of a host of new technologies that are available to provide warnings. None of these systems are infallible. However, for businesses or individuals operating or working in high-risk areas, they can provide advance warning of danger before a storm can be seen or heard and can provide the margin between life and death.

Satellite detection of lightning activity in the longer term is a very promising method for monitoring global lightning activity. If future detection systems can improve resolution and can monitor storm direction and speed of movement, satellites may be able to help improve lightning warning capability.

Figure 20: Lightning Strike at Kennedy Space Center

In summary, despite advances in lightning detection technology, lightning remains a real danger to humans, livestock, forest lands, buildings, sensitive equipment, and transportation and infrastructure systems. Claims that any detection equipment can "predict" a lightning strike should be viewed with considerable skepticism, since history shows repeatedly that lightning will strike when least expected, may fail to strike when conditions seem right, and in a totally capricious manner may jump to seemingly innocuous or safe items to reach its victims. The best policy is to heed the warning signs and take shelter if a lightning strike is possible. You alone are responsible for your own safety.

9

The Bell Ringer's Deception

U ntil the middle of the 18th century, church bells were rung at the approach of a thunderstorm in the belief that this would fend off lightning. Since bell towers were tall structures, they were frequently struck, and experience showed that a bell ringer's life expectancy during a major storm could be abruptly truncated. Franklin commented on this ecclesiastical approach to protecting buildings in his correspondence to John Winthrop, observing:

> "...the lightning seems to strike steeples of choice and that at the very time the bells are ringing; yet still they continue to bless the new bells and jangle the old ones whenever it thunders. One would think it was now time to try some other trick..."[1]

By this time Franklin understood the basic principles of lightning protection, had articulated them in his writings, and had seen several important buildings in Philadelphia outfitted with lightning rods in accordance with his design. His lightning rod design made use of two fundamental principles, arrived at by observation and experiment:

- Shielding—intercepting lightning so that it strikes the lightning rod and not the building or structure
- Dissipating—conducting the lightning current to ground

Still, this was protection, not prevention. Prevention, as Franklin well understood, involved knowledge of the origin and movement of thunderstorms. This was a subject that Franklin also studied, but his accomplishments were overshadowed by the attention given to his electrical work.

Since buildings and most infrastructure have fixed locations, "prevention" in the broadest sense is impossible. Prevention of lightning strikes on buildings and other fixed locations would require defusing the large electrical energy content of thunderclouds. Previous attempts by humans to modify natural weather conditions have generally ended in failure or met with limited success. Attempts from the 1960s to the 1980s to alter hurricanes by seeding them with dry ice or silver iodide particles ended in failure and eventually were abandoned. In part, the project—called *Stormfury*—was halted because of concern that the weather modification attempts might backfire. In 1974, when Hurricane Fifi hit Honduras, newspaper articles reported that the United States seeded the hurricane to direct it away from Florida, thus causing it to strike Honduras. In reality, no hurricane seeding missions had been conducted in 1974.[2]

However, as Chauncey Starr noted in Chapter 7, the subject of how one might defuse thunderstorms has not received any serious scientific investigation and is worthy of further research. Even if it turned out that discharging thunderclouds was impractical, research might shed new insights into the mechanism of lightning formation and make possible improved detection or early warning systems.

Diverting Lightning with Laser Beams
It may be possible to discharge thunderclouds using lasers. The method is being explored by Russian, Japanese, and American scientists. Some small-scale laboratory tests indicate that it might work, but so far it has not been demonstrated conclusively during actual thunderstorms, despite numerous attempts.[3]

As a laser beam passes through air, it creates a path of ionized particles. The amount of ionization, range of the beam, and ultimately the scattering (dissipation) of the laser beam depend on its frequency, power, and the composition of the air. Moist air can scatter and attenuate the beam more rapidly than dry air, as does denser air near sea level, compared to air at high altitudes.

When rockets are used to trigger lightning, they typically reach an altitude of roughly 650 to 1,300 feet, so the range of a laser capable of triggering lightning presumably need not be much greater than this. (Lasers have been used to reflect light from the moon, so a laser beam has the potential to travel a long distance.) The technical issue is whether the laser beam has sufficient intensity to create a strongly ionized path that persists for a sufficient period of time to trigger lightning. Experiments using rockets trailing conducting wires indicate that the ionized path need not be extremely long; it could possibly be as short as 33 feet (10 meters.)

Laboratory experiments have been performed whereby a laser beam was directed from one high-voltage electrode to another, causing a spark to jump 10 inches along the ionized path created by the laser.[4] While this laboratory test demonstrates the feasibility of the concept, deployment to the field for testing under realistic conditions is considerably more complicated.

First, the laser power needs to be increased, and portable units would be desirable. To protect a sensitive facility— such as a nuclear power plant—several laser installations would have to be located around the site and linked to the North America Lightning Detection Network. Upon receiving a signal indicating the approach of a thunderstorm, the system would be readied. It would also require electric field measuring instrumentation to sense when conditions were conducive to a lightning strike.

Laser beams would be deflected into the cloud by a mirror system. (Obviously it would not be a good idea to have the lightning flash follow the laser path back to earth and destroy the equipment.) The mirror installation would have to be placed in a safe location and grounded so the return stroke would hit it and be conducted to earth.

While this is an interesting concept, more research needs to be done to prove it can work in the field. In addition to building a practical system rugged enough to be used in the field, tests would be required to establish how such a system could be safely operated. Also it would be necessary to see if a laser system was economic. I spoke with Jean-Claude Diels, professor of Physics and Electrical Engineering at the University of New Mexico, to learn if researchers were ready to perform field tests of a laser system. He told me that research is ongoing but that additional funding is needed to further refine the laser equipment before field trials can be conducted. He stated that the power of the ionizing laser does not seem to be a problem; around 0.1 joule in the ultraviolet band appears to be adequate, and a source providing 1 joule pulses at a wavelength of 266 nanometers has been developed. The big challenge, however is maintaining an ionized channel for sufficient time for a discharge to occur.

Professor Diels said that the solution being attempted in his research is to follow the ultraviolet pulse with a visible, near-infrared pulse of sufficient intensity (say, 10 joules) to keep the channel ionized for about 10 microseconds. He believes that a lightning discharge can be triggered under these conditions.

False shutdowns of nuclear power plants are expensive, typically costing a utility hundreds of thousands of dollars in operating expenses and lost revenue. Utilities in areas prone to lightning strikes indicate that some nuclear plants are shut down several times per year as a precautionary measure, the typical cost of a shutdown being as much as $500,000 when labor costs and lost revenues are taken into consideration.[5] If the laser system worked and could be deployed at a reasonable cost, there would be a significant cost savings. Once the technology is proven, in addition to power plants, it could be used at refineries or other sensitive facilities, and also at stadiums or outdoor athletic events as well.

Improving Protection

While there might be a possibility of protecting buildings at fixed locations if lasers or some other means of directing thundercloud discharge proves to be feasible, it seems less likely that a means of deflecting lightning strikes from electric power transmission lines will be found. The evidence suggests that national electrical grids are still vulnerable to blackouts caused by lightning. A partial solution might be to surround substations located in high risk areas with Faraday cage enclosures. Improved lightning arrestors would also help reduce outages. Modern lightning arrestors are generally reusable, but some burn out and must be replaced. Ralph Bernstein, an engineer and EPRI program manager, introduced the concept that it may be possible to develop intelligent arrestors equipped with microprocessor controls capable of sensing conditions and adjusting the performance of the lightning arrestor as required.

By their nature, high voltage transmission lines have greater immunity to lightning strikes than lower voltage distribution lines. One means of protecting distribution lines would be to place them underground in specially-designed tunnels—sometimes referred to as *utilidors* (utility corridors). These also contain telephone cables, cable TV lines, and gas and water lines. While the initial cost is higher, the overall cost is reduced because multiple utilities are served. Protection is not guaranteed, however. There have been cases where lightning damaged buried utility cables, either through a direct strike or a ground strike that jumped to the cable. Overall, utility experts believe that the damage due to lightning strikes would be greatly reduced in well-designed, shielded, underground systems.

Lightning Safety Guidelines

So much for buildings and fixed locations. Preventing strikes on humans, animals, and transportation vehicles is virtually impossible due to the random and capricious nature of lightning. Therefore the only practical means of prevention is avoiding a lightning strike altogether. Given the recent advances in meteorology, lightning warning systems, and the establishment of the North American Lightning Detection Network, prevention of lightning strikes on aircraft, space vehicles, watercraft, and most importantly, people, should be feasible—if warnings are taken seriously and basic principles are observed.

The first principle of lightning safety is to avoid thunderstorms, the source of lightning strikes. Airlines route planes around thunderstorms. NASA cancels space flights when thunderstorms are imminent. Today, the prudent mariner is able to access weather fax information via shortwave radio and laptop computer, and chart his or her course accordingly to avoid major storms. The casual weekend boater should know enough to head for the boat ramp if thunderstorms are possible, just as the golfer should stay off the golf course. The key lesson here is that you need to take personal responsibility for your own safety.

Deadly Rugby
In June 2000, a rugby tournament took place not far from Annapolis, Maryland. The rugby matches involved more than 20 teams and began around 9 A.M. on a warm and muggy day when the weather forecast indicated possible thunderstorms. Later in the day, a thunderstorm approached the area at the start of the match between the Norfolk Blues Rugby Club and the Washington Rugby Football Club. Rain began to fall and thunder could be heard and lightning could be seen in the general area. By this time, the National Weather Service had issued a thunderstorm "warning" for the Annapolis area.[6]

Playing for the Norfolk Blues Rugby Club was Robert Patton, who came to the matches in the company of his father, Donald Patton. The elder Patton attended the tournament in the capacity of a spectator. As the Norfolk Blues-Washington

Rugby match progressed, rainfall increased, the weather conditions visibly deteriorated, and lightning flashed directly overhead. The younger Patton continued to play until the match was finally halted by the referee because of the weather.

At that point both Pattons left the playing field and retreated to a nearby area beneath some trees where they had left their belongings. As they were leaving the area to seek shelter in their nearby automobile, both were struck by lightning. Donald Patton died as a result of the strike and his son Robert was injured, but subsequently recovered.

Several years later, Judith Patton, the wife and mother of the victims, sued the United States of America Rugby Football Union, Ltd, alleging that the rugby union was liable for the death of Donald Patton and injuries suffered by Robert Patton by failing to institute a policy regarding the safe evacuation of players and spectators from the field of play, by failing to provide adequate training for officials to ensure the safety of participants and spectators, and by failing to monitor and detect dangerous conditions occurring during the rugby matches. The circuit court in Maryland, which heard the case, dismissed it on the basis that the defendant (the rugby union) "did not owe a duty of care to Robert or Donald Patton."

In essence the court concluded that lightning is "a universally known danger created by the elements" and that in the absence of evidence that the defendant created a greater hazard than was brought about by natural causes, there was no duty to warn and protect against what should have been obvious to every player and spectator. Players and spectators were free to leave at any time; in fact, the court noted, many did leave.

The case was appealed. The appeals court found that there was no negligence because there was no duty owed to the players and spectators, and without a duty owed, there can be no negligence. In short, the appeals court upheld the decision of the lower court, citing *Hames v. State of Tennessee* and several other cases to the effect that in something as obvious as a thunderstorm accompanied by lightning, all persons are expected to assume the burden of protecting themselves and keeping out of harm's way.[7]

Guidelines for personal safety are published by the National Oceanic and Atmospheric Administration, the National Lightning Safety Institute, and other organizations.[8] First and foremost, before engaging in outdoor activities, find out if there is a possibility of thunderstorms and adjust your plans accordingly. The most important and basic principle of protection is simply to not put yourself at risk in the first place.

The idea that you have to take individual responsibility for protecting yourself in thunderstorms has been embraced by the courts as well as by lightning experts who have developed safety guidelines. There have been a number of cases in which individuals playing golf or other sports, or even spectators at such events, have sued the golf course or sports tournament operator, claiming that the operator had a responsibility to protect them. (Also see Chapter 8 for court decisions about lightning warning systems and shelters.)

In each of the cases I reviewed (approximately six in all), the courts ruled in favor of the defendant (the course or tournament operator). In rejecting the plaintiff's (the injured party's) claim, the court stated that the risks and dangers associated with playing or observing a sport in a lightning storm are obvious to most adults. And, a "reasonably prudent adult can recognize the approach of a severe thunderstorm and know that it is time to pack up the clubs and leave before the storm begins to wreck havoc."[9] One court went on to rule that it is one's own responsibility to protect himself from the weather, and that "it is unreasonable to impose a duty on the organizer of an outdoor event to warn a spectator of a condition that the spectator is fully able to observe and react to on his own."

In the case of *Hames v. State of Tennessee*, the widow of a golfer who was struck by lightning and killed on a state-owned golf course sued, claiming the state was responsible.[10] The Tennessee Supreme Court reviewed the case on appeal and dismissed the claim using the language cited in the preceding paragraph. In addition, the court ruled that the plaintiff had to pay the costs of the appeal. The *Hames* case was cited in many of the other cases I reviewed.

These findings of the courts seem to reinforce the first principle of the lightning protection guidelines: *check the weather and do not put yourself at risk if there is a possibility of thunderstorms!*

Next, if despite favorable weather reports, you hear thunder or see lightning, seek shelter immediately. This is basic—take shelter in a substantial building or vehicle when thunderstorms threaten.

The 30/30 Rule No Longer Recommended
The 30/30 rule has previously been used to define a lightning threat. The thinking was that if you heard thunder, look for a lightning flash. When you saw a flash, count the seconds until you heard thunder. If the count was 30 seconds or less, it meant that the strike was 6.4 miles (10.3 kilometers) or less distant and you were in imminent danger.[11] You should take shelter immediately. The other part of the 30/30 rule meant do not leave shelter until 30 minutes after the last flash or sound of thunder.

Today we recognize several problems with the 30/30 rule. The first is the impracticality of associating thunder with a specific lightning flash, especially when there are multiple flashes. Next, what do you do when you hear thunder but do not see the flash? The average lightning strike travels 5 to 10 miles; however, strokes as long as 60 miles or more have been recorded. So, while you are standing around counting to 30, you are already in danger. Occasionally, as a storm passes, lightning will backflash from the trailing edge of the storm when least expected—the so-called "bolt from the blue." This is the reason for the 30-minute delay before leaving shelter.

For these reasons, the 30/30 rule has been replaced with a more succinct guideline: **"When Thunder Roars, Go Indoors."** This phrase has been adopted as the slogan of National Lightning Awareness Week.

Sometimes when thunderstorms threaten you may find yourself in the open with no safe shelter—a building or an automobile, for example—nearby. To put it bluntly, this is not a good situation. However, there are several things that you can do to minimize the risk of being hit by lightning. A common tendency is to seek the shelter of trees when rain begins to fall. Trees may actually provide some measure of safety during a thunderstorm under certain conditions. Avoid very tall trees and in particular a single tall tree. Also avoid such other tall objects as light poles, flagpoles, or utility poles. If possible, find a dense group of small trees surrounded by taller trees or find a dry cave, ditch, or depression in the ground. The guidelines warn of dangerous areas to avoid: open areas, areas beneath trees, areas near water, and those nearby metal posts or antennas, et cetera. If you should feel or observe your hair standing on end, skin tingling, or any sensations resembling static electricity, you should immediately assume the lightning safety crouch. These are indications that the electric field in the air near the surface of the earth where you are currently located has reached a value at which a lightning discharge could occur.

In the lightning safety crouch position, your feet should be close together (touching each other), your body in a squatting position and your elbows pressed against your knees, your hands covering your ears, and your head as low as possible. Do not lay flat. The idea here is to minimize your body surface area and maintain the lowest elevation possible. Your feet should be in contact with each other, to minimize the possibility of a step voltage from a ground strike.

The purpose of assuming this position is to present the lowest profile possible to the charged atmosphere in hopes that the flash will occur elsewhere. If you happen to be the unlucky target, survivability is enhanced if the lightning strikes your back (rather than your head) and jumps to the ground, rather than flowing to ground through your body and feet. Clearly this is a last-ditch proposition, reminiscent of elementary school drills in the 1960s during which students were instructed to take shelter under their desks in the event of an atomic bomb attack. One wonders, what thought processes would go on as you waited for the sledgehammer blow of a 20,000 ampere lightning strike on your back?

A group of people who are caught without adequate shelter should not huddle together, but rather should spread out, so that if there is a lightning strike and someone is incapacitated, others will be able to render immediate assistance. Here, the key word is *immediate*. As noted in Chapter 4, many lightning victims initially suffer cardiac or respiratory arrest. The recovery rate for such victims is high if cardiopulmonary resuscitation (CPR) is started immediately. A common misconception is that lightning victims may carry a residual electrical charge. This is false. CPR can be started immediately without any danger to the person administering assistance. Of course, if time and conditions permit, it is advisable to move the victim to a safer location, but do not delay CPR to do so.

As an important final note, the guidelines describe first aid measures for lightning victims. The most important one is to treat the dead first. All lightning strike deaths are caused by cardiac arrest or cessation of breathing. Those who *appear* to be dead can often be revived, if aid comes quickly enough. Cardiopulmonary resuscitation should be attempted immediately on comatose victims: only a few minutes delay can spell the difference between survival and death or permanent disability.[12] Treatment can be safely delayed for victims who are not unconscious.

Another approach is to use one of the lightning detection devices described in Chapter 8 to warn of dangerous conditions. These instruments—particularly the personal warning devices—should be used with caution. The inexpensive ones are little more than AM radios. There is no substitute for the human ear and eye. If you hear thunder or see lightning, you should immediately seek shelter.

Lightning protection guidelines are summarized in Table 6.

Table 6: Compilation of Lightning Safety Guidelines

Prepare a Lightning Safety Plan:
- Know the weather forecasts.
- Make alternate plans if necessary.
- Have a "weather eye" out for lightning and listen for thunder.
- Select a safe place to retreat to if thunder is heard or lightning seen—and include the time to reach it in the plan. Also include additional time if you are responsible for a group of people such as a group of ball players or scouts out on a hike.

If a Thunderstorm Is Likely, Seek Shelter:
- Postpone outdoor activities. If time permits, move pets or farm animals to protected shelters or barns. If you see lightning or hear thunder, seek shelter immediately. (If you can hear thunder you are already in danger.)
- Take shelter in a fully enclosed metal vehicle (cars, buses, trucks, enclosed farm vehicles). It is important to roll up windows and avoid contact with metal or conducting surfaces outside or inside the vehicle.
- Seek shelter inside a substantial building—any home or building with plumbing and electrical wiring (a school, church, or office building, for example).
- CAUTION: Some structures, such as golf shelters, park shelters, bus stops, et cetera, may be "lightning protected" to prevent structural damage and fires but that does NOT provide personal protection. They may have lightning rods on the roof, but you could be exposed to a side flash if the structure is struck.
- Remember, rubber-soled shoes and rubber tires provide NO protection from lightning. However, the metal body of a hard-topped vehicle provides increased protection if you are not touching metal.
- Stay away from metal sash windows, metal door frames, fireplaces, metal bed frames, other metal objects inside buildings.

Table 6, continued
- Avoid showering, bathing, washing dishes, et cetera. Plumbing and bathroom fixtures can conduct electricity.
- Use hard-wired (corded) telephones only for emergencies. Cordless and cellular telephones are safe to use.
- Unplug appliances and such other electrical devices as computers before the storm approaches. Surges from lightning can cause serious damage. Generic surge suppressors protect neither people nor equipment from lightning damage. If you live in a high lightning risk area, it may be worth the extra cost to purchase surge protection devices that are rated for lightning.
- Use a battery-operated weather radio for updates from local officials.

Avoid Being Isolated or Standing Near Tall Objects:
- Avoid being isolated (as in alone in an open field) and definitely avoid remaining near an isolated tall object (a double whammy!).
- Avoid natural lightning rods—any tall structure such as a tall, isolated tree in an open area, towers, flagpoles, or light poles.
- Avoid hilltops, open fields, golf courses, sports fields, parks, school yards, playgrounds, the beach, indoor or outdoor swimming pools, or a boat, canoe, kayak or surfboard on the water.
- Avoid isolated sheds or other small structures in open areas or gazebos, fences, shelters, baseball dugouts, athletic field bleachers.
- Avoid tractors, farm equipment, motorcycles, golf carts, golf clubs, and bicycles—equipment not completely enclosed in a metal body.
- Avoid being near water—because this generally means you are isolated and taller than the surroundings (like on a beach, in a boat, et cetera).

During a Thunderstorm:
- There is no excuse for being caught in a thunderstorm. Usually this is the result of not following lightning safety guidelines, making incorrect decisions when faced with bad weather, or being in an environment or situation (such as an isolated fishing camp) where you should both: 1.) Be aware of the risk; and 2.) Realize that you are accepting the risk simply by being there.
- In a forest: Seek shelter in a low area under a thick growth of small trees.
- In an open area: Go to a low place such as a ravine or valley. Be alert for flash floods.

Table 6, continued:
- If in a small boat, on a surfboard, or swimming in open water, retreat to land and find shelter immediately.
- In a large boat, go below and stay clear of electronic devices and metal rigging.
- If you feel your hair stand on end or hear a buzzing sound (indications that lightning is about to strike), you are in extreme danger. Run as fast as possible for the nearest shelter. If no shelter is available within miles, the last DESPERATE thing you can do is squat low to the ground, feet together. Place your hands over your ears. Make yourself the smallest target possible and minimize your contact with the ground to the single point where your feet are located.
- DO NOT lie flat on the ground (step voltage danger).

Following a Thunderstorm:
- Observe the second part of the 30/30 Rule. Do not go outside until 30 minutes have elapsed since the last sound of thunder or sight of lightning flash.
- If someone is injured, call for emergency medical assistance as soon as possible. (In the United States, dial 911.)
- Check breathing; make sure the victim's airway is clear.
- Note: Mouth-to-mouth resuscitation is no longer recommended due to hepatitis and HIV risks.
- Check heartbeat: If the heart has stopped, administer chest compressions in accordance with the latest guidelines of the American Heart Association.
- If the victim is conscious and breathing, look for other possible injuries such as nervous system damage, broken bones, loss of hearing and eyesight, or burns.

While there is no guarantee that these guidelines will prevent injuries, experts consider them to be the most likely ways of minimizing the chance of lightning injury based on the latest research and experience.[13]

Two Who Are Making a Difference

I have included many examples of lightning strikes throughout this book to illustrate the diverse ways in which individuals can be killed or injured. This is but a fraction of the examples you can find by scanning books, magazines, and newspaper headlines. While some circumstances repeat over and over—individuals taking shelter under a tree when rain begins to fall, or failing to leave a golf course soon enough—it is still remarkable that individuals have been hit in almost every conceivable location, both indoors and out.

The lesson we can draw from this is that protecting buildings against lightning strikes is important, but even more important is education. Two groups are doing remarkable and highly significant educational work, one focusing on prestrike, one on poststrike actions.

Struckbylightning.org, Inc.

Michael Utley, a highly successful and busy broker with PaineWebber, volunteered to take time off from work to participate in a charity golf tournament to raise money for the YMCA. As his foursome approached the 10th hole, a warning horn sounded and the group stopped playing and walked away from the hole, Utley a few steps behind the others. There was a bright flash and loud bang.

Thirty-eight days later, Utley opened his eyes, saw the roof of an ambulance, various tubes and intravenous bottles, and asked "Where am I?" He later learned that he was in an ambulance, being transported from an intensive care unit to a rehabilitation hospital. His story is remarkable. When he was struck on the golf course, his heart stopped. One of the players knew CPR and got his heart started. It stopped again in the ambulance on the way to the emergency hospital, but the medics got it restarted again. In the intensive care unit, he was in and out of a coma. He has no recollection of what transpired during the 38 days he was hospitalized. His physicians advised his wife that his future condition was problematic—that he would "most likely be a vegetable, a quadriplegic, unable to do anything for himself." But Utley defied the odds; he not only survived but began the laborious process of rebuilding his body and his mind.

When I spoke to him, he described the enormous challenges he faced very matter-of-factly, with characteristic good humor. At one point he told me that he shared a very special relationship with his young daughter that few fathers could claim: "We both got out of diapers at the same time."

During his lengthy recovery Utley thought a lot about his experiences. After attending a meeting of lightning strike survivors he realized that he was not alone. He came to the realization that the victims of lightning strikes are far more numerous than generally known. He thought about trying to help victims, much as he had been helped himself. Then an idea flashed into his mind: what if there were no more victims? He saw that most strikes could be avoided if individuals refused to place themselves at risk. He saw education as the key, and further study convinced him that it was necessary to start at a young age, so the ideas and practice of lightning safety would be ingrained and automatic. From this realization he went on to develop a unique educational program.

Utley's remarkable program encompasses lectures, publications, and a dramatic video to bring home its message. He finds that his ideal target audience is 7- to 11-year-olds— second-graders to fifth-graders. They are curious, interested, and able to understand the message. Utley believes that by the time kids become teenagers, his message is no longer "cool." Teenagers, with the unique wisdom of that age, believe that they know all that is important to know, and it is difficult to get them to focus their attention on something as remote and unlikely as a lightning strike.[14]

LS&ESSI—Lightning Strike and Electric Shock Survivors International, Inc.

When the idea of this book was first suggested to me by my agent, Ron Goldfarb, I began some research to see if such a book had already been written, and perhaps more importantly, to see if there was a need. I accumulated a great deal of technical information, and in the course of doing so, stumbled across the Web site *lightning-strike.org*.[15] I accessed this and discovered that it was an organization dedicated to alerting people to the dangers of lightning—and perhaps most important, functioning as a support group for lightning and electric shock survivors.

Lightning Strike and Electric Shock Survivors International, Inc., or LS&ESSI as it is called by most members, was created in 1989 by Steve Marshburn, Sr., himself a lightning strike victim. In spring 2004, I called Marshburn and asked him about the organization and how it came into being. He told me the following story.

Steve Marshburn: "I worked in a bank near Jacksonville, North Carolina. The bank had interior teller's cages and one drive-up window. It was a busy fall day— Friday, payday—and people were lining up in the bank as I went to open another teller's window, one that happened to be next to the drive-up window. The drive-up window had a speaker system so the teller could communicate with people in the vehicle outside. As I took my station, the teller at the drive-up window had momentarily stepped away, leaving her microphone pointed in my direction. The weather was clear, the sky blue.

"As I greeted the first customer, I heard a loud noise and felt a terrific pain in my back, as if someone had hit me with a baseball bat. I later determined that lightning from a thunderstorm about 10 to 12 miles away had struck the drive-up window. From there it flashed from the speaker system to the inside microphone and hit me in the back. Amazingly, while I was in pain and stunned, the shock did not knock me off the stool and I actually kept working, although I knew something was wrong.

"The next day I was in considerable pain and went to see the local doctor. He did not know what to do other than give me a prescription for some pain killer medicine and referred me to a neurologist. This was just the first of many doctors I was destined to see over the next 15 years as my condition slowly grew worse—lack of energy, memory loss, coordination loss, disorientation, and never-ending back pains and headaches. After 15 years I was fortunate to find another doctor who had experience with a previous lightning survivor and was finally able to get me started on the care that I needed. Finally a doctor who listened! In the meantime I had been corresponding with other lightning strike survivors who had many of the same symptoms I'd had and who also were told by their doctors that 'There is nothing wrong with you.' At last I knew that we were not all crazy.

"My neurologist advised me that I could no longer work on a public job, especially as a banker where figures and numbers are all-important. At this point I decided that my new purpose in life would be to help others. So, in 1989—20 years after I'd been hit, I formed LS&ESSI."

Following my initial conversation with Marshburn, I decided to attend the next LS&ESSI annual conference, which took place in June 2004, in Orlando, Florida. This was the 14th annual meeting of the organization. As I mention in the preface of this book, the conference had a profound effect on my thinking. There were a number of informative speakers, including several medical professionals who were very experienced in dealing with lightning-related injuries. During the conference the attendees (there were more than 100 from a number of different countries) had an opportunity to meet informally in small groups to share their experiences. I attended one such meeting. After attending it, I knew I had to write this book.

A LS&ESSI Discussion Group

Sixteen men sit in a conference room. Fourteen of them have been struck by lightning; two have come in contact with high voltage. They have all lived to tell about their experiences. They are survivors. They all suffer from the after-effects of their electrical encounters.

One by one they told their stories: "The power was supposed to be turned off." "It was a clear day; I was standing next to a building when the lightning struck." It was four years ago, or six, or ten.

One still experiences sleep apnea; an air breathing apparatus is never far away. Tinnitus—ringing in the ears—is a common complaint. One man notes an oddity—he can hear whispered comments across the room, but has trouble with nearby conversations.

The men are united by adversity; they share a common bond unknowable by family and friends. "I know what you're feeling," is a statement that evokes a bitter response. "You cannot know what I feel," they say, unless you happen to be one of the men in the room.

They all agree that they have been changed by the experience: "I am not the person I used to be. I am reconciled to the idea that I can't do what I used to do."

One says: "You have to be your own advocate; no one is going to come forward to help you. You have to be smarter than the doctors, and tell them what to do. They don't know how to treat your problems; sometimes they don't even believe you have a problem."

The room becomes very quiet as one man describes how close he came to killing himself—actually finding himself on a deserted beach one night. He credits the group with saving his life; his wife for aiding his recovery.

Around the room, heads nod in agreement and understanding as each man describes the limitations he has come to grips with. One says: "I can't remember things; I've got a short fuse." Another says: "I can't sleep; I roll around a lot." Others: "I can't drive." "Sometimes for no reason, my leg will just buckle under me." "My sense of balance is impaired." "I have weird dreams." "I take medicine for the side effects caused by the medicine I take."

For those knocked unconscious by the strike, their hearts stopped in a potentially fatal arrhythmia, and it was only the timely intervention of CPR or defibrillation that brought them back into the world of the living. Others—those who did not lose consciousness, or who had no visible burn marks—told of being sent home from the hospital after a few hours or perhaps a day. Then a week later, or a month later, medical problems began to surface—first one thing then another as the effects of burned nerves and tissues became more apparent. Some of the damage healed, but much of it was permanent, or slowly grew worse over time. At some point the men realized that they were damaged; there were things about them that would never be the same. This was the first step in a long process of ultimate survival and recovery.

What sustained them? Their sense of humor along with a fierce determination to recover as much of their former selves as possible. Most drew support from a wife, mother, husband, child—and especially from this group. Without some support, they say they might not have made it.

Each of the lightning strike survivors I've interviewed has a unique and dramatic story. Marshburn, working in a bank, was hit as he sat at a teller's window; a woman, struck sitting at her desk in an office building while speaking on the telephone; another man, who ran outside in a thunderstorm to roll up the windows in his car, disabled for life. They were all victims who had lasting injuries and disabilities, some whose lives were so disrupted that they were driven to the point of suicide.

These and other case studies serve to illustrate the nature of injuries caused by lightning, the medical treatment victims received, and the circumstances under which they were struck by lightning. It is by understanding the propagation of the lightning strike that we can best avoid the risk of injury or death.

More Education Needed
There is a critical need for a global program of lightning education and awareness, especially in countries and regions with a high level of thunderstorm activity. It need not be costly or complicated. Recently, the U.S. National Weather

Service established the National Lightning Awareness Week with the slogan "When Thunder Roars, Go Indoors." This slogan, accompanied by some simple graphics, could be printed on posters and displayed in community centers, schools, rural agricultural cooperatives, wherever people at risk might congregate.

A simple graphic—a jagged lightning bolt—might be developed and added to the universal symbol inventory registered with the International Organization for Standardization (ISO) and used to identify buildings or shelters with certified lightning protection systems that can be used as refuges during thunderstorms.

Holding National Lightning Awareness Week during the month of June—just before the summer lightning season begins—is a good first step. For the first time, a major government agency, in recognition of the societal cost of lightning, has initiated a program to mitigate lightning risk.

Educating Medical Practitioners

My discussions with lightning strike survivors revealed many instances in which the victims felt that medical practitioners they consulted had minimized their symptoms or overlooked injuries that later proved to be serious. In a sense, this is understandable because lightning strikes are rare events in comparison to other diseases and ailments that physicians diagnose and treat, and there is only so much that can be included in medical school curricula. In addition, practicing doctors have little time to do research.

Medical practitioners must in some way be made more aware of symptoms that indicate potentially debilitating lightning strike consequences. This should begin with the emergency room specialists who are often the first to examine patients with lightning injuries. When lightning symptoms are observed, referral to competent specialists—especially cardiologists and neurologists—with expertise in the treatment of lightning strike survivors should be automatic.

Dr. Mary Ann Cooper is on the faculty of the University of Illinois (Chicago), in the Department of Emergency Medicine. She is known worldwide for her work with lightning survivors. She is also on the board of directors of LS&ESSI and is one of the most knowledgeable lightning medical specialists in the United States. Dr. Cooper and Dr. Christopher J. Andrews in Australia are representative of physicians who have written extensively about the unique aspects of lightning injuries.[16] When I first met Dr. Cooper at an LS&ESSI meeting, I saw that her empathy and understanding for patient concerns was extraordinary, and knew that at some point I had to talk to her.

Two years later she graciously agreed to be interviewed. I asked her how she became interested in lightning.

Dr. Cooper: "I had a life altering experience some 20 years ago in Louisville, Kentucky, when I was contacted by the wife of a man who was injured on his farm 15 years before. She wanted help for her husband; she was not suing anyone or looking for any compensation. He wanted to be able to keep working, and this more than anything brought home the significance of the neurocognitive and chronic disability issue to me personally.

"For a number of years, I supported a lightning research program here at the university, mostly from personal funds. We eventually closed the lab when my best students graduated and the research building housing my lab space was torn down. And, frankly, I became tired of funding the effort myself. Funding was always a problem because the National Institutes of Health and the Center for Disease Control haven't budgeted monies for lightning injury research, perhaps because the victims are not as numerous as those with major diseases. This is in part politically driven, when you consider the vast constituencies that support cancer research, heart research, and AIDS research—big lobbying groups and big pharmaceutical company research dollars. Another factor is probably the fact that many of those injured by lightning are blue-collar workers and do not represent a strong political force."

Many of the lightning survivors I met in the course of my research felt that their physicians were not familiar with lightning injuries and really had not helped them. I asked Dr. Cooper if she thought this situation was improving.

Dr. Cooper: "No, I do not think the medical profession is more aware of lightning injuries today. Part of the problem, however, is how patients see their illnesses and their expectations of their doctors.

"For example, if you sprain your ankle, it will be painful at first but will feel better after a few days. Still, as a doctor, I know that it will take at least six weeks to heal—but patients don't understand this and expect nearly instant relief ('MacDonald's Medicine'). If not instant medical relief, they at least want to hear about some milestone (as 'when the swelling goes down,' or 'when the redness goes away' that they can look forward to as a positive indication that they're back to 'normal.' Most physicians are not familiar enough with lightning injuries to be able to give patients answers that satisfy.

"A lightning injury can lead to a variable amount of pain. It can be relatively minor or intense, but generally the source of pain is nonspecific and it's hard to put a finger on it. Doctors can provide medicines that will furnish a degree of pain control. But sometimes the pain doesn't go away.

"After a while, if the pain doesn't go away, the patient goes through a sequence of five stages of loss. The first is usually denial, 'Oh no, this didn't happen, this can't be me.' Another phase is bargaining, 'If I just find the right doctor, the right pill, do the right exercise, I will be better tomorrow/next week/next month.' Another phase is anger—often displaced to family or physicians since there is often no one to blame in lightning accidents. Another phase is depression when the pain and cognitive changes do not resolve in the expected 'reasonable' amount of time, it starts looking like it's never going to resolve and the patient becomes hopeless: 'The pain doesn't get any better, it causes sleep deprivation and depression, a fear that it will never go away.' The fifth and last phase is one of acceptance, 'Okay. I can learn to live with this and get on with my life.' This usually occurs at about 2 to 3 years and not all survivors achieve it. By the way, there isn't necessarily a clean order and sequence to these stages. They can interact; patients can bounce back and forth between stages.

"Back to your question about doctors and familiarity with lightning injuries. In terms of diagnosis, different medical specialists have their own personality, differences in training, and different perspectives when it comes to looking at injuries. It would not be unusual for a neurologist to perform tests looking for results that are abnormal. If the abnormality occurs at a single point, then he or she would be more inclined to consider it a neurological problem. If abnormalities appeared at multiple points, their tendency is to think of it as a psychiatric problem. Neurologists will acknowledge that auto accidents can cause brain injuries, but so far seem less inclined to consider that lightning can cause the spectrum of brain injury that we consistently see. This may require an attitude shift in neurology, which will not come easily because of the background and training undergone by neurologists. One thing that might bring about the shift would be if we find significant brain changes with the functional MRI (fMRI) research that we are doing.

"At the university, we now have the most powerful MRI research units in the world. Our neuropsychologists have developed a test that focuses on one of the major deficits that lightning and electrical shock survivors have that we can test for with the fMRI. As with any research there are problems with subject selection. One limitation is that subjects must be 'clean,' meaning no previous drug dependence (including excessive use of alcohol), no previous brain injury, blunt head trauma, psychiatric history, or other things that could cloud the results. I think that this new tool holds promise.

"Disability, not death, is the main problem with lightning injury. Disability and the inability to maintain a job can be a real fact of life with lightning injuries. Many victims have trouble getting Social Security or Workman's Compensation to recognize their disability. Some defects or injuries seem to lie dormant for a while, but most disabilities appear within a few days to weeks, perhaps months. There has been a tendency for lightning survivors to have disability or workman's compensation claims denied because lightning was not considered a work-related injury. The situation has changed since Ron Holle documented that nearly one-third of lightning injuries occur on the job.

"Lightning injuries and the recovery process put a tremendous strain on the individual and his or her family. In some cases the emotional burden becomes so great that it leads to divorce. The victim's spouse reaches the point where it is no longer possible to cope with the constant care giving, the aggravation of memory loss, sleepless nights, anxiety, and often, the anger and hostility displayed by the victim.

"Sexual dysfunction is another real problem. It has taken at least 10 years before this became an open topic of discussion. I think it applies to men and women alike, but men have a harder time of it because a performance problem is much more obvious with a man. Both men and women report a lack of desire, which may be due to nervous system injuries, spinal cord injuries, side effects of medication used for pain, and other problems, or simply the pressures due to loss of a job, sleep deprivation, personality changes, and financial pressures. Some patients report that they 'can't stand to be touched,' no hugging or touching in bed, and so on. This clearly would be a barrier to intimacy and to comforting or loving between partners.

"At the moment there is no good way of stopping or mitigating the cascade of injury that starts when someone is struck by lightning. I hate to end my comments on such a negative note, so let me add that naturally we need to continue research and hope that medical science can come up with better treatment options.

"In the meantime, however, our best chance is to prevent injury in the first place. I'm currently focusing my efforts on working with the United States National Weather Service to broaden public awareness and education against further injuries.

"Since the early 1990s the death rate has been dropping. We think that is at least in part due to efforts of Ron Holle, me, and others working with local news media, as well as Discovery Channel and NOVA TV programs, other documentaries and news programs, and broad-based educational efforts. We think that a big step forward was the establishment of the National Lightning Safety Awareness Week. Lightning safety guidelines are now in place in the golfing industry, little league, backpacking and camping groups, park managers, swimming pool literature, soccer and many other venues, and the dangers of lightning injury have become much more broadly disseminated. Given the high societal cost of lightning injuries—loss of income and lifelong medical expenses— these educational programs are a great value to society. And if they help a hundred or even just a dozen people avoid the lingering trauma of a lightning injury, I'll feel my efforts have been worthwhile."

How can lightning strike survivors locate physicians with lightning strike experience? Dr. Cooper told me that there is no single source. One way might be to contact LS&ESSI and ask for the names of LS&ESSI members who live in your area. They might be able to refer you to an experienced physician. The internet may be a source of information that will help. For example, the American College of Emergency Physicians has a patient fact sheet on lightning injuries that includes a brief summary of medical effects of lightning and early treatment and diagnostic measures.[17] For a general source of information on lightning injuries, as well as descriptions of various diseases and a medical encyclopedia, the United States National Library of Medicine and the National Institutes of Health maintain a Web site called "Medline" that can be searched for information on specific topics.[18]

A central lightning medical information database, accessible by the Internet, would also be useful, much like the database on poisons and poison antidotes operated by local and national poison control centers.[19] Perhaps a better analogy is the United States Center for Disease Control and Prevention Web site operated by the United States Department of Health and Human Services. The existence of such a national database might also provide a convenient means for doctors to voluntarily file lightning strike incident reports, using a standard form that would list date, time, and location of strike, as well as major medical consequences using a multiple-choice "check off" sheet similar in format to the reports filed by airline pilots and flight engineers. Another important step would be to provide lightning injury treatment training as a part of the Continuing Medical Education programs that many physicians take part in to renew their licenses.

In a more positive vein, nearly all lightning deaths and injuries are preventable through better education and public awareness. Simply by paying greater attention to weather patterns the risk of a lightning injury can be reduced. Understanding the concepts described in this book and applying them to protect lives and property can do much to eliminate human suffering and economic loss.

Michael Utley, Steve Marshburn, Dr. Mary Ann Cooper, and a handful of others are examples of caring people who have dedicated their lives to understanding and eliminating or at least reducing the trauma of lightning strikes. Hopefully by following their example and improving public awareness and education in all countries of the world with frequent thunderstorms, infrastructure damage and human injury and loss of life by nature's death ray can be steadily reduced to the point at which such incidents are truly rare occurrences.

Appendix 1: Units of Measure, Conversion Factors, Data

Multiply:	By:	To get:
Coulomb/second	1.0	Ampere
Bar	14.5	Pounds/square inch
Electron volt (ev)	1.602×10^{-19}	Joule
Cubic feet	0.0283	Cubic meters
Feet	0.305	Meters
Feet	12	Inches
Grams/cubic centimeter	1.0	Metric tons/meter^3
Horsepower	746	Watt
Inches	2.54	Centimeters
Kilocalorie	4.19×10^3	Joule
Kilowatt hour	3.6×10^6	Joule
Kilometer	0.621	Statute miles
Miles/hour	0.447	Meters/second
Meters	3.281	Feet
Meters	39.37	Inches
Metric ton	2,205	Pounds
Mile	1.609	Kilometers
Mile	5,280	Feet
Pounds (force)	4.448	Newtons
Pounds	0.454	Kilograms
Pounds/square foot	47.9	Pascal
Pounds/square inch	6,890	Pascal
Pounds/cubic foot	0.01602	Metric ton/meter^3
Short ton (2000 pounds)	0.907	Metric tons

Data

Speed of sound in dry air at standard temperature and pressure = 331.4 meters/second or 1,089 feet/second

Speed of light = 2.998×108 meters/second

Charge on the electron = $1.602 \times 10-19$ Coulomb

Pascal = Newton/square meter

Siemens = unit of electrical conductance, = amperes/volts

Appendix 2: Glossary of Special Terms

air terminal. Metallic rods on the roofs of buildings or other tall structures used as part of a lightning protection system.

arborescence. A fern-like pattern of burns on the skin frequently observed on victims of a lightning strike.

bremsstrahlung. X-rays produced as electrons slow down, literally, "braking radiation" (German).

Brontophobia. Fear of thunder.

cardiopulmonary resuscitation (CPR). A system for reviving patients whose hearts have stopped beating, consisting of clearing the air passages and compressing the chest, sometimes accompanied by breathing into the individual's mouth.

dart leader. The second phase of a lightning discharge. The dart leader follows the ionized path created by the stepped leader and precedes the return stroke.

earth terminal. See ground terminal.

dissipation array. A system of ground terminals that supposedly "discharges" thunder clouds and prevents lightning strikes. There is no scientific evidence that it works.

early streamer emission systems (ESE). A system of air terminals that supposedly enlarge the protected area, or otherwise create a "protective space charge. There is no scientific evidence that these systems work.

Electrocardiogram (ECG). A recording made by an instrument that senses the electrical signals from a beating heart.

Electroencephalogram (EEG). A recording made by an instrument that senses the electrical signals from the brain.

equivalent circuit. An electrical engineering technique for designing a circuit that will replicate the performance of some electrical system.

extremely low frequency (ELF). Radio signals in the frequency range of 3 to 30 Hz. These have wavelengths of 10,000 to 100,000 kilometers and find use as a means to communicate with submerged submarines.

Faraday cage. A lightning protection system that consists of a metal skin or system of closely spaced metal bars or conductors connected to a ground terminal and enveloping the building or object to be protected.

fault. In electrical engineering, any condition that causes an electrical circuit to short circuit or discharge to ground rather than to the intended load.

flashover. A condition where the electric current jumps to another conductor, object, or ground because the voltage is so high that the normal insulation (which might be air) is broken down and an ionized path is created.

fulgurite. Sand or other substance fused by lightning; typically tube-shaped.

fuzzy dissipaters. Air terminals terminated with many metallic bristles. See comments under *early streamer emission systems.*

graupel. Soft hail, small ice pellets.

ground fault interrupter (GFI). An electronic device that senses if an electric current is flowing improperly to ground (indicative of a hazardous condition). If a ground fault is detected, the ground fault interrupter quickly disconnects the circuit.

ground terminal. A system of metal rods or cables embedded in the earth to dissipate electricity by conducting it to the ground.

high frequency (HF). Radio signals in the frequency range of 3 to 30 MHz. These have wavelengths of 10 to 100 meters.

ion. An atom or molecule with a net electric charge due to the loss or gain of electrons.

ionosphere. An outer region of the atmosphere, 30 to 50 miles (50 to 80 kilometers) above the surface of the earth, characterized by ions and free electrons.

ionized path. A path or track in air, a gas, or another material where ions have been formed.

keraunophobia. Fear of lightning.

lightning rod. See *air terminal.*

outage. In electrical engineering, the condition when the normal supply of electric power has been interrupted.

shunt. A device to bypass the usual flow of electricity; a parallel path of current flow.

stepped leader. The initial stroke in a lightning discharge. The stepped leader creates an ionized path that initiates the lightning discharge.

step voltage. The potential difference between two points (usually in the earth) that results from a lightning discharge into the earth.

surge protector. A device for protecting electronic equipment from sudden high voltages.

thunderstorm day. A day in which one or more thunderstorms occur.

varistor. An acronym for "variable resistor"; an electronic semiconductor device whose resistance varies non-linearly with the applied voltage.

very high frequency (VHF). Radio signals in the frequency range of 30 to 300 MHz. These have wavelengths of 1 to 10 meters.

very low frequency (VLF). Radio signals in the frequency range of 3 to 30 kHz. These have wavelengths of 10 to 100 kilometers.

Endnotes

Preface

[1] Rakov and Uman (2003), 164. This is the radio frequency power; a smaller portion of the lightning energy is radiated as light, so the total power generated is actually greater.
[2] Ehrlich (1994).

Chapter 1 Thor's Anvil

[1] *The Holy Bible*, King James Version, Psalms 135:7.
[2] MacCurdy (1958), 392.
[3] Franklin, Benjamin. 1751. *Experiments and Observations on Electricity Made at Philadelphia in America—and communicated in several letters to Mr. P. Collinson of London, F.R.S.* London: printed by E. Cave at St. John's Gate.
[4] Franklin, Benjamin. Letter to P. Collinson, London, dated July 29, 1750. This letter had attached a description of Franklin's electrical experiments that was printed in booklet form by E. Cave in 1751. The letter and attachment have been reproduced in *The Papers of Benjamin Franklin*, Vol. 4: July 1, 1750 through June 30, 1753, p 9-33, eds. Leonard W. Labaree, Whitfield J. Bell, Helen C. Boatfield, and Helene H. Fineman, New Haven: Yale University Press, 1961.
[5] Cohen (1990), 127.
[6] Franklin, Benjamin. Excerpted from an article describing the kite experiment printed in *The Pennsylvania Gazette*, October 19, 1752. Also printed in Joseph Priestley, *The History and Present State of Electricity, with Original Experiments* (London, 1767), pp. 179-81, and reproduced in *The Papers of Benjamin Franklin*, Vol. 4: July 1, 1750 through June 30, 1753, p 360, eds. Leonard W. Labaree, Whitfield J. Bell, Helen C. Boatfield, and Helene H. Fineman, New Haven: Yale University Press, 1961.

[7] Franklin, Benjamin. An article describing lightning strikes on two homes printed in *The Pennsylvania Gazette*, August 6, 1752.

[8] Samuel Glasstone (1958), 156-160. *Sourcebook on Atomic Energy*, 2nd ed. Princeton, NJ: D. Van Nostrand Company Inc.

[9] Cheney (1993), 88-89.

[10] Ibid., 110.

[11] Ibid., 148.

[12] See www.esbnyc.com. Accessed July 10, 2006.

[13] Uman (1986), 47-48.

[14] Rakov and Uman (2003), 350-353.

[15] Ibid., 41-42.

[16] C.E.P. Brooks (1925), "The Distribution of Thunderstorms Over the Globe," *Geophysics Mem.*, 24:147-64, London: Air Ministry Meteorological Office.

[17] Captain Jerry M. Linenger (2000), 145. *Off the Planet*. NY: McGraw Hill.

[18] Isaacson (2003), 145.

Chapter 2 That Bolt from the Blue

[1] Andrews et al. (1992), 9-10.

[2] David M. Ludlum (1991), 95-99. *National Audubon Society Field Guide to North American Weather*. New York: Alfred A. Knopf.

[3] For a liquid to freeze, it requires an initial crystalline nucleus—usually a speck of dust or particle of material on which the liquid can condense. The trace impurities normally present in water provide this, so water freezes at 32 degrees Fahrenheit (0 degrees Celsius).With the very pure water in raindrops, in the absence of an initial nucleus, it is possible to lower the temperature below the freezing point without it freezing.

[4] Steve Chawkins and Monte Morin (2005), A1. "Lightning Kills Scout, Troop Leader in Sequoia," *Los Angeles Times*, July 30.

[5] Cooray (2003), 3. Also see Rakov and Uman (2003), 77-77.

[6] Cooray (2003), 19.

[7] Rakov and Uman (2003), 86-87.

[8] Magono (1980), 119.

[9] Ibid.

[10] Cooray (2003), 21-22 and Rakov and Uman (2003), 85.

[11] Cooray (2003), 19-26.

[12] Rakov and Uman (2003), 7.

[13] Marshall (1973), 4-5. See also Rakov and Uman (2003), 12.

[14] Chisti, Main Uddin (2007). "Bolt from the sky strikes jumbos dead—Freak accident claims five from a herd of 11 elephants in Alipurduar," *The Telegraph*: Calcutta, India. May 5.

[15] Lee et al. (1992), 6, or Westman, ed. (1956), 921. The range of values comes about because measurements are typically made between needle points (the lower voltage) or spherical electrodes (the higher voltage).

[16] Golde (1978), 9-10.

[17] Rakov and Uman (2003), 5.

[18] See Rakov and Uman (2003), 163, for a compilation of return stroke size measurements. The siemens (S) is the SI unit of conductance (the reciprocal of resistance) and replaces the older unit that was called the mho. Interestingly, "mho" is ohm spelled backwards.

[19] The lightning strike releases between 1 and 10 gigajoules. Rakov and Uman (2003), 12, 114. The energy content of a barrel of crude oil is around 5.8 million BTU or 6 gigajoules, where the preface giga equals 10^9.

[20] See for example Uman (1986), 123-33; Stenhoff (1999), and Hiroshi Kikuahi. "Ball Lightning," Chapter 2 in Volland (1995), Vol. 1, 167-185.

[21] Stenhoff (1999), 78.

[22] Randi Boyd, "Out of the Blue—Our Story," in Marshburn, ed. (2000), 83-85.

[23] Stenhoff (1999), 113-122.

[24] Laurence Bergreen (2004), 89-90. *Over the Edge of the World—Magellan's Terrifying Circumnavigation of the Globe*. New York: Perennial.

[25] Dwyer (2005), 65-71. See also, J. R. Dwyer, et al. (2004). "A Ground Level Gamma-ray Burst Observed in Association with Rocket-triggered Lightning," *Geophys. Res. Lett.*, Vol. 31, L05119, doi:10.1029/2003GL018771 and J. R. Dwyer (2004), "Implications of X-ray Emission from Lightning," *Geophys. Res. Lett.*, Vol. 31, L12102, doi:10.1029/2004GL019795, 2004.

[26] Rakov and Uman (2003), 6. See also Davies (1965), 413.

[27] Frederick E. Terman (1955), 803. *Electronic and Radio Engineering*, New York: McGraw Hill.

[28] Ibid., 825-26.

[29] Davies (1965), 413.

[30] Rakov and Uman (2003), 432-435.

[31] R. A. Helliwell (1965). *Whistlers and Related Ionospheric Phenomena*, Stanford, California: Stanford University Press.

[32] Hayakawa Masashi, "Whistlers," Chapter 7 in Volland, ed. (1995) Vol. 2, 156-189. This is a survey of recent research findings and theory of whistlers.

[33] Rakov and Uman (2003), 483.

[34] Blue light in the visible spectrum has a wave length of 4,800 to 5,200 Angstroms (0.48 to 0.52 microns), which corresponds to the predominant spectral emission lines of doubly ionized nitrogen and singly ionized oxygen.

[35] Rakov and Uman (2003), 485.

[36] Rakov and Uman (2003), 546-547. Note: this reference, Chapter 16, provides an excellent in-depth critical review of the extensive literature pertaining to extraterrestrial lightning. See also Volland, ed. (1995) Vol. 1, 214-229.

[37] Rakov and Uman (2003), 536.

[38] For Venus, the closest approach to earth is 25 million miles, while Mars, the next closest planet, has a minimum approach distance of 35 million miles.

[39] Rakov and Uman (2003), 536.

Chapter 3 When Lightning Strikes Twice

[1] Lyons (1997), 142. In a personal communication to Craig Smith, Prof. Martin Uman noted that this area of New York is probably subject to 3 strikes per square kilometer per year, so 1/3 square kilometer would get a strike every year.

[2] Andrews et al. (1992), 6. See also Rakov and Uman (2003), 52.

[3] Rakov and Uman (2003), 40.

[4] Ibid., 44 – 46.

[5] Ibid., 50.

[6] This account is based on Lynn Rosellini (2004), 165-184. "We've Been Hit!" *Readers Digest,* June, 2004.

[7] Golde (1978), 186.

[8] Cooray (2003), 10.

[9] Volland, ed. (1995), Vol.1, 148.

[10] Cooray (2003), 10-11.

[11] Rakov and Uman (2003), 43.

[12] Ibid., 26-31.

[13] Steve Levin (2005) "Lightning Injures Dozens at Venango County Family Reunion," *Pittsburgh Post-Gazette*, Sunday, July 17.

[14] Based on published data, the lightning flash density F_d is approximately related to thunderstorm days by the equation $F_d = 0.04 T_d^{1.25}$, where F_d is the flash density in flashes per square kilometer per year and T_d is the number of thunderstorm days. Using this equation, there is 1 flash per square kilometer per year for an area that experiences about 13 thunderstorm days per year, or 1 flash per square mile for a region that experiences 28 thunderstorm days per year. See Rakov and Uman (2003), 35-36.

[15] Typically there is approximately 0.04 – 0.05 lightning flashes per square kilometer per year for each thunder hour. In a region having 100 thunder hours per year, one could expect

4 to 5 ground flashes per square kilometer per year, or 10 to 13 ground flashes per square mile. See Rakov and Uman (2003), 36-37.

[16] Rakov and Uman (2003), 38.

[17] Ibid., 39, 41.

[18] Lyons (1997), 153.

[19] Andrews et al.(1992), 6.

[20] Ibid., 44.

[21] Rakov and Uman (2003), 43-47.

[22] Andrews et al. (1992), 40.

[23] Ibid., 41.

[24] Anonymous (2004), 1 "Lightning Claims 500 Lives, Damages Property of Several Hundred Million Dollar (sic) a Year," *The Bangladesh Observer*, Monday, December 20.

[25] R. E. Lopez and Ronald L. Holle (1998), 2070-2077. "Changes in the Number of Lightning Deaths in the United States During the Twentieth Century," *Journal of Climate*, Vol.11.

[26] U.S. National Climatic Data Center. *Storm Data*. Ashville, NC: National Oceanic and Atmospheric Administration (NOAA).

[27] See National Oceanic and Atmospheric Administration website at http://www.nws.noaa.gov/om/severe_weather/04-30year.gif.

[28] Mary Ann Cooper (2005), "Fact Sheet: Medical Aspects of Lightning," http://www.lightning safety.noaa.gov/medical.htm. Accessed April, 2006. See also E. Curran et al. (1997), Section 2.

[29] Frazier (1979), 81.

[30] http://www.sirlinksalot.net/lightning/html.

[31] See Andrews et al. (1992), 41-45 and Curran, et al. (1997).

[32] For example, a century-old church was destroyed by lightning on November 15, 2005. The Charter Oak Church near Churubusco, Indiana was hit on the bell tower, causing a fire that eventually caused the roof to collapse. No one was

injured, but the church was a total loss. Then, on August 27, 2005, Lightning struck the bell tower of the Corpus Christi Church in Lawrence, Kansas, at around 3:30 A.M, causing the electronic bells to toll for more than an hour. A few weeks earlier, on August 8, lightning struck the Calvary Baptist Church in Hilltown Township, Pennsylvania. Children attending a day camp had been brought inside the building when the storm arrived. Lightning hit the church chimney, showering bricks onto the roof and punching a hole into it. No one was injured. A similar incident caused minor damage to the famous Lichfield Cathedral in Staffordshire, England. The cathedral, dating from 1200 A.D., was struck on July 5, 2005. The cathedral precentor was quoted as saying that church-goers were repeating their prayers when there was a loud bang, a flash, and the building shook. No one was injured. Church goers at a Lutheran church in Imbonggu, near Mendi in central Papua New Guinea, were not so fortunate. Lightning struck the church just after the service ended on September 7, 2004, splitting the building in half, killing one woman and injuring 35 other worshippers. See www.sirlinksalot.net/lightning.html on the dates indicated for original news articles. Accessed April 14, 2006.

[33] Andrews et al. (1992), 52-53.
[34] Curran et al. (1997), Section 11, "Location."
[35] Trevino, Lee and Sam Blair (1982), 3-9. *They Call Me Super Mex*. NY: Random House
[36] Curran et al. (1997), Section 3.
[37] Ibid., Section 8.

Chapter 4 Crabs and Lions Beware: Health Impacts of Lightning

[1] Lee et al., (1992), 7. Marshall (1973), 101, gives values that are approximately twice as high as those given by Lee.
[2] Resistors are color coded to indicate the value of resistance in ohms, with each color signifying a number between 0 and 9.

Black is zero, brown is 1, red is 2, orange is 3, yellow is 4 and so on. Gold and silver bands signify the tolerances (5% and 10%). Generations of electrical engineers have been taught to remember the color codes by a mnemonic device: "bad boys ruin our young girls but violet gives willingly."

[3] Anonymous (2005), "7-year-old Startled as Lightning Strikes her Mattress – Child was Sleeping when Bed Caught on Fire," WKMG-TV6, www.Local6.com/news/467256/detail.html, accessed April 17, 2006.

[4] Robert Ireland, "The Incident," in Marshburn, ed. (2000), 10-17.

[5] Isaacson (2003), 69.

[6] Gem L. Poe in Marshburn, ed. (2000), 86-88.

[7] Golde (1978), 177.

[8] Cooray, ed. (2003), 554-556.

[9] Ibid., 556-557.

[10] Ibid., 554.

[11] Andrews et al. (1992), 30.

[12] Cooray, ed. (2003) 559-561.

[13] Ibid., 557-559.

[14] BBC Online Network (1998) "Footballers Struck by Lightning," October 26, 1998, and "World: Africa Lightning Strike Kills Football Team," October 28, 1998, http://newsbbc.co.uk/1/hi/world/africa/203137.stm, accessed April 14, 2006.

[15] See www.sirlinksalot.net/lightning.html on the dates listed. Accessed April 14, 2006.

[16] Andrews et al. (1992), 53-107.

[17] Golde (1978), 173-174.

[18] Andrews et al. (1992), 53-57.

[19] Ibid., (1992), 53-54.

[20] Go to http://www.americanheart.org and follow the cues to the self-learning modules.

[21] Golde (1978), 177.

[22] Andrews et al. (1992), 58-59.

[23] Lee (1992), 37-44.

[24] Andrews et al. (1992), 108.

[25] Lee (1992), 34-35.

[26] Ibid., 44.

[27] Andrews et al. (1992), 62; Lee et al. (1992), 85-86.

[28] Anonymous (2003) "Lightning Blows Teen's Tongue Ring Out of His Mouth," as reported by Denver's ABC7 News, August 26, http://www.thedenverchannel.com/news/2433342/detail.html. Accessed April 5, 2004.

[29] Andrews et al., (1992), 63-66, 107-108; Jellinek (1955), 25.

[30] Andrews et al., (1992), 62.

[31] Ibid., 58-59.

[32] Ibid., 60.

[33] Ibid., 59-60.

[34] John Corson (2004), Quoted in "Perspectives," *Newsweek*, August 2, 2004, 21.

[35] Andrews et al. (1992), 60.

[36] Dane Lanken (2000), "Struck by Lightning," *Canadian Geographic Magazine*, January. See www.canadiangeographic.ca/Magazine/JA00/lightning/lightning.html. Christine Fram's story is as reported by Dane Lanken in this article.

[37] Lee et al. (1992), 61.

Chapter 5 Reasons for Keraunophobia

[1] Lyons (1997), 155.

[2] Andrews et al. (1992), 137-138.

[3] Jeff Stevens (2006). Personal communication with Craig B. Smith.

[4] Sarie Van Niekerk (2003), "Lightning Kills Cop," news24.com, July 12, http://www.news24.com/News24/South_Africa/News/0,,2-7-1442_1456257,00.html. Accessed April 5, 2004.

[5] Meera Vijayan (2006), "Lightning Kills Anglers," *The Star* (Malaysia), April 10; anonymous (2006) "Lightning Strikes Man in Malaysia," April 11 http://www.metoffice.gov.uk/cgi-bin/newsid?article=17092276&epoch=1144761283. Accessed April 12, 2006.

[6] Apfelberg et al., in Andrews et al. (1992), 50-51.

[7] Ravitch et al., in Andrews et al. (1992), 51-52.

[8] Bob Ruffolo, "Lightning Strike," Marshburn, ed. (2000), 220-21.

[9] Leona Lewis (1986), "Horses Hit by Lightning in 1911 During a Thunderstorm Near Glacier Point in Yosemite Valley were Ordered Burned on the Spot," *Merced Sun Star,* March 1. (Thanks to Howard Wells for forwarding this information.)

[10] Anonymous (2003), "Lightning Strikes Two Moscow Nudists," *Independent Online,* July 11. See http://www.int.iol.co.za/general/news/newsprint.php?art_id=ct 20030711231101151N3232.

[11] Associated Press (2005), A24, "Lightning Kills Boy Scout, Injures 3 Others on Utah Mountain," *Los Angeles Times,* August 4.

[12] Betty L. Smith, "Zapped," Marshburn, ed. (2000), 80-82.

[13] Mary M. Frederick, in Marshburn (2000), 91-98.

[14] Catherine Oshanek (2005), "Lightning Strike Sets Car on Fire, Driver Unhurt," *Cochranetimes.com*, June 15, http://www.cochranetimes.com/story.php?id=1666970.

[15] Anonymous (2005). "Lightning Strikes Car Traveling on Turnpike," NBC6.Net, September 5, http://www.nbc6.net/news/4936711/detail.html.

[16] Anonymous (2006),"Truck Struck by Lightning on Alligator Alley," *Local10.com, South Florida's TV news web site,* http://www.local10.com/news/8592386/detail.html.

[17] Associated Press (2006) "Lightning Hits Firetruck," April 27, *KnoxNews,*

http://www.knoxnews.com/kns/cda/article_print/0,1983,KNS_
348_4654648_ARTICLE-DE.
[18] *The Holy Bible,* King James Version, *Psalms* 18:14;
Revelation 4:5.
[19] Sources: Anonymous (2005). "Man Killed by Lightning at
Funeral," *Herald Sun,* Victoria, Australia,
http://www.heraldsun.news.com.au. June 24; Levi J. Long
(2005), "Lightning Kills Father Visiting his Son's Grave,"
Arizona Daily Star, May 30,
http://www.azstarnet.com/dailystar/dailystar/77459.php;
Anonymous (2006), A16, "Lightning Kills 5 Youths Praying
at Metal Cross," *Los Angeles Times,* April 26; also see
Associated Press (2006) "Lightning Kills Five Children
Decorating Metal Cross in Mexico," April 24, as reported on
http://www.foxnes.com_story/0,3566,192868,00.html;
Anonymous (2003), "Preacher Seeks Sign, Gets Zapped by
Lightning," *WorldNetDaily,* July 4,
http://www.worldnetdaily.com/news/article.asp?ARTICLE_I
D-33422.
[20] Anonymous (2003), "Lightning Strike Kills Nine in
Church," Sydney Morning Herald, December 14,
http://www.smh.com.au/articles/2003/12/14/1071336800605.h
tml.
[21] Associated Press (2004), "Lightning Strikes Jesus on
Gibson's Christ Film Set," *Ananova,* April 5.
http://www.ananova.com/entertainment/story/sm_831648.html
?menu+entertainment.latesthead.

Chapter 6 The Lights Flickered and Then Went Out

[1] U.S. Federal Power Commission (1967), 13-14. "Studies of
the Task Groups on the Northeast Power Interruption," Vol.
III of *Prevention of Power Failures—An Analysis and
Recommendations Pertaining to the Northeast Failure and the*

Reliability of the U.S. Power Systems, Washington D.C: U.S. Government Printing Office.

[2] Anonymous (1977), 12-18 "Night of Terror," (the New York blackout of July 13, 1977), *Time* Magazine, July 25.

[3] National Lightning Safety Institute Web Site at: www.lightningsafety.com.

[4] Cooray, ed. (2003), 479-495, Chapter 9 "Lightning and EMC" has a detailed discussion of lightning effects (referred to as electromagnetic compatibility, or EMC in this book).

[5] MacCurdy (1958), 388.

[6] Franklin, Benjamin. Excerpted from an article describing lightning strikes on two homes printed in *The Pennsylvania Gazette*, August 6, 1752. Franklin's ongoing interest in the effects of lightning on buildings is further evidenced by a letter his son William sent him a year later (July 12, 1753.) In it William describes how lightning preferentially sought out metal in its path to the ground. Letter reproduced in *The Papers of Benjamin Franklin*, Vol. 5: July 1, 1753 through March 31, 1755, p 4-7, eds. Leonard W. Labaree, Whitfield J. Bell, Helen C. Boatfield, and Helene H. Fineman, New Haven: Yale University Press, 1962.

[7] Jean Marie Mayfield (2004). "Bolt of Lightning Tours Family's Home," *The Times Picayune* (New Orleans), January 8, http://www.nola.com/news/t-p/index.ssf?/base/news-3/1073546006250290.xml.

[8] Lisa Cunningham, "The Mystery Condition," Marshburn, ed. (2000), 113-119.

[9] Anonymous (2005), "19 People Hurt as Lightning Strikes Grain Silo," April 15, http://www.expatica.com/source/site_article.asp?subchannel_id=81&story_id=19131&na.

[10] Anonymous (2003), "Lightning Fire Destroys over a Million Gallons of Jim Beam Bourbon," WNDU 16 News Center, South Bend, Indiana, August 4, http://www.wndu.com/news/082003/news_21177.php.

¹¹Bailey Greene-Kouri, "The Day My World Was Forever Changed," Marshburn, ed. (2000), 228-234.

¹² Anonymous (2005) "Seven Injured by Weekend Lightning Strikes," July 25, http://www.nbc6.net/weather/4764540/detail.html.

¹³ Associated Press (2004), "Lightning Strikes High School Football Team, 40 Injured," September 15, http://www.kirotv.com/news/3732185/detail.html.

¹⁴Barry W. Smith "He Died to Save Our Son," Marshburn, ed. (2000), 64-65.

¹⁵ National Interagency Fire Center (2005) "Wildland fire statistics," http://www.nifc.gov. Accessed May, 2006.

¹⁶ Associated Press (2004), A19, "Alaska Wildfires burn 80,000 acres," *Los Angeles Times*, June 22.

¹⁷Andrews et al. (1992), 27-29.

¹⁸ The reader should know that these dimensions are "nominal." The standard 2"x 4" today is actually 1.625 inches x 3.25 inches and this particular one was 92.3 inches long and weighed 12.63 pounds. To make the measurements I inserted a brass wood screw in each end of the board and applied either an alternating current (120 volts) or a direct current (13.85 volts). I found that the equivalent circuit was a 330k ohm resistor shunted by a 0.7 nanofarad capacitor in the wet or green condition. After letting this board dry at room temperature in my office for 3 months I found that it had lost 3.32 pounds and now weighed 9.31 pounds. The resistance increased dramatically by a factor of over 30 to more than 10 megohms for both alternating and direct current test conditions. The shunt capacitance was negligible, or at least beyond my measurement capability.

¹⁹ I thank Jim Workman for bringing the petroglyphs to my attention and for providing the following reference: Arlene Benson and Floyd Buckskin (date unknown), 53-63, "Magnetic Anomalies at Petroglyph Lake," *Rock Art Papers,*

Vol. 8, Ken Hedges, ed., San Diego, California: San Diego Museum Papers No. 27.

[20] Anonymous (2005) "Lightning Caused Rio Bridge Fire," January 4, http://www.ekathimerini.com/4dcgi/_w_articles_politics_1000 26_01/04/2005_54688.

[21]Robert L. Davidson "My Unfortunate Accident to a New Life," Marshburn, ed. (2000),18-20.

[22] Barbara Watson (2001), 4, *Virginia Thunderstorms and Lightning*, April 21, http://www.erh.noaa.gov/er/lwx/lightning/va-lightning.htm.

[23] Adam Morton, and Chee C. Leung (2005), "Lightning Causes Havoc, Sparks CONNEX Probe," *The Age*, http://www.theage.com.au/news/national/lightning-causes-train-havoc-sparks-connex-probe.

[24]Captain Fatty Goodlander (2004). "On Watch—God's Own Ax," *Cruising World*, December, 17-19.

[25] Anonymous (2005), 8-10. "Lightning! Flash, Bang, Your Boat's Been Hit—Now What?" *Seaworthy*, the BoatU.S. Marine Insurance and Damage Avoidance Report, Vol. 23, No. 3 July.

[26]Char Griggs, "Out of the Blue," Marshburn, ed. (2000), 235-237.

[27] Op. cit. Anonymous (2005), 10. "Lightning! Flash, Bang! Your Boat's Been Hit-Now What?"

[28] United States Coast Guard (1979). *Marine Accident Report: Explosion and Fire on Board the SS Chevron Hawaii with Damages to Barges and to the Deer Park Shell Oil Company Terminal, Houston Ship Channel*, September 1, 1979. See also http://spills.incidentnews.gov.

[29] Diane Rinehart and Eric Malnic (2005). "All 309 Aboard Air France Jet Survive Toronto Crash Landing," *Los Angeles Times*, August 3, p. A-1.

[30] James Gamble (1881), 7. "Wiring a Continent—The making of the U.S. Transcontinental Telegraph Line," *The Californian*

magazine, as reproduced on http://www.telegraph-history.org. Accessed May 7, 2006. Interesting note: Western Union ceased telegram messaging services as I was writing this book, in January 2006. Thus Mr. Gamble's incredible accomplishment of stringing the telegraph lines over rugged mountains was finally doomed 145 years later, not by Indians or weather, but by cell phones and e-mail.

[31]Bonnie J. Bartos, "An Enlightening Experience with Medicine," Marshburn, ed. (2000), 123-131.

[32]David Smith, "My Lightning Story," Marshburn, ed. (2000), 64-65.

[33] Andrew Flower (W0ZUX) (2003), 21, "What's Loud and Bright and Lasts a Fraction of a Second?" *QST Magazine,* February, American Radio Relay League.

[34]Gerrie Catolane, "My Story," Marshburn, ed. (2000), 62-63.

[35] Dave Bell (2005). Lightning Causes Tank Fire," *The Leader-Union*, Vandalia, Illinois, March 31. See http://www.leaderunion.com/articles/2005/04/01/news/news00 .txt.

[36] Josephine Covino, Chairperson, Lightning Protection Review Committee, United States Department of Defense Explosives Safety Board, quoted in Kithil (2004), iii.

[37] Ron Wooten (2006), "Report of Investigation into the Sago Mine Explosion Which Occurred January 2, 2006," Charleston: West Virginia Office of Miner's Health, Safety, and Training. The United States Mine Safety and Health Administration (MSHA) web site at www.msha.gov/sagomine.asp is another source of information about the Sago Mine disaster and rescue attempts. See also http://www.wvminesafety.org.

Chapter 7 Dodging the Electric Bullet

[1] Gaster (1959), 66, 607-608, 633-634.

[2] See International Electrotechnical Commission (2006), *Protection against Lightning,* 1st ed. International Standard

IEC-62305. This international standard is available in English, French and Spanish language versions and currently consists of 4 parts: General Principles, Risk Management, Physical Damage to Structures and Life Hazard, and Electrical and Electronic Systems within Structures. A fifth part (only partially complete at the time this book was written) will deal with electromagnetic compatibility issues. Refer to www.iec.ch for details. In the United States, a basic standard for buildings is: National Fire Protection Association, (2004) *Standard for the Installation of Lightning Protection Systems,* NFPA 780. Refer to www.nfpa.org for details. Richard Kithil, National Lightning Safety Institute, has compiled a list of more than 20 lightning design codes and standards for various United States government agencies such as the Department of Defense, the Department of Energy, and others, as well as British, South African, Australian, and other international standards. Copies are available for purchase. See www.lightningsafety.com.

[3] Thompson Lightning Protection Inc. St. Paul, Minnesota is a major manufacturer of lightning protection equipment.

[4] Marshall (1973), 37.

[5] Electric Power Research Institute (2003), 4-13, *TFlash User's Guide, Version 2.09,* TR-113808, Palo Alto, California: Electric Power Research Institute.

[6] After Golde (1978), 86.

[7] Marshall (1973), 41.

[8] Rakov and Uman (2003), 1813.

[9] Ibid., 1813-1815.

[10] Ibid., 1815.

[11] Ibid., 1817-1818

[12] Lightning Protection Institute (1987), 25-27, *Standard of Practice LPI-175, 3rd ed.,* Maryville, MO: Lightning Protection Institute. See also Lightning Protection Institute (2004), *Standard of Practice for the Design-installation-*

Inspection of Lightning Protection Systems, LPI-175, 2004 ed. See http://www.lightning.org.
[13] The best reference I know is Martin Uman's new book, *The Art and Science of Lightning Protection*, Cambridge: Cambridge University Press, 2008. Two other useful sources of information are the Lightning Protection Institute, http://www.lightning.org, Maryville, Missouri, (800) 488-6864 and the National Lightning Safety Institute, http://www.lightningsafety.com , Louisville, Colorado, (303) 666-8817.
[14] Anonymous (2005), "Timberrr! Lightning Slices a Fairway Landmark," *The New Zealand Herald*, December 23. http://www.nzherald.co.nz/section/story.cfm?c_id+1&0bjectI D=10361233.
[15] The National Collegiate Athletic Association 2005-06. *Sports Medicine Handbook*, "Guideline 1d-Lightning Safety." See also the National Lightning Safety Institute website, www.lightningsafety.com for additional information on indoor pools.
[16] Richard Kithil and Kevin Johnston (2007). *Lightning and Aquatics Safety: A Cautionary Perspective for Indoor Pools*, Louisville, Colorado: National Lightning Safety Institute.
[17] For additional safety information specific to agriculture consult the National Ag Safety Data Base, operated by the Center for Disease Control within the National Institute for Occupational Health and Safety. Refer to www.cdc.gov/nasd.
[18] Garry Rudd, "My Own Story in My Own Words," Marshburn, ed. (2000), 207-216.
[19] Golde (1978), 184; Marshall (1973), 110.
[20] The National Oceanic and Atmospheric Administration (NOAA) has posted the image on its web site at http://www.crh.noaa.gov/pub/ltg/plane_japan.php. The image is provided courtesy of Zen Kawasaki, Department of Electrical Engineering, Osaka University.

[21] A description of testing procedures and test laboratory equipment is available from Lightning Technologies Inc. at http://www.lightningtech.com .

[22] The procedure for aircraft testing and certification is quite complex. For readers interested in details, refer to the Federal Aviation Administration (FAA) website at http://www.faa.gov. The basic regulation in the United States is found in FAR Part 25 Section 25.581, "Lightning Protection," which mandates lightning protection but gives no details as to how it is to be accomplished. SAE International Aerospace Practice (ARP) 5777, "Aircraft Lightning Direct Effects Certification," has been endorsed by the FAA as an acceptable method for complying with Section 25.581.

[23] Anonymous (1996), *Lightning Protection*, Standard E-4 revised December, 1996, Edgewater, MD: American Boat and Yacht Council.

[24] Anonymous (2005), 8. "Lightning! Flash, Bang, Your Boat's Been Hit—Now What?" *Seaworthy*, the BoatU.S. Marine Insurance and Damage Avoidance Report, Vol.23, No. 3 July.

[25] For additional details on lightning and sailboats, see Thomsen, Ewen M. (1992). "Lightning and Sailboats," Sea Grant Project No. R/MI-10, July, Gainesville Florida: University of Florida. Also refer to http://www.marinelightning protection.com, (a web site maintained by Ewen Thomsen) for additional data and links to other sources of information.

[26] Ralph Bernstein (1997), 9. *Performance Evaluation of the National Lightning Detection Network in the Vicinity of Albany, New York*, Report TR-109544: Palo Alto, CA: Electric Power Research Institute.

[27] T. A. Phillips , et al. (1967), 949-967. "Influence of Air Density on Electrical Strength of Transmission Line Insulation," *IEEE Transactions on Power Apparatus and*

Systems, August, Vol. PAS-86, No. 8, New York: Institute of Electrical and Electronic Engineers.

[28] Electric Power Research Institute (2003), 3-1, 3-2, *TFlash User's Guide, Version 2.09*, TR-113808, Palo Alto, CA: Electric Power Research Institute.

[29] Sadly, as this book was being finished, Dr. Chauncey Starr died peacefully in his sleep a few days after his 95th birthday.

[30] Ralph Bernstein, et al. (1996), 12-1, "Lightning Detection Network Averts Damage and Speeds Restoration," *IEEE Computer Applications in Power*, April, Vol. 9, No. 2, New York: Institute of Electrical and Electronic Engineers.

[31] For details, refer to R. Dean Straw, ed. (1997), 4-13 *The ARRL Antenna Book*, Newington, CT: The American Radio Relay League.

[32] See Kithil (2004), 105-116.

[33] Marshall (1973), 115-123.

[34] Kithil (2004), 150.

[35] Golde (1978), 133-135.

[36] A useful general source for information concerning mines is the United States Department of Labor, Mine Safety and Health Administration. See http://www.msha.gov.

Chapter 8 Predicting the Unpredictable

[1] See *Sall v. T'S, Inc., d/b/a Smiley's Golf Complex*, 34 Kan.App.2d 296, 117 P.3d 896 (2005).

[2] For example, in addition to Sall, cited in this chapter, see: Jaffe v. City and County of Denver, 15 P.3d 806 (2001); Grace v. City of Oklahoma City, 953 P.2d 69 (1997); Davis v. The Country Club, Inc., 53 Tenn. App. 130, 381 S.W.2d 309 (1963).

[3] If you have questions or require legal or other expert advice, you should seek the advice of a competent attorney or other professional.

[4] Information on these products can be found at: http://www.strikealert.com, http://www.comm-omni.com, (for

SkyScan detector), and http://www.spectrumthunderbolt.com for ThunderBolt Pro.

[5]For example, see http://www.ambientweather.com.

[6] See http://www.comm-omni.com, (for SkyScan detector), http://www.weathershop.com/FMLA-1000.htm (for the FMLA-1000 system), and http://secure.sciencecompany.com/Lightning –Detectors-C608.aspx for the SkyScan EWS, and to http://www.blasterstool.com for information on all three instruments.

[7] See http://www.thorguard.com for product details and information.

[8] See http://www.boltek.com for product details and information

[9] See http://www.rabunlabs.com for product details and information.

[10] Personal communication, Ron Holle November 8, 2004.

[11] For the United States go to http://www.nws.gov and follow the menus to thunderstorms. For the United Kingdom, go http://www.meto.gov.uk; for Europe, (26 countries participating) go to the European Center for Medium-Range Weather Forecasts at http://www.ecmwf.int.

[12] See http://www.weatherdata.com.

[13] See http://www.intelecast.com.

[14] See http://www.accuweather.com

[15] Contact Vaisala at (520) 806-7300 or thunderstorm.sales@vaisala.com for pricing or more information.

[16] Refer to thunder.msfc.nasa.gov/validation/instruments.html.

[17] H. J. Christian, K. T. Driscoll, S. J. Goodman, R. J. Blakeslee, D. A. Mach, and D. E. Buechler (1996), 368-371, "The Optical Transient Detector (OTD)," *Proceedings of the 10th International Conference on Atmospheric Electricity*; Osaka, Japan; June 10-14, 1996.

[18] See http://trmm.gsfc.nasa.gov/.

[19] Steven Businger, et al. (2002) "A New Lightning Prediction Index that Utilizes GPS-Integrated Precipitable Water Vapor," *Weather and Forecasting,* American Meteorological Society, October.

Chapter 9 The Bell Ringer's Deception

[1] Franklin, William T., ed. (1817), *Memoirs of the Life and Writings of Benjamin Franklin, LL.D., F.R.S., &c,* B. Franklin letter to John Winthrop dated July 2, 1768 in vol.3, p 370-74. London. Also reprinted in *The Papers of Benjamin Franklin,* Vol. 15: January 1, 1778 through December 31, 1768, p 166-68, eds. William B. Willcox, Dorothy W. Bridgwater, Mary L. Hart, Claude A. Lopez, and G. B. Warden, New Haven: Yale University Press, 1972. See also Isaacson (2003), 137.

[2] Sheets and Williams (2001), 175.

[3] Rakov and Uman (2003), 296-298 has a review of research related to the use of lasers to trigger lightning.

[4] Jean-Claude Diels, et al. (1997), 50-55, "Lightning Control with Lasers," *Scientific American,* Vol. 277 No 2. August .

[5] Bernstein, et al. (1996), 15, "Lightning Detection Network Averts Damage and Speeds Restoration," *IEEE Computer Applications in Power,* 12-17, Vol. 9, No 2, April.

[6] Patton v. United States of America Rugby Football Union, ltd, 381 MD. 627, 851 A.2d 566.

[7] See Hames v. State of Tennessee, 808 S.W.2d 41, April 8, 1991.

[8] The Federal Emergency Management Administration (FEMA) has guidelines concerning lightning risks and provides guidelines for what to do (and not to do) before, during, and after a thunderstorm. See: http://www.fema.gov/hazard/thunderstorm/ A number of other sources have compilations of lightning safety guidelines, including the National Oceanic and Atmospheric Administration (NOAA) and the American College of Emergency Physicians. In this table I have drawn from several

sources to make the tabulation as complete as possible and to correlate with the actual case histories included in the text.

[9] Hames v. State of Tennessee, 808 S.W.2d 41, April 8, 1991.

[10] Hames v. State of Tennessee, op.cit.

[11] The speed of sound in air under typical atmospheric conditions is 1,129 feet per second (344 meters per second), so in 30 seconds sound travels 33,870 feet or 6.4 miles.

[12] Sadly, today medical experts shy away from recommending mouth-to-mouth resuscitation due to the risk of contacting hepatitis or HIV. Emergency medical kits contain devices that can be used to reduce the risk, but it is the rare situation where they would be available. If the victim is a relative or known individual the risk may be minimal. So far I have found no evidence of an individual contacting hepatitis or HIV after giving CPR.

[13] For additional details www.lightningsafety.noaa.gov has the best website on lightning safety.

[14] Following his injury Michael Utley created Struckbylightning.org, Inc., a non-profit corporation headquartered in West Yarmouth, Massachusetts. See http://struckbylightning.org or call (508) 364-4208.

[15] The URL for the Lightning Strike and Electric Shock Survivors International, Inc. is http://www.lightning-strike.org. LSESSI is a 501c3 non-profit organization.

[16] Andrews et al. (1992).

[17] For information, access: http://www.acep.org/webportal/PatientsConsumers/HealthSubjectsByTopic/SeasonalSafetyandWellness/FactSheetLightningInjury.htm

[18] Access this web site http://www.nlm.nih.gov/medlineplus/encyclopedia.html and then use the search tool and search under "lightning injuries."

[19] In the United States, poison control centers are regional. In California there are several regional services accessible 24 hours per day by telephone or e-mail, for example

http://www.calpoison.org. When I accessed this organization
and searched on "lightning," there were no entries. There is
also the American Association of Poison Control Centers,
http://www.aapcc.org that can be used to locate a state or
regional office. Other countries have a single source for
poison information.

Annotated Bibliography

Andrews, Christopher J., Mary Ann Cooper, Mat Darvenizia, and David MacKerras, eds. 1992. *Lightning Injuries: Electrical, Medical, and Legal Aspects.* Boca Raton, FL: CRC Press. A comprehensive treatment of the medical aspects of lightning injuries.

Anonymous. 2006. *Protection Against Lightning.* IEC Standard 62305-1, Geneva, Switzerland: International Electrotechnical Commission. The basic European standard for lightning protection.

Anonymous. 2004. *Standard for the Installation of Lightning Protection Systems.* NFPA 780. Quincy, MA: National Fire Protection Association, Technical Committee on Lightning Protection. First published in 1904 as *Specifications for Protection of Buildings Against Lightning,* this is the latest edition of the basic lightning protection standard in the United States.

Cheney, Margaret. 1993. *Tesla: Man Out of Time.* New York: Barnes and Noble Books. Biographical study of Tesla the man, his life, and his inventions.

Cohen, I. Bernard. 1990. *Benjamin Franklin's Science.* Cambridge MA: Harvard University Press. A definitive, carefully researched survey of Franklin's work on electricity, lightning, and other scientific fields.

Cohn, Ellen R., et. al. eds. Various dates. *The Papers of Benjamin Franklin,* Vols. 1-39. New Haven: Yale University Press. This massive compendium of Franklin's writing and correspondence covers his early life, his scientific experiments and research, and his activities as a diplomat and senior statesman for the United States.

Cooray, Vernon, ed., 2003. *The Lightning Flash.* London: The Institution of Electrical Engineers. This is Volume 34 in the IEE Power and Energy series. It is a handbook with detailed treatment of the science and physics of lightning, from its origins to its effects on infrastructure and humans, as well as methods for protection.

Curran, E. Brian, Ronald L. Holle and R. E. Lopez. 1997. *Lightning Fatalities, Injuries and Damage Reports in the United States from 1959-1994.* National Oceanic and Atmospheric Administration Technical Memorandum NWS SR-193. Washington D.C.: U.S. Government Printing Office. Note: The report is available at http://www.nssl.noaa.gov/papers/techmemos/NWS-SR-193/techmemo-sr193.html. Accessed April, 2006.

Davies, Kenneth. 1965. *Ionospheric Radio Propagation,* National Bureau of Standards Monograph 80. Washington D.C.: U.S. Government Printing Office. A broad treatment of radio propagation, including characteristics of the ionosphere and ionospheric disturbances. Chapter 9 discusses the propagation of low and very low frequency waves, including those caused by lightning.

Dwyer, Joseph R. 2005. "A Bolt Out of the Blue," *Scientific American* May, 65-71. In this fascinating article, Professor Dwyer summarizes the latest research concerning the complex origins of lightning and the physical processes that occur when lightning is created. Among the new findings described are the radiation releases that accompany a lightning strike.

Ehrlich, Gretel. 1994. *A Match to the Heart.* New York: Pantheon Books. A detailed and moving first person account of what it is like to be struck by lightning and the lengthy recovery process that followed.

Fink, Donald G., ed. in chief, John M. Carroll, associate editor. 1999. *The Standard Handbook for Electrical Engineers,* 14th ed. New York: McGraw-Hill. The basic reference handbook for electrical engineers.

Frazier, Kendrick. 1979. *The Violent Face of Nature-Severe Phenomena and Natural Disasters.* New York: William Morrow and Company. In this book Frazier discusses all types of natural disasters, from weather-related severe phenomena such as tornadoes and hurricanes, to earthquakes and volcanoes. He discusses forecasting, warning, and prediction as well as the increasing vulnerability of modern societies to specific types of disasters.

Gaster, Theodor H. ed., 1959. *The New Golden Bough—A New Abridgement of the Classic Work by Sir James George Frazer.* New York: Criterion Books. This classic work of anthropology links primitive magic, taboos, and religion to the evolution of modern cultures around the world. To the ancients, the weather, in particular lightning and thunder, reflected the omniscient power of the gods and gave rise to many fascinating superstitions.

Geddes, Leslie A., ed. 1995. *Handbook of Electrical Hazards and Accidents*, Boca Raton: CRC Press. A comprehensive treatment of the causes and consequences of electrical shock, due to either lightning or commercial electricity.

Golde, Rudolf H. 1978. *Lightning Protection.* London: Academic Press. Although dated, this book touches upon lightning protection for aircraft, bridges, mines, petroleum storage facilities, and facilities for storing explosives.

Gray, William R., Tee Loftin, Tom Melham, Cynthia Russ Ramsay, and Judith E. Rinard. 1978. *Powers of Nature.*

Washington, D.C.: National Geographic Society. This book has a description of weather-induced natural disasters and volcanoes.

Isaacson, Walter. 2003. *Benjamin Franklin—An American Life.* New York: Simon & Schuster. A detailed biography of Franklin from childhood to his death in 1790. Provides an overview of his scientific work, but has greater emphasis on his role as statesman, diplomat, and philosopher.

Jellinek, Stefan.1955. *Atlas Zur Spurenkunde Der Elektrizatät.* Vienna: Austria: Springer-Verlag. (In German). An atlas of nearly 200 photographs and drawings of damage or injuries caused by electrical shock or lightning. Shows characteristic damage to trees and building materials, as well as wounds to humans.

Kithil, Richard, Jr. 2004. *Lightning Protection for Engineers— An Illustrated Guide for Critical High Value Facilities in Accord with Recognized Codes and Standards,* Rev. 2006. Louisville, CO: National Lightning Safety Institute. This is a practical handbook for engineers and others interested in lightning protection of structures, communications facilities, and high risk facilities containing sensitive electronics or explosives. It has hundreds of illustrations and an overview of various codes and standards.

Kithil, Richard, Jr. 2006. *Introduction to Lightning Safety and Risk Management of the Hazard.* Louisville, CO: National Lightning Safety Institute. An illustrated training manual covering the physics of lightning formation and the basics of lightning risks and protection methods.

Lee, R.C., E. G. Cravalho, and J. F. Burke, 1992. *Electrical Trauma: the Pathophysiology, Manifestations and Clinical Management.* Cambridge: Cambridge University Press. This book describes injuries due to electric shock and lightning, as well as their treatment.

Lyons, Walter A. 1997. *The Handy Weather Answer Book*, 2nd ed. Detroit: Visible Ink Press. A detailed reference with questions and answers for basic weather phenomena.

MacCurdy, Edward. 1958. *The Notebooks of Leonardo Da Vinci*. New York: George Braziller. Da Vinci's notebooks are amazing for the breadth of his studies and observations on topics ranging from human anatomy and art to weapons and warfare and weather, including lightning.

Magono, Choji. 1980. *Thunderstorms*. Amsterdam: Elsevier Scientific Publishing Company. A detailed scientific treatment of the atmospheric physics of thunderstorms and lightning.

Marshall, J. Lawrence. 1973. *Lightning Protection*. New York: John Wiley and Sons. This book deals with lightning protection and safety. It has some interesting sections on camping and outdoor activities and on the lightning protection of communication towers and sytems.

Marshburn, Steve, ed. 1998. *Life After Shock—58 LS & ESVI Members Tell Their Stories*. Jacksonville, NC: Lightning Strike & Electric Shock Survivors International, Inc. First person accounts of being struck by lightning, symptoms and disabilities, and the process of medical treatment and recovery.

Marshburn, Steve, ed. 2000. *Life After Shock, Volume II—49 LS & ESVI Members Tell Their Stories*. Jacksonville, NC: Lightning Strike & Electric Shock Survivors International, Inc. Additional first person accounts of being struck by lightning, symptoms and disabilities, and the process of medical treatment and recovery.

Martin, Thomas C. 1995. *The Inventions, Researches, and Writings of Nikola Tesla*, 2nd ed. New York: Barnes and Noble Books. This is a reprint of the first compilation of Tesla's work on high frequencies, high voltages, and polyphase currents that was first published in 1883. Tesla had a dramatic impact on the commercialization of electric power by demonstrating that alternating current could overcome many of the disadvantages of direct current.

Rakov, Vladimir A. and Martin A Uman. 2003. *Lightning: Physics and Effects*. Cambridge: Cambridge University Press. The most current, definitive and complete technical compendium on the engineering and physics of lightning.

Reynolds, Ross. 2000. *Cambridge Guide to the Weather*. Cambridge: Cambridge University Press. Explains atmospheric conditions that cause different weather conditions, weather forecasting and hazardous weather conditions including locations and incidence of thunderstorms.

Schiffer, Michael B. 2003. *Draw the Lightning Down— Benjamin Franklin and Electrical Technology in the Age of Enlightenment*. Berkeley, CA: University of California Press. This book surveys the history of electrical research in the 17th century, with discussion of Franklin and other important scientists, but also discusses many obscure and quirky uses of static electricity, including electric canons, toys, electrical treatments for menopausal women and so on.

Seeger, Raymond J. 1973. *Benjamin Franklin: New World Physicist*. Oxford: Pergamon Press. An overview of Franklin's research in electricity, lightning and other physical phenomena.

Sheets, Bob and Jack Williams. 2001. *Hurricane Watch—Forecasting the Deadliest Storms on Earth.* New York: Vintage Books (Random House). Bob Sheets is the former director of the United States National Hurricane Center and has flown in aircraft through numerous hurricanes. Chapter 7 of this book, titled "Controlling Storms," tells the story of Project Stormfury and predecessor attempts at weather modification.

Stenhoff, Mark. 1999. *Ball Lightning—An Unsolved Problem In Atmospheric Physics.* New York: Kluwer Academic/Plenum Publishers. A technical treatment of ball lightning, including various theories, reports of observations, effects on aircraft and other structures, risks.

Straw, R. Dean, ed. 1999. *The ARRL Handbook for Radio Amateurs—2000,* 77th ed. Newington, CT: ARRL—the National Association for Amateur Radio. The ARRL is the organization of radio amateurs and over the decades has rendered a valuable public service by providing emergency communications during natural disasters. This book includes a section on protection of radio equipment from lightning.

Uman, Martin A. 1984. *Lightning.* New York: Dover Publications. A detailed description of lightning physics and theory by one of the leaders in lightning research.

Uman, Martin A. 1986. *All About Lightning.* New York: Dover Publications. A non-technical book in the format of questions and answers about lightning physics.

Uman, Martin A. 1987. *The Lightning Discharge,* New York: Academic Press. A technical monograph detailing the physics of lightning discharges, properties, associated electric and magnetic fields, and including a discussion of lightning discharges on other planets.

Uman, Martin A. 2008. *The Art and Science of Lightning Protection,* Cambridge: Cambridge University Press. A new and definitive treatment of lightning protection.

Volland, Hans, ed. 1995. *Handbook of Atmospheric Electrodynamics.* Boca Raton: CRC Press. This detailed 2-volume handbook has chapters dealing with the physics of lightning flashes, ball lightning, whistlers and other atmospheric phenomena, extra-terrestrial lightning, and lightning protection.

Westman, H. P., ed. 1956. *Reference Data for Radio Engineers, 4th ed.* New York: International Telephone and Telegraph Corporation. A handbook with extensive technical data for radio and electronics engineers.

Permissions, Credits and Acknowledgments

As in the case of all my books, I am indebted to many people for help and encouragement. First, I especially want to thank Professor Martin Uman, who besides writing the Foreword to the book, generously shared his expertise, answered my questions, and opened both his home and his research facilities to me.

To those who shared their personal or family lightning stories with me—my thanks: Bonnie J. Bartos, Randi Boyd, Gerrie Catolane, Frank Coffman, Lisa Cunningham, Bob Davidson, Susan Woods Evans, Mary M. Frederick, Char and Ron Griggs, Robert Ireland, Todd Kolber, Bailey Green-Kouri, Dana Larson, Antoinette Palmisano, Gem L. Poe, Ted von Rosenvinge, Garry Rudd, Bob Ruffolo, Barry Smith, David Smith, Betty Smith, Jeff Stevens, Howard and Mitzi Wells, Jim Whitehead.

Among the many technical experts and scientists I met with, I am especially grateful to those at the Electric Power Research Institute who assisted me and provided access to EPRI's research results: Dr. Chauncey Starr, chairman emeritus, Dr. Clark Gellings; Ralph Bernstein, and Judith Mills, librarian. At Stanford University, Julia Hartung and Margaret Kimball assisted my research, as did Professor J. C. Diels at the University of New Mexico. I am especially indebted to Ron Holle at Vaisala and Richard Kithil Jr., National Lighting Safety Institute, who were most generous in sharing information and resources. Jim Workman provided information on the links between lightning strikes and prehistoric rock art. Karen Manos helped me understand the legalities of lightning protection. An old friend and former classmate, Richard Thompson, helped me understand some of the early testing of electric transmission lines.

A very special thanks is owed Steve Marshburn, founder of Lightning Strike and Electrical Shock Survivors International, and to Michael Utley, founder of Struckbylightning.org, who, besides sharing personal stories, introduced me to other lightning strike survivors and gave me an entirely new perspective on just how terrible are the human consequences of being struck by lightning.

Dr. Mary Ann Cooper, Professor of Emergency Medicine at the University of Illinois at Chicago, and one of the foremost authorities in the world on the medical effects of lightning injuries, kindly reviewed several sections of the manuscript. My good friend Dr. Morris Hasson, Director of Executive Health at the University of California, Irvine, School of Medicine, kept me straight on medical terminology.

The staff at the Balboa Branch of the Newport Beach Public Library (Phyllis Scheffler, librarian, assisted by Barbara Zinzer and Michael Payne), as usual were an exceptional resource in helping me track down information from obscure sources. I thank Kurt Mueller for providing the illustrations, Anne Elizabeth Powell for her usual insightful manuscript review. As always, my wife Nancy freely gave her support, in book design, proof-reading, and research assistance.

Finally, to my agent, Ron Goldfarb, who suggested the topic and provided wise counsel, my gratitude.

My thanks to Simon & Schuster, New York, for permission to quote from pages 69, 137 and 145 in *Benjamin Franklin: An American Life*. Copyright © 2003 by Walter Isaacson. Bodley Head. Reprinted by permission of Simon &Schuster, Inc.

Photo credits are as follows: plates 1 and 9 and book cover: Dev Gregory; plate 3 and 11: Greg Geffner; plate 7: Long horizontal cloud lightning flash, often called spider lightning, over Norman, Oklahoma on July 7, 1994 at 2305 CDT. Photo copyright 1994 by Ronald L. Holle; plate 12: Frank Coffman; plate 13: Three cloud-to-ground lightning flashes viewed from Oro Valley, Arizona on July 23, 2003 at 2107MST. Photo copyright 2003 by Ronald L. Holle; plates 2, 4, 14 and author photo: Andy Ryan; plate 5: Fred Muzic. Plate 8 courtesy of Vaisala, Inc. with a special thanks to Ron Holle.

All illustrations are by Kurt Mueller, based on sketches by the author.

INDEX

A

aborescent burns · 101
act of God (definition) · 200
air pressure · 30, 186
airline crashes attributed to lightning
    · 144
American College of Emergency
    Physicians · 242
American Heart Association · 98
Ampere, Andre-Marie · 31
Andrews, Christopher J. · 238
Apollo 12 · viii
arc welder · 30
Aristotle · ix
athletic fields · 90, 171, 208
attachment process · 35, 36
avalanche of electrons · 31, 41
Avalon Harbor, Catalina Island ·
    138

B

balloons · x, 12, 14, 24
Bartos, Bonnie J. · 149
bell towers · 70, 217
Bernstein, Ralph · 192, 221
blackout of electric power · 121,
    122, 190, 195
blizzards · 59
blue jets · 47
Boyd, Randi · 38
Boys, Charles V. · 11, 33
Boys' camera · 11, 34
breakdown · 6, 12, 27, 30, 32, 34,
    84, 85, 87, 132, 133
bremsstrahlung · 42, 246
brontophobia · 109

C

Camp Blanding · *See* International
    Center for Lightning Research
    and Testing
Camp Steiner, Utah · 114
capacitive coupling · 123
capacitor · 3, 6, 10, 43, 77, 85, 89,
    98, 123, 152, 163
cardiac arrest · xii, 136, 227
Catolane, Gerrie · 150
Caviezel, James · 120
Center for Disease Control · 238,
    243
Chevron Hawaii (oil tanker) · 141
cloud electrification theories · 23
cloud lightning flash · 17, 32, 36, 52,
    144, 204, 205, 213
cloud-to-cloud · See cloud lightning
    flash
cloud-to-ground · See ground
    lightning flash
Coffman, Frank · 151
conductivity · 35, 43, 77, 164
convective theory · 26
convective thunderstorm · 20
Cooper, Mary Ann · 238, 243
corona discharge · 26, 40, 166
Corson, John · 104
cosmic radiation · 31
cosmic rays · 26, 28, 31, 44
coulomb · 31
Coulomb, Charles Augustin · 31
CPR cardiopulmonary resuscitation ·
    85, 96, 227, 246
cumulonimbus clouds · 7, 12, 15,
    19, 20, 21, 23, 27, 47, 55, 58,
    166, 205, 218, 246
Cunningham, Lisa · 126

D

D'Alibard, Jean-Francois · 4
dart leader · 36, 246
Davidson, Robert · 136
DaVinci, Leonardo · 2
Deer Park Shell Oil terminal · 141
defibrillators · 98
diameter of lightning channel · 35
dielectric · 3, 28, 29, 43, 100, 123,
    152, 163
dielectric strength · 30
Diels, Jean-Claude · 220
dipoles · See cloud electrification
    theories
direct strike · 55, 83, 87, 91, 123,
    157, 185
direct strike with a flashover · 83
Dwyer, J. R. · 15, 32, 40, 41

E

earth terminals · See grounding
    system
effective height of a structure · 54
Ehrlich, Gretel · xii, 109
Eiffel Tower · 53
electric field · x, 12, 15, 17, 25, 28,
    30, 35, 40, 41, 53, 84, 91, 124,
    129, 132, 164, 166, 198, 204,
    205, 208, 219, 226
electric field strength · 28, 166, 205,
    208
Electric Power Research Institute ·
    122, 190, 191, 192, 193, 194,
    200, 210, 211, 221
electrical building codes · 75
electrical conductivity · 28, 35
electrical power system outages ·
    185, 189
electrical resistance · vii, 76
electricity danger levels · 74
electrocardiogram · 95, 97, 246
electrocution · 75
electromagnetic compatibility
    (EMC) tests · 177
electromagnetic coupling · 148, 185

elephants · See West Bengal
ELF (extremely low-frequency) · 43
elves · 48
Empire State Building · 12, 13
epithelial cells · 81
EPRI · See Electric Power Research
    Institute
equivalent circuit · 83, 85, 90, 246
Etruscans · 1
extraterrestrial lightning
    Jupiter · 49
    Mars · 50
    Mercury · 50
    Saturn · 50
    Venus · 49
ExxonMobil tank farm, Indiana ·
    153

F

Faraday Cage · 165, 177
Faraday, Michael · 165
fatalities · See lightning fatalities
    data
Federal Aviation Administration ·
    14, 16, 147, 166
Federal Emergency Management
    Agency · xvi
Federal Power Commission · 121
flashover · 84, 85, 87, 89, 100, 101,
    123, 133, 144, 148, 181, 185,
    188, 198, 247
Flower, Andrew · 150
forest fires · See wildland fires
Fram, Christine · 105
Franklin, Benjamin · ix, 2, 23, 35,
    79, 124, 156, 217
Frederick, Mary · 116
frequency of lightning strikes
    northern hemisphere · 57
    southern hemisphere · 57
    tropical regions · 58
Friction Pitch · 54, 55
frontal thunderstorm · 20
fulgurites · 2, 16, 135

G

Gamble, James · 147
gamma rays · 32, 41
Gannon, Christopher · 201
Gardisky Lake · 19, 22
global flash rate · 18
global warming · 58
golf courses · vii, 71, 120, 170, 171,
   201, 202, 208, 231
Goosen, Retief · 71
Grand Teton National Park · 54
Grand Teton peak · 54
graupel · 25, 57, 247
Greene-Kouri, Bailey · 127
Griggs, Ron, Char, and Linsey · 140
ground flash incidence rates · 63
ground lightning flash · 32, 48, 53,
   59, 157, 204, 205, 207, 211, 213
ground wave · 43
grounding system · xiv, 156, 157,
   158, 159, 161, 162, 168, 169,
   170, 196, 197

H

hailstones · 25
Hames v. State of Tennessee · 223,
   224
Hams · *See* radio amateurs
Harrison, Jeff · 109
Helliwell, R. A. · 46
HF (high-frequency) · 43, 44, 46,
   77, 85, 124, 150
Holle, Ron · 210, 241, 242
hurricanes · 59, 68, 212, 218

I

ice particles · 26, 27
impedance · 76, 77, 85, 157
inductive mechanism theory · 25
injury rate · 68, 69

International Center for Lightning
   Research and Testing · 15, 16,
   193, 205
intracloud · See cloud lightning flash
ion · 6, 247
ionization · 6, 28, 29, 31, 32, 167,
   189, 218
ionosphere · 28, 29, 44, 46, 47, 48,
   247
   critical frequency · 44
   D-layer · 28, 44
   E-layer · 44
   F1-layer · 44
   F2-layer · 44
Ireland, Robert · 78

J

Jacob Riis Park · 52
Jupiter · 1, 49, 50

K

K'awil · 2
Kazakhstan · 38
kelong (fish platforms) · 111
Kennedy Space Center · 214
keraunophobia · 109, 115, 117, 248
kite · ix, 3, 5
Kithil, Richard · 205
Kolber, Todd · 182
Krider, Phillip · 210

L

Lamarck Col · 22
Larson, Dana · 87
Leadville, Colorado, · 186
Leyden jar · 3
Lichtenberg figures · 101
lightning arrestors · 70, 189, 194,
   195, 221
lightning casualty rates · 66
lightning detection

advanced systems · 213
area warning devices · 207
legal aspects · 200
personal warning devices · 207
principles of operation · 204
subscription warning services ·
    212
system types · 206
lightning detection and warning
    systems
    risk of litigation · 203
Lightning Detection Network · 193,
    219
lightning detection systems · x, xvi,
    13, 17, 62, 203, 206, 209, 214
lightning education · 236
lightning fatalities data · 56, 65, 66,
    67, 68, 69, 120, 144
lightning flash counters · 62
lightning flash density · 62, 64
lightning protection
    air terminals · 12, 156, 157, 158,
        159, 161, 165, 167, 168, 176,
        196, 246
    aircraft · 177
    antenna towers · 196
    avionics · 144, 177
    boats · 181, 184
    bridges · 176
    copper ground plate · 162
    critical soil ionization potential ·
        163
    dissipation arrays and charge
        transfer systems · 165
    down conductors · 156, 165, 181,
        196, 197
    early streamer emission (ESE) ·
        166
    electrical transients · 167
    Faraday cage enclosures · 221
    fuzzy dissipaters · 182
    ground fault interrupters · 75
    ground rods · 161
    hazardous materials and
        explosives storage facilities ·
        197
    induced currents · 127, 169, 177
    intelligent arrestors · 221

lightning rods · 4, 6, 9, 15, 156,
    166, 217
mines · 199
nuclear power plants · 220
public assembly buildings · 169
risk assessment · 160
rolling sphere method · 158
soil resistivity effect · 162
surge protection devices · xiv,
    157, 168, 169, 195, 199, 206
television and radio stations · 196
typical system components · 157
lightning safety · 171, 222, 232
duty to protect oneself · 224
guidelines · 224
lightning safety crouch · 226
Lightning Strike and Electric Shock
    Survivors International, Inc · 87,
    232
lightning strike prediction · 204
lightning strikes
    Boy Scouts · 22, 114, 175
    camping and backpacking · 174
    churches · 119
    economic losses · 122
    global patterns · 17, 57, 58, 213,
        214
    height effect · 53
    horseback riding · 113, 130
    motor vehicles · 117
    motorcycles · 136
    nudists · 114
    penitentiary · 116
    rugby field · 223
    seasonality · 64
    television · 78
    wildland fires · 131
lightning types
    ball lightning · xi, 37
    bead lightning · xi, 37
    ribbon lightning · 37
    sheet lightning · xi, 36
lightning victims-age and sex · 69
lightning victims-deadliest day · 70
lightning, effects on
    agriculture · 172
    airplanes · 142, 143, 147, 176
    antennas · 150
    avionics · 144

boats · 138, 140, 178, 183
bridges · 176
bridges and highways · 135
buildings · 124
chimmneys · 168
explosive and munitions storage
    facilities · 153
football fields · 130
green wood · 132
high voltage transmission lines ·
    186
high-rise office building · 127
manufacturing plants · 127
microelectronics · 123
oil storage tanks · 151, 153
personal computers · 168
pipelines · 153
railroads and train controls · 137
soil and rock · 134, 164
swimmers · 128, 129, 172
telecommunication systems · 148
telecommunications and electric
    power lines · 147
telephones · 149
underground mines · 155
wooden power poles · 133
lightning, medical effects of
abdominal injuries · 102
arrhythmia · xiii, 96, 98, 235
asystole · 83, 96, 97
brain injury · 97
burns · 56, 71, 86, 89, 100, 101,
    102, 103, 111, 112, 131, 173,
    176, 246
cardiorespiratory arrest · 85, 96,
    99
cerebral depolarization · 98
congestive heart failure · 69
disability · 241
electroporation · 100
erythema · 101
fractures · 100
on ears and eyes · 102
on heart and lungs · 93
on livestock · 92, 130
on muscles and bones · 100
partial paralysis · 99, 103
post-traumatic stress disorder ·
    103

psychiatric and psychological
    impacts · 103
puncture wounds · 100
sexual dysfunction · 241
short-term memory loss · 88, 150
tinnitus · 102
Linenger, Jerry · 18
LS&ESSI · See Lightning Strike and
    Electric Shock Survivors
    International, Inc., See Lightning
    Strike and Electric Shock
    Survivors International, Inc.
Lucretius · ix

M

Magellan, Ferdinand · 40
Marshburn, Steve · 233, 243
Marx Generator · 10
Marx, E. · 10
Maxwell, James Clerk · 50
metal oxide varistor · 189
meteors · 44
Mont Saint-Michel · 169
Monte San Salvatore · 13
Mount Tioga · 19
Mount Vesuvius · x
Mount Whitney · 22

N

National Aeronautics and Space
    Administration · 14, 166, 206,
    213
National Collegiate Athletic
    Association · 171
National Institutes of Health · 238,
    243
National Lightning Awareness
    Week · 226, 237
National Lightning Safety Institute ·
    205
NCAA · See National Collegiate
    Athletic Association

North American Lightning
    Detection Network · xi, 13, 64,
    154, 193, 194, 200, 210, 211, 222
Northeast Blackout · 122

O

Occupational Health and Safety
    Administration · xvi
Ohm, Georg S. · 76
Ohm's law · 29, 76

P

Patton, Robert and Donald · 222
PET scans (positron emission
    tomography) · 106
Petroglyph Lake, Oregon · 135
petroglyphs · See lightning, effects
    on soil and rock
phase conductors-transmission lines
    · 185
Pliny the Younger · x
Poe, Gem L. and Mary Louise · 80
Pompeii · x

R

radio amateur · 42, 150, 195
resistivity · 76, 81, 82, 91, 129, 163,
    164, 181, 196, 198
return stroke · x, 15, 17, 35, 36, 42,
    219, 246
Richman, G. W. · ix
rockets · x, 14, 15, 17, 31, 219
Rogan, David · 59
Rudd, Gary · 172
Ruffolo, Bob · 112
runaway breakdown · 41, 42
Ryan, Harris J. · 185

S

safety · See lightning safety
Sago mine disaster · 154, 199
Saint Elmo's fire · 40, 146
Sall, Patrick · 201
satellites · 17, 49, 52, 57, 213, 215
Sentry Box Experiment · 4
Sequoia National Park · 22, 114
sferics · 45, 46
Shango · 2
Shriner, Kaylee · 78
side flash · 87, 89, 125, 133, 140,
    175, 184
skin resistance · 81
Smiley's Golf Complex · 201
Smith, Barry W. · 130
Smith, Betty · 115
Smith, David · 150
snow · 1, 23, 25, 26, 174
space station Mir · 18
spark gap · 10, 197
spark plug · 30, 189
spider flash · 63
sprites · 48
Stanford University · 46, 185
Starr, Chauncey · 190, 191, 192, 218
static electricity discharge · 28
step voltage · 56, 90, 92, 129, 164,
    226, 248
stepped leader · x, 12, 34, 35, 41, 42,
    246, 248
Stevens, Jeff · 109
streak camera · 12, 34
Struckbylightning.org, Inc. · 231
Summers, Clinton and Erica · 55
sunspot activity · 44
supercooled · 21, 27
surfing · 109
swimming pools · 128, 129, 242

T

Tahiti · 109
telephone lightning injuries · 89
Tesla Coil · 7, 8
Tesla, Nikola · 7

The 30/30 rule · 225
Thompson, Richard · 187
Thomsen, Matt · 101
Thor · 1
thunder · viii, ix, xii, xiii, 1, 2, 8, 14,
   17, 19, 20, 27, 36, 38, 39, 52, 55,
   60, 62, 78, 109, 110, 115, 128,
   130, 140, 143, 150, 172, 174,
   183, 195, 206, 222, 225, 228, 246
thunderclouds · *See* cumulonimbus
   clouds
thunderstorm cell · 21
thunderstorm days · ix, xiii, 21, 60,
   61, 62, 64
thunderstorm hour · 62
thunderstorms · ix, x, xi, xiii, 14, 19,
   21, 22, 26, 28, 29, 41, 44, 53, 54,
   57, 58, 60, 66, 80, 110, 113, 115,
   117, 120, 128, 129, 130, 136,
   139, 144, 149, 160, 170, 171,
   172, 175, 177, 192, 195, 203,
   208, 217, 218, 222, 224, 225,
   226, 237, 243, 248
   discharge using lasers · 218
transcontinental telephone line. · 147
transmission line faults · 75, 188,
   189, 247
transmission tower insulators · 186
treatment of lightning strike victims
   · 106
Trevino, Lee · 72
troposphere · 47

U

Uman, Martin · 15, 41, 194, 210
underground structure · xiv
undergrounding (of electric utilities)
   · 192
United States Air Force · 14, 197
University of New Mexico · 220
upward flashes · 53
urban heat island effect · 65
utilidors (utility corridors) · 221
Utley, Michael · 203, 231, 243

V

Vaisala · 210, 213
Van de Graaff generator · 10
Van de Graaff, Robert J. · 9
ventricular fibrillation · xii, 75, 83,
   90, 96, 97, 98
VHF (very high-frequency) · 44
VLF (very low-frequency) · 43
Volta, Allesandro · 23
von Rosenvinge, Ted · 178

W

water resistivity · 81
waveguide · 46
Wells, Howard · 149
West Bengal · 29
whistlers · 46, 47, 49, 50
Whitehead, Jim · 146
wildland fires · 131, 132, 175, 210
Wilson, C. T. R. · 6
Woods, Susan · 174

X

X-ray bursts · 15, 42
X-rays · xii, 32, 40, 41, 42, 246

Y

Yosemite National Park · 19, 113,
   131
Youngquist, Andy · 138

Z

Zeus · 1, 119
zinc oxide lightning arrestor · 194
zippers · 80, 86, 101